Sarah Josepha Buell Hale

Mercedes

A Story of Mexico

Sarah Josepha Buell Hale

Mercedes
A Story of Mexico

ISBN/EAN: 9783742897589

Manufactured in Europe, USA, Canada, Australia, Japa

Cover: Foto ©Thomas Meinert / pixelio.de

Manufactured and distributed by brebook publishing software
(www.brebook.com)

Sarah Josepha Buell Hale

Mercedes

MERCEDES

MERCEDES,

A STORY OF MEXICO.

BY SARAH HALE.

LOUISVILLE, KY.
BAPTIST BOOK CONCERN.
1895.

TO MY FATHER,

WITH LOVING RECOLLECTIONS

OF MY MOTHER,

THIS STORY IS AFFECTIONATELY DEDICATED,

BY THE AUTHOR.

PREFACE.

THE recollection of my own **ignorance before I came to** Mexico, of its social and **religious condition, and the** astonishment I have often felt since **at the incorrect state-** ments made in newspapers published **in the** United **States.** have induced me to write this story. I have attempted **to** represent the every-day life of the people as I have **seen** it during a residence here of six years.

A great many **of the** incidents related have come under my own **observation; as, for** instance, the conversation about the painter, **Señor Ramon Sagredo,** the courting scene in which Teodoro's **parents figure, and** the conversation between them in the **street** a year afterward; others were related **to me** by friends, so that I know them **to** be true; the crimping of the Virgin's hair is one **of** these. I have described journeys and places and landscapes and public **events, such as** the opening **of** Congress and the burning **of Judas, just as I** have **seen** them myself. The story of **Doña Benigna's** conversion is told just **as she** herself told it **to me;** the same **is** true of Doña **Susana's.** In Mercedes' conversion, **also,** "I tell the tale as 'twas told **to me."** All the language used by Teodoro on pages 306 and **307 is** faithfully translated from conversa- tions which took place between myself and one of our Mexi- can ministers **at my** dining table not long ago, when he was conducting **a** series of meetings **in our** church. In fact, I have hesitated to mention any **one** thing as the report of an eyewitness lest I might seem to exclude others, for really the book might almost be said to be made **up of** true incidents strung on a slender thread of a story.

After the manuscript **of** the book **was** finished I learned some additional facts about the Ladies' Church Society, one of which **I wish to** mention: on certain days in the week they visit the poor and the sick, being driven to their houses in their carriages if possible; if the carriages cannot go to the houses by reason of the narrowness or unevenness of the alleys in which the poor live, they are driven as far as the vehicles can go, then walk the remainder of the way. They supply them with bedding, clothing, food, and medicines. Of course we know the teachings of the Roman Catholic Church about the reward for such "good works"; nevertheless I could not help heartily echoing the sentiment expressed by one of our Mexican ministers when I related to him these facts: "If they are so good as Catholics, what would they not be if they knew the gospel!"

Friends of the United States who are sending the gospel to Mexico, your labor of love is bestowed on an intelligent, generous, warm-hearted, high-spirited, liberty-loving people.

I wish to express my gratitude to the friends, both Mexican and American, who, at my request, have kindly read the manuscript of this story and given me their opinion of it as a representation of life in Mexico.

If this simple story should inspire any of the people of my native land with greater zeal in the work of giving the Word of God to the inhabitants of Mexico, I shall have my reward.

SARAH HALE.

GUADALAJARA, MEXICO,
November 27, 1894.

MERCEDES,

A STORY OF MEXICO.

CHAPTER I.

OUR LADY OF ST. JOHN.

IT was an afternoon in July, about seven years ago, in the
town of Salta, in the northern part of Mexico. The
whole country wore a parched and thirsty appearance, for
the rains had been delayed. There was much suffering
among the poor in all parts of the country. In this town
there was not so much as in most other places, for a supply
of crystal water was brought from the mountains now, as all
the year, for the use of the people, and to irrigate the gardens and orchards in the town and the country around it.

A sort of awing mystery always seemed to me to hang
around the sources of this water, these "eyes of water," as
the people call them, away off in the Sierra Madre, something like that which, for the ancients, hung over the springs
of the Nile. But whether it came from the silent store houses
of the earth, from a river, or from a lake—"a picture of silver
in a frame of emerald" nestled in the bare, rugged mountain
like the memory of mother and childhood in the heart of
hardened age—here it was, the rushing, dancing, laughing,
life-giving water. Along the side of the town nearest to the
mountains it ran, in the channel provided for it. From this,
smaller channels were opened to convey the water to the
small gardens and orchards in the city and to the fields beyond. The people who lived in the unsightly *adobe* houses
on either side of the principal stream were said to live on the
Orilla del Agua (Oreya del Awa), the Border of the Water.

But notwithstanding the fact that these eyes of water did not seem to be affected by the long drought, there was much sighing for rain in Salta. The vegetation was parched; the figs, grapes, tunas, peaches, pears, and pomegranates were not so abundant as in former years, neither were they so large and sweet. The low shrubs on the mountains, their only vegetation, were not so green as usual.

So deeply was felt the need for rain in all parts of the Republic that the Catholics had, through one of the daily papers of that faith published in the City of Mexico, besought their Illustrious Prelate, the Archbishop, to order "that the prayers of the faithful, directed by His priests, should be addressed with one accord to the Almighty to appease divine justice if such should be his holy will."

"In other times," continues the writer, "and with the Christian faith which characterizes the Mexican people, and which fortunately we still possess, we have had recourse in similar calamities to Our Most Holy Mother, the Virgin Mary, in her sanctuaries of Guadalupe and of los Remedios.

"The images of the noble Lady are in her sanctuaries waiting to hear our public and fervent petitions."

We learn from the same paper that being thus urged "the Illustrious Señor Archbishop of Mexico, in order to obtain from heaven a remedy for the necessities that were afflicting in so great a degree the inhabitants of the capital and of the whole nation on account of the want of rain, ordered that in the Cathedral, the Colegiata, the Profesa, and the Paroquias of that city a three days' service should be held. The first day was to be dedicated to the sacred heart of Jesus; the second, to Our Lady of Guadalupe; the third, to the Holy Guardian Angel of the Mexican nation.

"With regard to the foreign parishes, his Eminence, taking into account the few resources at their command, abstained from ordering this three days' service, but he desired that the Señores Pastores, together with their congregations, should do what they well could to implore the mercies of God, our Lord."

Moved by this request of the **Archbishop the** people of **Salta, the** Sunday before **our story begins, had sought to secure the** intercession **of the Virgin of** St. John. **This image belonged** to a wealthy **family who** resided **in the town. They owned an** Hacienda, **that is, an** immense **farm with a hand-**some house on it, **about** three miles from **town. In** the chapel in the **yard of this** house the Virgin **spent the** greater part of the **year. It had become customary** in times of drouth to bring **her in** and **place** her **in the** principal church of **the** town **that** prayers for rain might **be addressed** to her.

Accordingly this very religious family had sent out their elegant carriage, drawn **by a** splendid span **of** sorrel horses, to bring in the image. They were accompanied by many of **the common** people, **some on shabby horses,** and hundreds on **foot. A fat,** dark-**faced priest, clad in** sacerdotal robes, **seated** himself **in the carriage** and took **Our** Lady in **his** lap. **She, or it,** is an image **about a** foot high. **Her** dress is much **adorned** with gold or **gilt, probably the latter.** How it came **to be believed that the** bringing **in of this image** had any in-**fluence in** securing rain I **am** not **informed. I** suppose that **in some** time of drouth **the people resorted to one** after **another of** their "saints," **and in turn to this** one; rain was **given soon after, so they concluded that it** was through her **influence.**

I do not **know either why she** is called the Virgin of St. John; but it is **probable that** she appeared miraculously (through **the assistance of the Holy** Fathers) in some place that is **called St. John. There are so** many virgins they must be distinguished **in some way.** In Mexico alone there are the Virgin **of** Guadalupe, **Our Lady** of Solitude, Our Lady of Mercy, Our Lady of Lourdes, and **a** multitude of others. An educated Catholic **would** explain to you that they all repre-sent the same person, the mother of our Lord, each one com-memorating **some** phase of her character or of her real or traditional life.

It would be **gross enough** idolatry to worship the mother of the Lord; but **that the** people worship the images themselves, just as pagans in oriental countries worship **their** idols, is proved by the fact that, **though** they all represent the same person, the Virgin Mary, nevertheless it is believed that more miracles are wrought by some images **of** her than by others.   The same is true of the images of **all the saints.** **The** people will **say frankly that** they worship the images unless the questions **that** are put to them **on** the subject remind **them of the** absurdity of such a practice.

On **the way to** the **town a** dozen men, dressed in grotesque costumes, danced in front **of** the carriage.   The Spanish priests, **when** they reached this country three centuries ago, saw before **them the** task of changing the religion of a whole **people.**   For the accomplishment of that purpose there were armies of Spanish soldiers whose cruelty seems incredible, and the "Holy Inquisition" with all the instruments of torture that Satan himself could devise; they added **to** these yet another means, **a** more merciful one, and **one which the** "unchangeable Church" **had** no scruples about **using: they** combined Romanism **with the** paganism of the Indians, **and** thus **the** war-dances **of the aborigines became** a part of the worship of the Holy **Apostolic Roman Catholic** Church in Mexico.

In the suburbs of the **town the** procession[1] was met by other hundreds of **the common** people, with now and then a well-dressed woman among **them.**   They unhitched the horses **from the** carriage, **tied two** long ropes to the axle, and as **many of** them as **could** conveniently seized **the** ropes and drew the carriage through the town to the church.   There Our Lady was deposited with all due solemnity.

Three days had passed and still it had not rained; but these good Catholics were in no danger of losing faith in their saint.   **They** complacently **quoted** their proverb, "What God does not will the saints **cannot do,**" without a thought **of** appealing to him who **"sends his rain on** the evil and on the good."

---

[1] *Nota.*—Religious **processions and, in** short, all religious ceremonies in the **open air are forbidden by the** law in Mexico, but in many towns they **are still tolerated.**

CHAPTER II.

SALTA.

THIS town is, as **I have** said, in the northern part of Mexico. If the curious reader should desire more accurate information about its situation I must recommend **him,** as a Spanish writer might **do,** to consult the "moral map" of Mexico, **as** it is not probable he will find it on any other. But he can **find** a number of others that will answer very **well** to the description.

Looking down the street in one of these small towns, towns of about twelve thousand inhabitants, one sees two unbroken lines of walls plastered and whitewashed or painted yellow, green or blue. One house is distinguished from another **by a** difference of a foot or two in the height of the **walls or by its color.** Occasionally are seen fantastically painted houses reminding one of bright spring calicoes and ginghams, and more rarely there is one of a rich, handsome brown color. They are nearly all of one story. The dwelling-houses are built around **one or** two courts, and **often** have gardens at the **back,** inclosed by a wall ten **or** twelve feet in height, continued from the wall of the house.

The stables **are at the** back of the second court, so that the horses and cows are always said, and truthfully, to be in the house; but they are **as** far removed from the family as could be **desired.** Around the second court are the kitchen and the rooms for servants. There are no front yards; whatever of flowers and shrubbery they have are in the first court.

Mexicans are not prodigal of windows. In the better class **of** houses there are usually two large windows in each of the two front rooms. They have vertical iron or wooden bars over them; in the large cities these are often substituted by an ornamental iron railing about three feet high at the bottom of the windows. The rooms which open on the courts often receive all their light from the folding doors, but sometimes each large room has a window.

Passing along the street one sees sometimes elegantly draped windows and handsomely furnished rooms, and hears the soft, rich notes of a piano, and sees groups of well-dressed ladies and gentlemen in conversation; or he sees through the great front doors a court full of flowers and vines, the greenness contrasting with the white pillars of the corridor which runs around the court.

The streets are favored with such names as "The Reform," "The Holy Spirit," "St. Domingo," among others of a patriotic origin. The stores of various kinds bear such fanciful names as "The Doves," "The Pretty Blue," "The Fountain," "Concord," "The High Waves," "The Future," "The City of London," "The Trojan Horse." Sometimes the suggestive names of "The Delights," "The Current of Life," "The Little Hell" are seen over saloon doors.

The scenes in the streets are curious enough to a foreigner. Here come some immense bundles of green cornstalks or hay wriggling and bumping along the street; presently one discovers four little donkey legs under each and he knows that the patient little animal's body is buried in the bundle. Women sit, scorning chairs or stools, on the sidewalk with their fruits spread out before them; a little farther on are children gambling with pennies. Here go rumbling ox wagons, each with two thick wooden wheels whose diameter is equal to the height of the driver. These drivers wear wide white pantaloons and tall, bell-crowned, broad-brimmed straw hats, sandals, and often, even in this warm weather, red woolen blankets. Often the clothing of the men of the common class is conspicuously parti-colored. Here are beggars crossing themselves on the forehead, lips and breast, according to the directions of the Church, and importuning the passers-by, in the most studied whines, "By the sacred passion of Christ, and for the love of God and His Most Holy Mother, to succor them with a blessed charity." Now and then a handsome carriage dashes by, and well-dressed gentlemen and ladies, the latter always bareheaded, **pass** one **on the** sidewalk. So much for the **better** part of town.

Often **the** houses of **the poor,** like these **on the** Orilla **del** Agua, **for** instance, have no windows even **in** the front rooms. When they have them **they** are small and covered with **un**painted wooden **railings.** Many of the houses are not **plas**tered on the outside, **but** instead of **the** plaster and soiled whitewash, display **the bare** *adobes.* **But not** for this **ugli**ness does impartial **Apollo** neglect **this quarter of town;** there is the **same glare of** white sunlight **on streets and** walls.

Salta has a history **which is** probably **not** very unlike that of **most** other Mexican towns. The story goes that about **three** hundred years ago a Spanish captain, accompanied by **some** Indian families and a Jesuit priest, coming from Saltillo, found their way through the intervening deserts and wildernesses to this place, and flattering **the** Indians **whom** they **found** here with the promise of protection from **their** enemies, **secured their** co-operation and founded this **town.**

Soon after this, as we learn from **the** "Notes for the History of** Coahuila and **Texas," written by a Mexican gen**tleman, who was probably **himself a** Jesuit, **some** Jesuit **priests,** prompted by zeal **"for the** extension of Our Holy **Mother** Church" and the "greater glory of God and His Most Holy Mother," came up from Guadalajara, and established many missions in these states. In this town was one of their most **important missions.** He speaks with enthusiasm of the self-**denial and holiness of** these "eminent gentlemen."

He says: "The early religious teachers, possessed of the most ardent faith, **and** courage which amounted to heroism, crossed unknown deserts and immense forests, leaning on rough staffs which they improvised from shrubs, **or** the branches ,**of trees,** barefooted and covered with coarse sackcloth; resting in their pilgrimages, now in the caves of the forests, now in ravines or swamps, reclining sometimes their fatigued heads on the hard rocks. The gentleness and resignation of those **eminent gentlemen,** in facing all kinds of dangers, suf-

ferings and hardships, overcame the ferocious instincts of
the savages.   Men clothed with so many virtues, without
fondness for riches or the luxuries of life, filled the barbari-
ans with astonishment and admiration; they drew near the
priest with respect and veneration.   Not understanding at
first the dialect of the Indians, they spoke to them by means
of signs, showing them the crucifix and the heavens, and indicating to them that their mission was one of peace and
charity.   When they had succeeded in acquiring some knowledge of the native language, they began by making them
understand the existence of an infinite Being, the supreme
Author of the creation, and also the immortality of the soul.
They preached to them against their superstitions, their wandering life, the shedding of human blood, and their immoral
customs.   The religious teachers who came to Coahuila and
Texas treated the aborigines with a tenderness truly paternal,
defending them from the molestations and oppressions of
their conquerors."

So well did these savages "advance in the knowledge of
the catechism" that it sometimes happened that "within a
few days the priests had as many as five hundred Christians
in their company." They received the Holy Father with em-
braces and kisses and hung on his neck; they sacrificed their
lives to defend him—that is, if we are to take this historian's
word for the statement.

I take pleasure in laying before you this description of the
character and doings of these "illustrious gentlemen." The
Lord forbid that I should do them an injustice; judging from
their history in all nations they have enough to answer for
before God and man if the truth is told in its mildest form.

Here in Mexico they taught the doctrines of their order.
just as they teach them everywhere they are tolerated: That
it is right to steal, to lie, to murder, to commit any crime
whatsoever if only the interests of the Church are to be
served by it; they introduced the inquisition; they subverted
the liberties of the people; they established monasteries and
convents all over the land; yea they went out like the very
spirits of the devil to deceive the nation.

When Mexico awoke to the terrible state of things she investigated their deeds and their influence, and her Congress, the Roman Catholic Congress of a Roman Catholic nation, you will remember, for the purity of the people and the protection of the family, abolished monasteries and convents and banished their founders from the realm.

"Why," said to me one day a gentleman who had lived here a good many years, "the passages run like a cobweb under this town. Formerly there were openings to the top of the ground for ventilation; around these openings were little chimneys. But since the passages are no longer used these have been thrown down and the holes are closed up. I went down into a passage one day. They are only wide enough for one man to walk in them, but every few yards there is a niche large enough for a man to stand in, so that if two of the Fathers met they could pass. They are full of human bones now."

"Bones!" I exclaimed, "Whose bones?"

"Oh! bones of Indians," so accustomed to the horrible thoughts he was suggesting that they made little impression on him. "You see if they did not believe what the Holy Fathers taught them they just murdered them and put them down there." One of these passages runs under the room adjoining the one in which I write this afternoon.

We read in the history which I have mentioned that the "Jesuit College" in this town "acquired rich possessions." It is a way they have, these Roman Catholic institutions! Notwithstanding the sublime meekness, resignation and self-denial of their founders, notwithstanding, as in this case, the half-clothed and unhoused savages by whom they were surrounded, they seldom or never failed to become very rich in a short time.

This monastery, the College, as it is called, was confiscated to the state with all the other church property when the monasteries and convents were abolished. When I first visited it it was used as a tenement-house. On the right-hand side of the hall as we entered was an arched recess large enough for three men to stand in it. It had recently been discovered in the smoothly-plastered and whitewashed wall. It was opened and the bones were taken out. A similar recess has been discovered on the other side of the hall; they had taken out the bricks, revealing the arch, but it still held its secret. How many such secrets does the house hold! We went to the door of the underground chambers from which the passages start which run under all the town, but it was locked. There were a great many bones in them, they told me. Even on the surface of the ground there were bones everywhere in the courts of that awful house.

Whatever mistakes may be made as to the history of this monastery, the Jesuit Fathers who occupied it stand condemned in the court of posterity. People went to the College to confess and were never seen nor heard of again. Wild, fearful stories of death by fire and hanging and starvation are commonly told and believed. O these holy Catholic priests!

CHAPEL OF THE HOLY WOOD.   Page 23

CHAPTER III.

AT THE CHAPEL OF THE HOLY WOOD.

IT was five o'clock in the afternoon of that July day, as well as one could judge by the clock on the Jesuit College, which, however, was not very reliable since, as the people declared, it "ran with the wind." The *siesta* (an afternoon nap) was over and the people were again passing to and fro in the streets. From one of the houses on the Orilla del Agua a woman and a girl came out, and drawing their faded blue cotton scarfs closely over their heads and shoulders, went off down the street.

The former wore a scanty, faded calico dress and very shabby shoes; the latter a factory dress, also faded and scanty and much worn, and shoes that rivaled the woman's in shabbiness. Reaching the shade they threw back their scarfs from their heads. The features, complexion and straight black hair of the woman marked her as a pure Indian. She was deeply scarred with smallpox, and one of her eyes had been put out by that dreadful disease. Her hair was arranged in two short, scanty braids which were tied together at the ends. Her face wore a complaining, ill-natured expression that was evidently habitual to it.

The girl's features were more European in their type, indicating the presence of some Spanish blood; it had come to her from her mother's side of the house. Her complexion was lighter than that of the woman; her hair was straight, black and abundant; she wore it parted in the middle, combed smoothly back and arranged in two long braids which hung down her back. Her mouth was somewhat large and her teeth white and regular. Her eyes were large, dark and bright, with an expression which indicated intelligence and vivacity; but sometimes they looked up at one with the hopeless, unexpressed appeal of a dumb animal. She was not

2

pretty nor handsome; yet a close observer would probably reflect that "some of these common people might amount to something if they only had a chance."

Her name was Mercedes Gonzales y Robledo. But you are not to suppose from this imposing array of names that this girl in the faded cotton dress was a descendant of a noble family, a princess in disguise, as it were. Mercedes was the name her parents gave her; it meant "mercies;" but it was bestowed on her with no thought of its sweet, quaint, suggestive meaning, but merely because it was a common and convenient name. Gonzales was the name of her father, and Robledo was her mother's maiden name.

For example, my dear Miss Mary, your father is Mr. Jones, and your mother was before her marriage, Miss Smith; then if you lived in a Spanish-speaking country you would be "Miss Mary Jones and Smith," or the Señorita (Sanyoreta) Maria Jones y Smith. Then if you should marry a Mr. Tompson, you would drop your mother's name but retain your father's, so that you would be "the Señora (Sanyora) Maria Jones de (of) Tompson." You would very rarely be called by your husband's name; only a dignified acquaintance would allude to you as "the Señora de Tompson." "Give up my father's name for a husband's! Never!" exclaimed a Mexican young lady, looking up at me with her great brown eyes full of astonishment.

Titles are much less used in Spanish-speaking countries than in the United States. You would not be Miss Jones before your marriage, neither would you be Mrs. Tompson nor the Señora Jones de Tompson after your marriage except in writing and in the conversation of mere acquaintances; from your cradle to your grave all your friends, including gentlemen and tiny children would call you, notwithstanding your connection with Mr. Tompson—just Mary Jones.

If Mr. Tompson should die before you, you would drop his name entirely except in legal documents and other papers of importance, and for purposes of explanation, when you would be mentioned as "Mary Jones, widow of Don Tomas Tompson." Your servants would call you "Doña (Donya) Maria," or "the Señora." You, in turn would give the title, Doña, to an elderly serving woman whom you wished to treat with respect. The titles Don and Doña are used only before given names; they do not, at present, as they did formerly in Spain, indicate high rank.

Your father, who in the United States is known as Mr. John Jones would be, supposing that his mother's maiden name was Brown, Señor Juan Jones y Brown; but for convenience he would generally be called Señor Jones, or Don Juan.

The name of the woman was Maria de los Angeles (Mary of the Angels) de Guerrero de Urriegas. The *de* preceding her maiden name seems to be more a matter of euphony than anything else. The baptismal name, "Maria de los Angeles," was in its origin an overflow of religious feeling, after the Catholic fashion.

In Mexico among the most common baptismal names are Jesus, Trinidad (Trinity), Maria de Jesus, Alta Gracia (High Grace), Jose-Maria (Joseph-Mary)

As they went along this favorite of the angels began to talk to the girl in her usual fault-finding tone:

"Come along! Why don't you walk faster? We shan't get there before dark. I reckon you want to pretend that you are tired from that walk on Sunday. That was nothing for a girl of fourteen. I am thirty years older than that, and I didn't mind it."

Mercedes thought that she was a great deal stronger, too, and that she had not worked so hard since, but she said nothing, for she had learned by long experience that such replies as she could make did no good. Maria de los Angeles was not the only woman who ever forgot or wilfully disregarded the fact that people are not necessarily strong because they are young.

"O, you are the very skin of Judas!" she went on growing bitterer. "You don't care anything for religion, nor for anything good. Think of a girl of your age who has never

confessed! You will never see purgatory! And your father
upholds you in all this wickedness; he'll get his reward.
How do you suppose I feel to think you didn't want to go
with me to the chapel to pray for my poor Mordicai?" and
her voice died away in a whimper.

"I didn't say anything about not wanting to go, aunt,"
replied Mercedes, trying very hard to avoid a sullen tone.

"But I know you didn't. You never want to do anything
that is right. You only want to devour those worthless
books your father allows you to read. The Fathers say it is
best for such as you not to know how to read, and I believe
it."

"Of course you do since the priests say it," thought the
girl, trying to repress a smile, in which, however, there was
more of bitterness than of merriment   These taunting allu-
sions to her books, accompanied, as they often were, by the
threat to burn them, were the hardest to bear of· all the unkind reproaches of her aunt. The books were Don Quixote,
the History of Mexico, and a Missal. These were the only
books she had ever had opportunity to read except Father
Ripalda's Catechism. The humorous and the poetical passages in Don Quixote were always a new delight to her; and
its fair ladies and gallant gentlemen were to her as familiar
friends. Her reading of the history of her country had developed in her the intensest patriotism; it had prepared her
to act the part of Joan of Arc if the necessities of her native
land should ever call for such a heroine.

From these books she had learned her letters, with a little,
a very little assistance from her father. Some children learn
the alphabet from the Bible, standing by a mother's knee
and feeling the caressing touch of a mother's hand on their
heads, and seeing the mother-love in the face above them,
and the saint's anxiety that they may gain the true wisdom,—
learn them beginning over there where the sweet, wonderful
story begins: "Now when Jesus was born in Bethlehem of
Judea, in the days of Herod the king;" and it is not strange
that in the minds of such, through all the hot and dusty and

weary days of life-travel, that story, intertwined with the weird fancies and indistinct recollections of childhood, rings now near now far off, sweeter than any anthem of angels, sweeter even than the lullaby of a mother.

This girl had no such recollections. If her mother had lived she would have taught her nothing of the Bible, of course, for she was a Roman Catholic, and hence, knew nothing of it. But she had died when her daughter was only four or five years old. Mercedes always clung to the belief that she remembered her. Some homely, loving face had bent over her in that dim, early time, some voice had spoken tenderly to her; the face and voice must have been her mother's.

Since that time she had known nothing of tenderness. Her home had been with her father's step-sister, Maria de los Angeles. In her early childhood, when she was permitted to put down the heavy baby she must bring water, carrying it in a heavy jar on her head. As she grew older nearly all the work of the household fell on her; the cooking of the *frejoles* (dried beans), the grinding of the corn for *tortillas*, the washing of the clothing of the family in the stream I have mentioned.

Notwithstanding all her efforts to please her elders, she could not remember ever having received a word of commendation from them. It probably seemed to them that it would make her indolent or presumptuous to be praised. Her aunt was not wilfully unkind, but she was a coarse, stupid, indolent woman, and she was placed in a position which would be dangerous for many people with better principles than her own—with almost absolute power over a helpless fellow-creature whom she did not love and could not understand. The girl's incomprehensible taste for reading and her lack of devotion for the Church made her aunt half believe sometimes, in the depths of her superstitious soul, that she must be bewitched. Her father treated her with comparative kindness. She knew it was through fear of him that her aunt dared not destroy the books. Once he said to

her suddenly: "You look like your mother, child," and then
turned away as if he were ashamed of betraying so much
emotion.   Another time he noticed her with the missal in her
hand and he said, "Take good care of it; it was your mother's." These two sayings of her father's she cherished, going
over them often as she lay on her pallet while the various
other occupants of the room were snoring.   She generally
concluded by saying to herself, "I believe he does love me!"
And in return for this, having no one else to love, she loved
him with an almost worshipping devotion; but she dared not
express it.   She saw other parents of her own class caress
their children, plan for them and try to educate them, and
she wondered often what were the feelings of such children.
She was very different from them, her aunt said, and Mercedes believed it because her aunt said it, and because the
circumstances seemed to prove it.

The girls of her own age sometimes invited her to go with
them to the *plaza* (small park) to promenade and listen to the
music of the band on the evenings of national and church
celebrations.   But though she longed with all the ardor of
youth to go, she seldom went.   She had no holiday attire as
they had; they would be ashamed of her.

She felt this difference of dress between herself and others
with an inexpressible shrinking.   She often wondered if she
would look as other girls did if she were dressed as they, in
dainty, stiffly starched print dresses and black shawls.   Her
imagination even soared higher than that, and she dared to
fancy herself clad in the lovely, soft garments and silken
scarfs in which she had seen the daughters of the rich, talking and laughing in low musical voices that sounded like the
chirping of birds, as they passed in elegant carriages.   And
she wondered vaguely if she were so clad if there would still
be about her any mark or deformity of face or figure that
would publish the fact that she was a peculiar creature, separated from all the common sympathies of humanity.

Thus separated by unkindness or carelessness from those
to whom she might naturally have looked for affection, and

from others by her own sensitiveness, she was in danger of becoming morbid. But fortunately there was in her composition some salt which preserved her from that. She was naturally of a gay disposition, and she had a keen sense of humor. No less keen was her appreciation of all the varied forms of nature about her; the peaceful murmur of the water, the songs of the birds, the beauty of the flowers, the picturesqueness of the rugged mountains, the rosy or golden or violet air which draped them of mornings and evenings, the clouds of sunrise and sunset. But of all her pleasures that half-stolen one of reading Don Quixote was the greatest.

By this time they had left behind them the narrow, dirty streets and unsightly houses of the outskirts of the town and were ascending the hill. These mountains among which the town is nestled are outlying ranges of the Sierra Madre (the Mother Range), a continuation of the Rocky Mountains. Their harsh outlines are softened by no vegetation except a few dwarfed shrubs. The great porous rocks among which their path lay stood up in all their bare picturesqueness.

They reached the top of this hill and walked perhaps a quarter of a mile on its almost level summit to a small, circular and very steep hill which arose abruptly from this elevated plane. On the top of this latter hill lay an immense circular rock, extending out on all sides beyond the apex of the hill. Perched on this rock was one of the "high places" of the Roman Church, a tiny white chapel. It could be seen for miles around, its outlines standing out sharply against the blue sky.

Slowly and laboriously they ascended the hill, panting and stopping now and then to rest. Sometimes Mercedes turned her head for a moment when her aunt was not looking to catch a glimpse of the town nestled among the green trees, of the valley and the encircling mountains.

When they reached the foot of the rock they passed around to the back of it and ascended the steps which had been made through it to the top. This rock, and, in fact, all these rocks and hills would be a worthy study for a geologist.

The last four or five steps Maria de los Angeles ascended on her knees; in the same manner she crossed the space between the top of the stairway and the door of the chapel, Mercedes spreading on the rock in front of her the two narrow pieces of coarse matting which she had brought along for that purpose. With difficulty she entered the chapel and crawled to a large wooden cross which stood in the floor. She remained kneeling in front of it weeping and counting her beads and whispering her prayers.

The girl made the circuit of the tiny room kneeling mechanically for a moment in front of the cross and the image of the Virgin, making the signs of the cross on forehead, lips and breast. She glanced as she passed at the coarse and ludicrous paintings given by those who had been healed of various infirmities through the virtue which dwelt in the Holy Wood, the cross before which her aunt knelt.

Most of these pictures represent the devotees crawling up the hill toward the chapel with lighted candles in their hands; in some of them the devotee is kneeling before the cross. One of the inscriptions reads thus:

"Higinio Garcia having suffered nine months from a disease perhaps unknown without having a moment of rest neither by day nor by night with sincerity of heart implored the holy Wood for mercy which was found for at the present if he is not well he is very much relieved and he dedicates this to it (the Holy Wood) for the justification of so great a myracle."

Another: "Jose-Maria Gerarda Gomes, i was seized by a disease i imboqued the holy wood and i was healed and for the greater beneration we dedicate this. Zenobio Zequndino."

Another: "the ninth day of the month of August of 1888 a horse thru the girl Benita Rodriguez breaking one of her arms. I the mother of this girl full of grief imboqued the holy wood asking for the relief of mi daughter and so it was in seven months she was well and sound and this made me with all my heart offur the present picture. Gabriela Rodrigues."

SALTA. (Page 25.)

The devotee before the cross had come to ask a similar mercy. Her son, Mordicai, had fallen from the scaffolding of a building, and though like any well instructed son of a Catholic mother he had cried to the Blessed Virgin for help she was not so propitious as in another case of the kind of which I have heard. In that, in answer to the man's cry of distress the Virgin held him in mid air till his companions brought a ladder on which he descended. This time perhaps the goddess was asleep or occupied with other matters; certain it is that Mordicai came down to the ground in a way which demonstrated admirably the geometrical principle that "a straight line is the shortest distance between two points;" and the result was a broken leg.

This cross has a history. The story goes that the priests when they came to establish a mission here, celebrated the first mass on this rock. Some time after that the Holy Fathers displayed to the people one morning a wooden cross about four feet in height which, they said, had been brought down from heaven the night before and placed on this rock. It was found to possess miraculous properties. The original cross decayed in a few years, but one night it disappeared miraculously and a new cross, also from heaven, took its place. This has happened several times in the course of the three centuries which have elapsed. A few years ago this tiny chapel was built to protect it. It has become celebrated, and the afflicted come now long distances to be healed by it. There it stands, a plain wooden cross, painted green, "at the orders of your Worship," as a Mexican would assure you, ready to heal you or yours of any infirmity.

Mercedes sat down on the low bench in the front of the chapel and looked at it all for a while, but listlessly, for she had seen it all before. Then she went out and sat on the low adobe wall which was built along the edge of the rock. The scene was oriental, as travelers have told us. There lay the town below her with its churches and low, flat-roofed houses, looking like Jerusalem after its glory had departed. One stately palm-tree standing alone waved its feathery foliage in the air.

She swept her eyes around the purple encircling mountains and over the town. They rested on the Jesuit College. The sight of that building always started a train of thoughts which tramped through her mind confused and troubled, like dark specters. The stories she had heard of it had had their natural effect on her lively imagination, on her susceptible spirit, nourished as it had been in gross superstition, brought up, as it were, on histories of witches, and restless spirits escaped from purgatory.

She had heard both sides of the story which I have told you of the lives and teachings of the priests, and both from persons whom all the loyalty of her nature compelled her to believe; the one side from her aunt and from the priests in the churches, the other from her father. She knew that what her father said about the wickedness of the Church and of the priesthood was true, but, on the other hand, her mother had been a devout Catholic.

Would that I could give you some idea of the confusion of mind of a thoughtful person who has been thus brought up! All her life long this girl had gone groping in the darkness, seeking some one to lead her by the hand. Was it right, really right, to lie and steal when the interests of the Church could be served by so doing? Was it right to do evil that good might come? Were miracles really wrought by these wooden crosses and wooden images? Could they really, in some mysterious way, hear prayers? Was it the real body and blood of the Lord which the priests and people drank and ate in the churches? What kind of Being was this Lord whom they ate, and for whom they named their children? And the Father, God, of whom they spoke so familiarly, was he the Great Spirit who created all things? Under what obligations was she to believe all these things? She was not responsible for the existence of such doctrines; she had found them in the world when she arrived here. Why must she have a religion at all? Was there, after all, any God, even an indefinite Being sitting away off in the heavens and taking no interest in the affairs of this world? Such a thought, if thought it might be called, it was so indistinct, frightened her; she sprang up and threw out her hands as if to fling it from her.

In restless haste and without thinking of what she was doing she unbraided her long, dark hair and threw it back over her shoulders. As she stood there with the wind plucking at her hair, her hands clasped tightly, her lips compressed, her shining eyes looking into space, her mind full of doubts and questionings suggested by the false teachings of others, her spirit palpitating with noble restlessness and longing for something higher and better, she might well represent the spirit of her country, this young republic that has suffered so much from the selfishness and wickedness of others, this nation which we behold struggling out of the darkness of Roman Catholicism, stumbling and falling and rising again in the road toward the realization of the high calling of nations.

Do not say rashly that common sense should have taught this girl what was right. Try to imagine how much you would have known if you had inherited Romanism from one side of your ancestry and paganism from the other. Remember how your errors in religious belief cling to you though you live in a land of which it might almost be said that the knowledge of the Lord covers it as the waters cover the sea.

Mercedes had never seen a Bible. Her case was not peculiar in that respect. There are comparatively few persons in Mexico who have ever seen it or have any distinct idea of the contents of such a book.

Read this extract which I cut from a religious paper, a part of a report of a speech made in a great religious convention in the United States by an American gentleman whose home is in Mexico:

"He alluded to the fact that it had been said by one preacher that our work in Mexico amounted simply to a proselyting from one phase of Christianity to another.

Then he proceeded to give us an idea of how much Christianity these Mexican Catholics have.

He said he went into a bookstore where a vast business is done. Of course the booksellers are conversant with books, necessarily acquainted with every book that is read by the people, for the books must be bought before they are read. He asked for a New Testament; none of the clerks knew what it was. The proprietor came up, and he did not know, but after searching around, brought an old dingy copy of the Old Testament in Spanish and seemed to think, as it was called 'old' that it was an old edition of the book that was asked for. The gentleman then took out of his satchel a New Testament in Spanish and showed it to the bookseller, who exclaimed, 'This is the New Testament! Well, I have had calls for it, but I never knew what it was before.' Of course he had had very few calls for it, for he would have ascertained what it was if his trade had demanded it.

At another time he went into another bookstore and asked for a New Testament. Failing to find it, he engaged in conversation with the bookseller in regard to the matter. The latter, resting his arm on the counter, leaned over and looked very earnestly into his face and said with much interest: 'Who is the author of this New Testament?'"

Others have had similar experiences. After reading such things as this can any one believe that Mexico is a Christian land?

Mercedes, however, had once read an extract from that mysterious book. A woman with a plain, kind face stopped her one day in the street and requested her to direct her to a certain house. When she thanked her for the information she gave her an advertisement card on which was a bright picture, telling her that the reading on the reverse side was an extract from the Sacred Scriptures.

It was that marvelous piece of word painting, the description of the Last Judgment, given in the twenty-fifth chapter of Matthew. So deep was the impression made on her mind that for weeks she seldom fell asleep without dreaming that she stood before the throne waiting with terror to hear her sentence. And she was always sent to the left-hand side.

Her imagination supplied all the details, the joy of the blessed, the anguish and despair of the accursed. It was a terrible strain on her childish mind. It was not in her power to do any of those good works by which, as it seemed to her, Heaven was to be bought. Besides, she had a depressing feeling that nothing she could do would be acceptable to God. As the months went by these impressions faded away; for more than a year they had troubled her only occasionally, but when they returned they always brought with them a vague feeling of unrest and of helpless terror.

Her contemptuous smile at her aunt's confidence in the priests had brought back this feeling of unrest. "It was very wicked of her to entertain a disrespectful thought of her religious teachers," she reflected. "Even if they did do things that in others would be great sins, as her father said they did, it was not wrong for them to do so; they were not subject to the rules that should govern other men; why, they had power like gods, like God himself, to forgive sins; they opened and no man shut, and shut and no man opened, the gates of the kingdom of heaven."

"Most Holy Mary," she said softly as she sat down again on the wall, "help me to think right thoughts!"

Many a time and more frequently as she grew older, life had seemed to be "closing in," contracting like the pitiless walls of a chamber of the Inquisition. That impression was very distinct this afternoon. Oh! how she longed to pass out beyond the amphitheater of hills and see the world which lay beyond. How she longed for some of the tender courtesies of life, for knowledge, for love! But there was no hope of anything better, she knew. There was no hope for her in the "Blessed Virgin," nor in God, nor in his Son, nor in any of the saints. The walls of the prison were coming nearer, the air was growing thick and foul; before her hopeless eyes surely, visibly, life was "closing in."

Just then she heard footsteps, and turning her head she saw a lady and a girl of about her own age, and a boy a year or two younger. They were all well dressed in the Parisian style; for the wealthy people in Mexico get their fashions directly from Paris. The lady wore a black dress of some soft, light material, and a thin black scarf, the daughter a light lawn dress and a silken scarf.

The former was a handsome matron of about forty. She had a clear brunette complexion, dark brown hair with a decided inclination to wave, and eyes of the same color. Her self-possession, her gait, the tone of her voice, the very set of her head marked her as a woman of wealth and aristocracy.

The girl's face reminded one of Raphael's St. Cecilia. There were the same curved outlines, the tender mouth, sweet alike in seriousness and in mirth, the innocent eyes. She had a clear, rich complexion like her mother's, and hair only a little lighter. It was a beautiful, girlish face, and better than that one felt at once that it indicated sincerity and good nature. The boy too was a handsome fellow with a strong resemblance to his mother.

They were almost out of breath with their climb to the top of the rock. They entered the church, knelt and crossed themselves before the various images, then the lady and her daughter sat down on one of the benches inside to rest. If they spoke at all it was in whispers because of the sanctity of the place and in order not to disturb the worshipper who was still diligently counting her beads.

The boy came out and after saying "Good evening" politely to Mercedes began to amuse himself by throwing gravels into the valley. Presently the lady and her daughter came out and stood looking at the view before them.

"Mama," said the girl in a low, musical voice which suited well the face and the unconscious air of high breeding which characterized every movement, "it is just eleven days now until we go to the City of Mexico."

"Yes, dear," replied the mother.

"Is the view from the hill of Guadalupe as pretty as this, mama?" went on the girl.

"O, yes, daughter," she replied, smiling, "this is nothing in comparison with that. I suppose there are few views in

Europe which surpass that. And we shall worship in the chapel of Guadalupe. You climb the hill to it by steps, too."

"Dear me! I hope it isn't as tiresome a climb as this," replied the girl with a low, rippling laugh.

"You should not speak of getting tired in the service of God, Magdalena," replied her mother in a gently reproving tone. "There is no merit in it when there is no physical suffering. Chapels and shrines are built on high, steep hills that we may mortify the flesh in reaching them and so be prepared to receive the grace of God. Come, it is time to go home," she added. "Come, Salvador (Savior), let's go," and they crossed the space in front of the chapel, saying "adios" pleasantly to Mercedes as they passed, and descended the steps on the side of the rock opposite to that where they had ascended. Mercedes watched them until they had disappeared, the boy and girl hand in hand merrily jumping down the steps.

A vision of loveliness they seemed to her; to see them was to have a glimpse of the world that she longed for. She had seen them before at a distance. The lady, she knew, was the wife of her father's landlord, the owner of the great *hacienda* on which all her kindred except her father had worn out their lives in the hopeless effort to pay ever-increasing debts.

"They do not seem to be such dreadful people," she thought; "they spoke very kindly to me. They have always been rich and happy. Of course they can't know how it seems to be any other way. I wonder how life seems to them."

Just then her aunt came out of the church, and Mercedes rolled up the matting and with aching limbs and an aching heart followed her down the steps.

CHAPTER IV.

A PEON.

MERCEDES' father was a *peon*. A peon is a man who owes a debt and is under obligations to work for his creditor till the debt is paid While the peon is actually employed the master furnishes him an insufficient quantity of corn for bread; he allows him also a miserable house free of rent.

In return the peon must work for his creditor, and for him alone until the debt is paid. The comity of the system forbids one master's employing the peons of another. The paying of the debt is made impossible by the prices at which his food and the other necessities of life are furnished him, for he must buy everything from his master, with whom an account was opened when he became his debtor. If the price of a peck of corn is 20 cents it is sold to the peon for 40 cents; cloth that would be sold to other men for 25 cents a yard is sold to the peon for 50 cents—that is to say that in that, as in all other cases, it is entered on the book that he has become a debtor to those amounts. This being the case it is clear that he can never discharge his debts.

The debts of the fathers do not extend to the children during their lives, nor are they inherited by them when the parents die. But the children become peons by force of circumstances. They must live; to live they must work; even if another master would employ them they would be in no better condition in his service; it is better to stay together; as soon as they are large enough for their work to be worth anything they open accounts with their father's master, thus becoming peons. If the master thinks the children are slow about entering into the father's or mother's state of servitude he has some very simple means of hastening that desirable consummation: he has only to oppress the parents more and the children must, for the subsistence of the family, open accounts with him. When an hacienda is sold, the peons, by means of their debts, are sold with it. When the children inherit the land they inherit the peons with it.

The great haciendas in this country are said to be about equally divided between Mexicans and foreigners. The latter are Spaniards, Frenchmen and Italians. These spend nearly if not all their time in Europe; and the Mexican owners of haciendas spend the greater part of the time either in Europe or in the cities. The administration of affairs is left to superintendents. If the *Senor* receives his regular supplies of money he probably gives himself little concern about the policy employed on his estate. If, by chance, a humane man should be employed as superintendent, and by virtue of his justice it should become possible for the peons to pay their debts they would leave the hacienda when these were paid, or go on working for reasonable wages; in either case there would be less money to send to the Senor; he would know at once that something was wrong in the administration of his affairs; he might not know exactly what it was, but, in short, as a matter of course, he would employ another superintendent.

There is, therefore, for the peon, no escape from slavery but through the gateway of death. In some respects it is worse than the slavery of the negroes in our southern States before the war. The slaveholder provided sufficient and wholesome food, and comfortable lodgings and clothing for his negroes on the same principle that prompted him to care for his horses and cattle. The master of peons provides for his slaves only while they are at work, and very poorly then; if they die he can get others for nothing. The negroes could be beaten for real or fancied delinquencies; the peons are not whipped, but with them other ways of punishment are used that are, perhaps, worse. When the superintendent thinks a peon is guilty of an offense he complains of him to the court, representing the case as he thinks proper. The superintend-

3

ent is generally on good terms with the judge, and the result is the peon is put into prison. There, of course, the oppressed man is making nothing; his wife and children, if they are unable to work, are suffering; if they can work they are entering deeper and deeper into the servitude of his master.

The system of peonage was abolished by the constitution of 1857, the constitution published by Benito Juarez. The theory was changed, in practice it is the same, the difference being that the peon cannot now be legally imprisoned for debt. It is, however, sometimes done illegally. The reason the system remains the same is this: Those who were then peons could never pay their debts for reasons which I have explained, and their children also became peons for reasons also explained. For some reason, however, perhaps owing to some little relenting on the part of some of the masters, there are not quite so many peons as formerly. Then, nearly all the humble class in some of the States were peons; now there are some even in the peon States who maintain a struggling, uncertain independence. In some of the States peonage does not exist.

There is one strip of country in Mexico in which the system has been considerably mitigated since the publication of the Constitution forbidding the arrest and imprisonment of the debtor. In the parts of the northern States which border on the United States the peon, knowing that he has over and over worked out his debts, flees from his master to Texas or to the other bordering States; or his sons escape to the United States and, finding employment, make money and pay the father's debts. It is said that this is the history of nearly all the Mexicans in Texas, and in the other States of the United States which border on the Rio Grande. They have escaped from centuries of bitter and hopeless slavery; will not this fact give you a tenderer feeling for the men and women whom you call by the ignominious name of "greasers"?

Some of these escaped peons have returned to the frontier of Mexico and have succeeded in buying small tracts of land, and by industry and economy have become prosperous.

These favorable conditions exist nowhere else but in the frontier. **The** peons of the haciendas farther toward the south—whither shall **they flee?** Ground down by ignorance, they know nothing **of the liberty** offered in the United States, **and if** they knew of **it their** poverty would not permit them to avail themselves **of it.** There is absolutely no alternative for them; they **and their wives** and their sons and their daughters after **them must** live and die **in** this cruel **slavery,** in ignorance and superstition and **poverty.**

The class of peons is very large, compared **with the** ruling class. The haciendas are immense, some of **them** being as **large** as the smaller of **the** New England States. On each hacienda there are hundreds or thousands of the peons, according to the extent **of** the estate **or** the ability of the owner to cultivate it. **There** is a **surplus of** field labor in **nearly** every State in the Republic.

On all public questions the laborers are kept in ignorance **and are influenced** to act as the Señor or superintendent **desires. In the** popular **elections,** for instance, the men all vote blindly as "mi Señor" directs them **to do.**

The remedies proposed for this evil are the **development** of other industries besides agriculture, such as mining **and** manufacturing—industries which **will give steady** employment to men **and** just remuneration, thus enabling them to maintain their **liberty and** perhaps buy that of some of their kindred. The establishment and support of common schools will also do **much to accomplish** their emancipation; but compulsory attendance on **the** schools **will** be necessary.

From that very interesting book, "Mexico: Our Neighbor," I learn that "in several of **the** more progressive States attendance at the schools is required and enforced by law; **and in** many localities where the parents of school children are obliged to labor in the fields or elsewhere during school hours nurseries are maintained with suitable attendants to care for the children under school age. The most encouraging information regarding **the** schools was the admitted fact that the Indian **children are** tractable and studious, learn rapidly, and soon become greatly interested in their studies, exhibiting quite phenomenal powers for memorizing and retaining, and fair capacity for the mastery and application of principles."

Of course, the breaking up of these great haciendas into smaller estates, which will inevitably result from the laws of inheritance in force in this country, will have a tendency to mitigate the evils of peonage. Real estate is here divided among all the children, instead of being given to the eldest son, as is the case in England. The children of these rich land owners, are, in many cases, rendered incapable or averse to attending to business by the idle and luxurious habits in which they are reared; therefore they, more easily than their fathers, sell parts of their estates. The result will be that as the poor man is enabled by mining and manufacturing operations to make and save a small sum of money he will invest it in land and become the independent owner of a farm. But this is at present little, if anything, more than a dream of the future.

Atanacio Gonzales had a fine mind, and with his energy and perseverance might, if he had been educated, have stood abreast of the most intelligent men of his country. But the policy of the Catholic Church in Mexico, as in all other countries in which she has had temporal power, has always been to keep the people in ignorance in order to keep them in subjection to herself. Through her influence there were no government schools in Mexico till after the publication of the present Constitution. It is said that before that there were few Catholic schools; but after the establishment of the government schools the Church also increased the number of her schools, and they were improved, she opining that if the people were to be educated it would be better for her interests for them to be educated in her schools. It is estimated that at present about sixty-six per cent. of the people cannot read.

In his youth Atanacio had been a Catholic: but in the army of Juarez he had imbibed liberal sentiments, and they had been strengthened by his **observations in** later years of the superstitions and absurdities **of Romanism,** and the corruptions **of** the priesthood. **His daughter** had been accustomed from her earliest years **to** hear him reiterate these facts **and** hurl maledictions against the Church. If he had said such things **in** a calm and moderate way they would have had far more effect on **her,** but the impressions she received against the Church were accompanied by an **indistinct** idea that her father himself, **the** being **she** most **loved,** was not quite as good **as** he **ought** to be, **and** that he **was** not, therefore, **a very good** judge of religion.

The consideration of the abuses of the Church, the disappointments **of** his life, and the long and hopeless struggle with poverty which he as **a peon** had had to wage, had hardened and embittered him. **Yet he** was **a** favorite with his companions; he had **always been** since the days when in Juarez' war camp he **read to his fellow** soldiers this volume of Don Quixote, **on which his** daughter now feasted, pronouncing **many** of **the words in a** way that would **have** been excruciating to the Spanish Academy.

CHAPTER V.

AN EVENING IN MERCEDES' HOME.

WHEN Maria de los Angeles and her niece reached home it was dark. They passed through the wide front entrance, crossed a dirty court and entered a long, white-washed room. It had no windows, the ventilation being effected through the door and a hole a little larger than that allowed for a stove-pipe near the top of the room, though, to tell the truth, this was generally closed with rags. Overhead instead of a ceiling were seen the bare, round beams. The canes which were laid over these to support the earth with which the house was covered were in such a state of decay that when the long-delayed rains should come there would be many a leak and it would be difficult to find dry spots on the floor for the pallets on which they slept.

A scaffold with a very thin mattress on which lay the afflicted lad, a high table with very slender legs, three high chairs, two of which had lost their backs, a chest for clothing elevated on a small frame like a table to keep it off the earthen floor and a low bench sitting against the wall, constituted ordinarily the furniture of the room. But in this time of affliction Maria de los Angeles had erected an altar at the end of the room opposite that in which lay the sick boy that he might have before his eyes continually the crucifix and the images of the saints with which it was plentifully furnished. It consisted of a scaffold or table about three feet high, four long and two wide, covered with soiled and ragged white cotton cloth. It was adorned with colored paper cut into fancy shapes, and with all the toys, crucifixes and images of saints which the devoted maternal relative of Mordicai could borrow from her neighbors, and rent from the priest. Before the image of Joseph,[1] the husband of the Virgin Mary, were burning wax candles.

A neighbor had been engaged to wait on the sick boy during Maria's absence. A great catastrophe had scarcely been averted. As Maria, after ascertaining the state of Mordicai's feelings, and learning that no miracle of healing had been wrought while she had been absent, sat down Turkish fashion on the floor to rest while Mercedes prepared the supper, Cipriana proceeded to relate the distressing narrative, Maria meantime showing her appreciation by plentiful exclamations of "Maria purisima," and other invocations which I prefer not to repeat. In her excitement the good natured Cipriana indulged in the high tones, violent gesticulation and strong, inverted constructions so common among ignorant people in southern countries.

"Awhile ago I went home to put on the coffee and frejoles for supper. I left Manuel asleep on the floor; Jubencia I left awake. There on the table was the candle lighted; the candle left I right there on the table lighted. Jubencia took the candle, lighted as it was, and set it on that box. There on that very box put Jubencia the candle lighted. The dress that you bought from Doña Antonia was hanging above the box just as you left it. It caught fire and burned up almost entirely, and not only that dress, but a dress of Jubencia's and other things. I was so sorry for the loss of that dress of Doña Antonia's, as you had wanted to keep it as a reminder of her; yes, the loss of the dress, how sorry I was of it! And the children, *Maria santisima!* they might have been burned alive! Alive might have been burned the children! But Jubencia screamed and my brother ran in and put out the fire."

---

[1] *Note.*—Monseñor Guame, Apostolic Legate and Doctor of Theology in Paris, France, says: "To this act of divine policy (the declaration of the Immaculate Conception of the Virgin Mary) Pius **IX.** adds another. He wishes the church of the Nineteenth Century to have for a defender the glorious patriarch whom Mary herself obeyed on the earth, and who in heaven has lost none of his authority over her and his divine Son. By a recent decree the Vicar of Jesus Christ solemnly declares St. Joseph protector of the Universal Church."

The three year old cherub, Manuel, had waked during the
excitement about the fire, and he continued to cry till
Mercedes gave him his supper.   It consisted of a teacupful
of *calabasa*, that is, sweetened pumpkin.   He sat on the dirt
floor, as did all the smaller children, to dispatch his meal.
This done he stretched himself out in as composed a posture
as if he were "laid out," thrust his hands into the pockets of
his pantaloons and resumed his crying, screaming lustily, "I
want to go to sleep," "I want to go to sleep."   Jubencia
joined him, and Cipriana's year old baby, also in pantaloons,
added his voice to the uproar.

"May all the saints help me!" exclaimed Maria.   "Manuel,
if you are sleepy why don't you go to sleep?   Don't hurry off,
Cipriana.   I am very much obliged to you for taking care of
them for me.   Jubencia, hush!   Mercedes, take up Manuel
and take off his shoes and put him to bed."

Just then Mercedes' father came in with an acquaintance.
They both wore white pantaloons, shirts of the same material, and sandals, that is, pieces of sole leather bound on
their feet with leather strings.

Mercedes' heart gave a leap of joy when she saw her father
lay down a new hat.   For two or three months he had worn
a hat that was so ragged it would not protect his head from
the burning rays of a semitropical sun; for a week he had
had none.   But the daughter did not know what the new one
had cost him; neither did he.   The superintendent had
ostensibly sold it to him for $.75, but he had written on his
account book $2.00 as the price of it.

Atanacio had sometimes had hopes of paying off those terrible debts before he died so that his daughter might not be
doomed all her life to grind corn, as it were, in the kitchens
of his masters, but he had more than once had reasons to
suspect such dealing as this on the part of the overseer.
There was no redress, as he knew; and the hope, which had
never had more than a struggling existence, went on through
the toilsome days dying a slow death.   Most of the peons
submitted quietly to their fate, but it was not in Atanacio's

nature to **bear** it in silence.   He **was in a good** humor to-
night, however.

He was **of** medium **height** and heavily **built.   His black
hair was** long and shaggy, **and** this with **the bushy eyebrows**
above his dark penetrating eyes gave him **an almost fierce**
appearance.

After the salutations **were** over he gave his **guest, Raimundo, a tall,** slender, mild-looking man, a seat at the table.
There was no table cloth, **but** Mercedes spread before **the**
guest **a** coarse, brown, cotton napkin **with** fringe **and a**
simple pattern of open work at each end.   **She** then brought
their supper of coffee, frijoles, tortillas and chile.   This latter delicacy **is** no more nor less than stewed red pepper.   I
have heard it said that in some parts **of** Mexico they make
coffee **fit for a** Sultan of Constantinople.   This beverage did
not belong **to** that class; it was strong and black, very **suggestive in smell and taste of the** burnt grains of which it was
made.   The coarse, brown sugar was cooked in **it.   They
partook of their supper without the** luxury of knives and
forks.

As the two men began **to sip** their **coffee they** plunged into
a discussion of the weather and its **influence** on the crops,
for having met only a few minutes before **in the street** they
had not had time to dispose **of** that topic.

"**If God does not** succor us with rain soon," said Raimundo, **loosening the Turkish** towel which **he** wore about his
neck, "there **will be more** suffering than any **of** us have ever
seen.   Why, **now in Saltillo corn sells** at seventy-five cents a
peck, and frijoles are still higher.   I thought as I came along
yesterday that the fields between there and here were drier
than I had ever **seen** them.   How are prices here?"

"O, about the same.   But we are expecting rain now."

"Why?" asked the visitor **in surprise.**

"They brought in the Virgin **of St. John last** Sunday," he
replied sententiously, with a glance **at** Maria de los Angeles
over his cup as he drank.   "That lady would not be so im-
polite as to leave us in misery after receiving all that attention.   You **are a good Catholic** still, are you, Raimundo?"

"Yes," replied that mild-looking person, scarcely knowing what to say, for he had seen the glance at Maria, and had also seen her face cloud with anger. "Yes, I have not gone back on the religion of my fathers yet."

"You go to mass every Sunday, confess at least once a year, do penance now and then, and repeat prayers with devotion to gain indulgences, just as our good Father Ripalda says we must?" went on Atanacio, for his politeness did not prevent his pursuing a subject that was disagreeable to his guest.

"Yes, I do all that. A man must have some religion, and what better can he have than that his fathers had before him?"

"Certainly," replied Atanacio with provoking coolness. "we are very religious ourselves. You have noticed our altar. Why in the last week Maria has burned more tallow under the nostrils of the *Senor St. Joseph*," he said with a quick motion of his thumb over his shoulder at the image of Joseph, "more than she will be able to pay for in a month with all the savings from her washing, not to speak of the rent she has to pay the priest for her idols. Three of those she has on the altar are rented from him at the rate of a dollar a month. And if Mordicai dies from that leg," he continued with a mischievous glance at the boy who was propped up on the bed, "if he should die, you know, it would take more money than Maria can earn all the rest of her life to pay the priests to pray him out of purgatory."

"Did you ever think," Raimundo," he went on, now under full headway, "did you ever count up what it costs a fellow to be saved by this Holy Apostolic Church?"

"No," said the visitor with dignity, "I've never counted it."

"Well, suppose we count it. Take the child of a poor man like me. First the baby must be baptized, because if it isn't it will be lost, certain. That costs $2.25. Now it is regenerated by this baptism, you know, and one who didn't know the Holy Mother Church might think that was the end of it. But it is only the beginning. When he is five or six years

old, for his greater security, he must be confirmed; that
costs $.25. He grows up and takes it into his head to be
married, just as if a poor man who doesn't know one day
where he is to get bread for the next had any right to a wife.
The Reverend Father says he will marry him for $15.00.[1]
Now the fellow makes about $.40 a day when he can get
work to do, which isn't all the time by any means. His food
costs at least twelve cents a day, the rest he must pay for
clothing and shelter, even if he has no kinsfolk to help on.
How long do you think it will take him to save the $15.00, eh,
Raimundo? even if his sisters should help him from their
little savings to buy his sweetheart's wedding dress?"

"He can never save it," reluctantly confessed the visitor.

"Hardly ever," resumed Atanacio, scornfully, "and so he
says to the good priest. And what does he reply? 'Well, let
another take the girl then.' So it is impossible for him to be
married by the Church, and the priest has taught him to
believe in no other. It is true that he can sometimes secure
the Church marriage by becoming a perpetual debtor to the
priest. But that might be a thing of the past but for the
superstition of Mexicans," he continued, glancing toward
Maria de los Angeles, who, having eaten her supper, had
seated herself sullenly on the low bench and, accompanied
by Mercedes, had taken up the usual occupation of the evening, the making of cigarettes. "He might now be married
by the civil law. That, in this part of the country, would
not cost him but $4.00.[2] But the trouble is the poor fellow
won't believe that that is marriage, he still wants 'the holy
sacrament of the Church' or nothing."

"Ave Maria purisima!" exclaimed the amiable hostess.
"That I should have to listen to such blasphemy against the

[1] *Note.*—This is a very low price. I know serving women whose husbands, with the help of their relatives, paid as much as $30 or $40. The
expense is in proportion to the elegance of the ceremony—the quantity
of holy water, incense, etc., that is used.

[2] *Note.*—According to the law civil marriage is free if the contracting
parties go to the office of the judge; but in some States, by an abuse of
authority, the judges charge according, they say, to the ability of the
groom to pay.

Mother Church! and in my own house, too!" She always spoke of it as her "own house," though she was indebted to Atanacio for that poor shelter. Her husband had left her about two years before without giving any account of his conduct either to the law or to the people. In this he only acted like a large proportion of the men of his class.

"You are very much mistaken. It is marriage by the Church that is not marriage at all. It is a mere farce."

The protege of the angels jerked angrily the painted wooden tray in which was the tobacco, spilling some of it into her lap.

Atanacio went on, "Well, he goes on through life, confessing and reciting prayers, paying for indulgences, crawling up church steps, whipping himself with knotted cords and thorny sticks, buying scapularies to wear around his neck, so that if he dies suddenly the Blessed Virgin will send the angels to take him straight to heaven, giving a few cents now and then to the beggars, as he can afford it, to pay his entrance into the celestial city; and at last he comes to die. Then notwithstanding his regeneration in his baptism at the beginning of his career, somebody must go flying off for the priest to come and hear his last confession and administer the extreme unction. Then the funeral in the church must be paid for, a good healthy sum for the masses, candles, etc., etc. He must be buried in consecrated ground, for it would break the hearts of his wife and children to lay him in unblessed earth. So the Father must be paid to bless it."

"You know how it was formerly; all the burying grounds belonged to the Church, and if one could not pay he could not bury his dead at all. When the bereaved family went to the priest and asked permission to bury in the Campo Santo (the cemetery) the reply always was, 'Where is your money?' 'I have none, Reverend Father,' said the widow, kneeling and kissing his hand. 'Then go and eat your husband,' replied the embassador of Christ."

"I remember when I buried my wife," he said abruptly, with a tremor in his voice. He bent his head on his hand for a few moments, raised it, attempted to go on, failed, got up, in his shame and confusion giving the table a push that set the cups and plates a rattling, and went out into the court. He was a rough man, you know.

Mercedes' head bent lower over the package of cigarettes she was putting up. In the silence that had fallen in the room the corn shucks in which they were wrapped rustled loudly. The visitor shaded his face with his hand; he, too, was ashamed of betraying emotion. He heartily wished that he could defend the faith of his forefathers, but he knew that much more of the same kind might be added.

Presently Atanacio came in and sat down. "O, the dead always were buried, I suppose," he said. "The relatives could go into the streets and beg the money; and thank God there always have been people with kind enough hearts to give for such a purpose. But the Constituent Congress put a stop to all that when they confiscated the lands of the Church to the State and provided burial grounds. That was in '59, you know," he was fond of being explicit on these points; "only it was a long time before some of the Catholics would accept this liberty. A man may bury his dead for nothing now, and if he cares for the priest's blessing and the holy water he can pay him to consecrate the ground."

"Now he is dead and buried, and just here one might say really begins the expense of his salvation. He is in purgatory suffering in the flames of torment. They are painted for the widow and children in lively colors by the compassionate spiritual adviser, compassionate, you see, to the poor soul in torment. Then if she is conscientious and really loves her husband, she will pay the priest all that she and the children can spare from their earnings to say masses for his release. And pay as much as she may the time of his release is always a little way in the future, after a little more or a good deal more money shall have been paid. This is what the Church makes off a poor man's soul, and she makes as much more off a rich man's as she can possibly wring from him during his life and from his wife and children after his death. How many fine houses can you think of, Raimundo, that have come into the hands of the priests from the widows and children of rich men, leaving them in poverty?"

"I know of one or two cases of the kind," replied the guest with some hesitation, and looking about him uneasily.

"I should think you did. I have not been about this world much, but I know of more than that myself. In one case a well-to-do man died and the priest told his widow he had not paid alms enough to secure his entrance into heaven. So the money was all paid to the priest, everything, till they came to the house. To save that they sent out to the streets and begged money to pay the alms that were still wanting. But that had to end, of course. The priests wanted the house, and they got it. The lady and her two daughters are now living in a common house in a back street and sewing for a living. I could tell you a good many more stories of the same kind."

"I think," said the visitor, gathering courage from his friend's boldness and glad to relieve himself and the others from the strain in which the conversation of the last fifteen minutes had held them, "the priests do catch themselves sometimes in the funniest way about these masses for the dead. You know Don Bartolo Ortis? Well, he is rich, you know, and so is his brother, Don Miguel. I tell you, Don Bartolo has everything fine in his house; they live like princes, and ride in a carriage worth $1,000. I know about it, for I worked on his hacienda a year. Well, his mother had been dead for I don't know how many years. But he and Don Miguel were still paying for the masses. But the curious part of it was that every year the priest asked for more than he had received the year before for the masses and the candles and the black ribbons and the holy water. Well, one day Don Bartolo and the old priest had been out driving in that $1,000 carriage. They had just got home and were standing under a tree. Two or three of us hands had been gathering *tunas* and were standing near. The priest asked for the money for the annual mass."

"'But, my dear father,' said Don Bartolo (you know he couldn't be anything but polite if he tried), 'you need more money each year than the year before. It seems that the more we pay the deeper in she goes. I think for her sake we had better not pay any more.' And neither he nor Don Miguel ever did pay another cent; I heard him say so a long time afterwards."

"Yes," said Atanacio, laughing, "I heard of a wealthy gentleman who paid for eighteen years to get his father out. At last he went to the priest and said, 'Father, it breaks my heart to think that my poor father is still suffering in purgatory. Tell me how much it will cost to say masses enough once for all to release him.' The priest remained very thoughtful for awhile with his head on his hand. At length he looked up and said, 'It will cost $1,000.' 'Well,' said the son, 'let the masses be said at once.' Then there was flying about the cathedral, and pretty soon the great organ was set agoing and the candles were lighted, and the priests with their robes on were at the altars, and the boys were waving the censers of incense, and the gentleman was kneeling and shedding tears in abundance. After all that had gone on for an hour or two, up comes the priest, and he says, 'Well, my dear sir, I am happy to inform you that your father is now delivered from purgatory.' 'And is there no danger of his ever returning?' asked the gentleman. 'None whatever,' replied the priest. The gentleman got up and threw his arms around the priest and thanked him; and then he walked off and left him, and the good Father is waiting to this day for that $1,000. I suppose the gentleman thought he had already paid him enough without that."

And so story followed story; but neither they nor the loud laughter with which they were accompanied were to Mercedes' taste. She slipped out after awhile into the court, trying not to hear the grunting of the shabby pigs, that were tied by her aunt's door and the neighbors', trying not to see the two or three lean, deformed dogs which came around her. Once she stretched her clasped hands upward towards the

sky, and an inaudible cry wrenched itself from her suffering
soul: "O God, have mercy on us!" But the heavens seemed
brass above her; the darkness settled down more heavily on
her spirit; there was no intimation in the stars, shining
brightly in the blue sky, no hint in the quivering air, that a
great change was at hand, that there remained to her only
one more night of her old, hopeless life.

So the changes in our lives often come. And sometimes
we do not recognize them even when they come; only in after
years we can look back and say: "That was a turning point."

CHAPTER VI.

A TELESCOPIC GLIMPSE OF ROYALTY.

ON a pleasant July morning, the morning after the visit of Mercedes and her aunt to the chapel on the hill, two ladies sat in their cool and shaded parlor.

Perhaps it was only pleasant in that parlor, one could not imagine that it was ever otherwise there. Even if you stepped out on the narrow front balcony where the bright plumaged parrot was screaming and scolding and laughing, you were beguiled from looking at the hot and dusty street by the sight of the plaza opposite, it was so cool, so shady, so pretty with its trees and rosebushes and other shrubbery. You could see and hear the great fountain in the center, from whose topmost basin the water fell in showers of diamonds, continuing its downward course, from basin to basin, till it reached the great basin whose fluted sides were painted the national colors, red, green and white. Over there, too, in full view, was that graceful oriental palm tree, so suggestive of cool oases and sparkling fountains in the desert.

This parlor was in the second story of the house, so that the noises from the street came to the inmates only in subdued undertones. There was a great deal of individuality about the room, or rather a great deal of two individualities; but they were so beautifully blended and harmonized that one could not discern where the one ended and the other began. There were some things in the room which suggested a love for literature, music and the fine arts, other things which were equally suggestive of a love for the beauties of nature and the practical side of life. But none of these things—neither the books, nor the pictures, nor the music, nor the exquisite fancy work—ever obtruded themselves on you; you only had a feeling that they were there.

4

There were chairs of several patterns and no two alike. The dainty wicker rocking chair invited you, a great upholstered chair held out its arms for you, a pretty, slender camp chair offered its services, a great easy sofa assured you of comfort. Here and there on the low tables was a choice book which had strayed in there from the well-filled bookcase that you knew instinctively was somewhere in the house. Over the windows were the daintiest and softest of lace curtains.

The two German ladies who sat in this room were in keeping with their surroundings. They were both somewhere in thirty. One of them contradicted race traditions, for she had dark hair, a dark complexion, and dark eyes. There was an independent, practical look about her, in her quick movements and in her position, whether she sat or stood. Her thin summer dress was dainty, to be sure; one enjoyed looking at it from the collar to the hem; but it was evident that the principal idea of the wearer in designing it had been to secure comfort and not to follow the latest fashions.

There was a streak of contradiction in her. If you remarked that the bird which she was painting on the velvet table scarf was beautiful, she would reply in the most nonchalant tone, " No, it is not pretty, but it suits this scarf." If, anxious to say something pleasant, you plucked up courage after that to observe that it must be a difficult and tedious task to paint it, she at once answered that, on the contrary, it was very easy indeed, and that she could paint it in an hour if she tried. If you even said it was pleasant in that room, she would respond that of course one could expect to be only comparatively comfortable in there when it was so hot outside.

Yet she was the best natured of people. She was a very interesting conversationalist if one left the talking entirely to her. She would give him quaint sketches of travel and and descriptions of people and customs, brightened by gleams of humor and emphasized by her own vigorous way of putting things. She had a delightful way, too, of keeping herself entirely out of her narratives, or at least in the background. You only felt that you were seeing people and things through the eyes of an original and practical person.

She had no religion, probably because she knew that by having none she could contradict more people than she could by adopting any of the many forms of Christianity or paganism. But to do her justice the tricks and shams and chicanery of Roman Catholicism were disgusting to her. Its wickedness and greed of filthy lucre were not unknown to her either. No form of Protestantism was known to her except Lutheranism, and of it she had never heard much. So far life had gone smoothly and she had felt little need of religion.

When she was only eighteen she had come alone across the ocean to marry the young German merchant, who had preceded her a year or two to make a home for her. She had three children. Her two eldest, who were boys, were in school in Germany; the youngest, a fair, winsome girl of thirteen, was with relatives in the United States, attending school. In the loving, practical letters which she sent every week to her children one found the best expression of her character.

The other lady was tall and fair, with blue eyes and fluffy, yellow hair. A nameless grace of manner, as undefinable as the faint perfume of flowers, a graciousness which was prompted by kindly feelings toward high and low, characterized all she said and did; they would have made her a charming woman even if her face had been homely.

She never contradicted. Neither did she always agree with what was said. If it was a matter of any consequence about which she differed from you in opinion she made you feel somehow that she thought differently, but with perfect delicacy and charity for your way of thinking, and with not the least assumption of infallibility on her part.

She was a Catholic; she told you so in a perfectly off-hand and well-bred way, as if it were a matter of course, or just as she would say, "I am a German," but with a little intangible something in tone and manner that made you feel that she would think, if she should think anything about it, that it was

very respectable to be a Catholic; but you never had any
fears that she undervalued you for differing from her in
religious beliefs.   But she had no images nor altars, except
that in her private room there hung a silver-mounted crucifix
over her quaint, old-fashioned bed, which, with the other
furniture, had been brought from the old country.

She went to church sometimes, but rarely, and when she
did go it was more to hear the music than for any other purpose.   She would have liked to hear an eloquent sermon now
and then merely for the eloquence of it.   She never had any
acquaintance with the priests, and if she had permitted herself to have a poor opinion of any one they certainly would
have been among those unfortunate persons.

She, too, could tell delightful stories of travel, but there
was the difference between her narratives and those of her
cousin Gretchen that there is between Longfellow's "Outre
Mer" and the narration of a brisk business man.

Both she and her companion were very popular with the
Mexicans, for, besides the possession of all the social and
domestic virtues, they were accounted to be ladies of great
learning.   It was rumored that besides their native German
and the Spanish language, they spoke also with ease and
elegance, French, English and Italian; and some were even
so wild in their assertions as to add Greek and Latin.
But public opinion was divided on this latter subject, some
affirming that only the tall, fair one possessed those accomplishments.

They numbered so many ladies of the best society among
their visiting acquaintances that with the exception of the
small circle of their most intimate friends, they seldom called
at the same place more than once a year; though to tell the
truth they made no great efforts to call on their friends often,
contenting themselves with saying, "Come to see us whenever you feel like it; we are always glad to see you.   But
don't wait on us; we have so many acquaintances we find it
impossible to visit them all often."   They never went to the
Sunday night balls, unless they had guests who wished to go:

and only occasionally did they go to the more select entertainments.

Frederica, one would not fail to learn, belonged to a highly respectable family in Germany, for in the course of one's acquaintance with her, some day when he was looking at her photograph album, for instance, and noticed some handsome young gentlemen in uniforms, she would remark that they were her nephews, that they were favorites of the young prince, the heir apparent to the crown of the empire, that through his influence they had been admitted to the best universities, and that recently when he made a tour through Bohemia and Hungary he had selected one of them to accompany him.

Nor was that all. On the wall hung two pictures of an old castle in a lake. One of them represented it as it looked in summer, the other as it looked in winter. Part of it was in ruins, but part of its massive gray walls still defied time. It was built by Charlemagne, and he had lived in it for awhile, she said.

It stood near Aix-la-Chapelle. It has its legend, of course. The great emperor once gave to his fair wife a ring, telling her that he would never forget her while she kept it. She died, and in her last moments she secretly put the ring into her mouth. The emperor could never find the talisman, but still it attracted him. He had her body placed in a glass case and he sat all the time by her side. At length the bishop found the ring, and took it, saying nothing to his master about it.

Then Charlemagne went always with the bishop—everywhere—till he, tired of his royal society, threw the ring into the lake. The emperor, under the spell of the enchantment, had an island made in the middle of the lake and built on it this castle and lived in it.

Frederica was born and brought up in this castle in the midst of the enchanted lake. As one listened, and looked from her to the picture, and from the picture back to her, he would experience something like the feeling of the woman

who said that she never saw Washington Irving herself, but
that she had once had the privilege of walking out of church
behind a woman who had seen him; with the difference that
the feeling would be as much more intensified, as royalty is
greater than genius. And such royalty! Ye sun, moon and
stars! (as Dickens might have said), think of a woman who
was brought up in a castle of Charlemagne's!

But though there was doubtless in her heart some very
natural pride in the aristocracy of her family of which this
castle was to her a representative, her womanly grace always
saved the listener from any painful feeling of inferiority.
He was always ready to believe that she had shown him the
pictures and given him all the information about her family
merely because they were matters that were curious and
interesting.

But whatever there may have been of pride in her heart,
there was far more of bitterness, which, however, no visitor
ever suspected. The shadow of this castle, representing, as
it did, the high respectability of her family, had darkened
her life.

When she was about twenty years old she had loved a
young gentleman whose family was equal to her own in
wealth and respectability. Her love was returned and they
were betrothed. The prospective marriage was very agreeable to both families, especially to the relatives of Frederica,
for it was evident that Herr Gaussen, though only three or
four years older than herself, would soon be recognized as
one of the leading merchants of the city in which he lived.

But just when things were at this happy stage Herr
Gaussen became acquainted with the Lutheran religion,
examined it, and adopted it. Then there was wailing in both
families. That one who was anything to them should be
infected with "that heresy of Martin Luther's" seemed to
them the greatest misfortune and disgrace that could befall
them. But in vain his sisters entreated him, in vain his elegant mother even knelt before him and lifted to him her face
bathed in tears, pleading by the respectability of his family,

by all his early recollections, by her mother-love. With all tenderness, but firmly, he told her that Lutheranism was more in accordance with the Sacred Scriptures than Romanism, and therefore he must be a Lutheran.

Useless, too, were the remonstrances of Frederica's family, her own tears and evident suffering, her refusal to marry him unless he would return to the fold of the church. One evening they stood in a deep window overlooking the lake on which the moonlight was dancing. He had come for his final answer. She had believed all the time that when he saw there was no other hope of their marriage he would return to the Church. Such obstinacy was unaccountable to her. But as the restless days and sleepless nights went by and there was no sign of yielding, hope had almost died in her heart. It was evident, however, that he suffered no less than herself.

"How can you do anything which brings so much suffering to us all?" she was saying.

"I cannot do otherwise, as I believe the Bible, the Word of God, Frederica. My salvation depends upon it."

"I never saw a Bible, but I know that there is no salvation outside the Church."

"I used to think so, but I have learned now from the Word of God that 'the just shall live by faith,' and not by the observance of the rites and ceremonies of the Roman Church. Let me show you what I have learned from the Bible, Frederica; you cannot fail to see that it is the truth. Will you not?"

There was a long silence while the girl stood, leaning against the window, with her face buried in her hands. A fierce struggle was going on in her mind. How could she give up his love and the joyful prospects which had brightened her life for months? But, on the other hand, how could she bring this shame on her family! How could she, a young girl, turn against the religion of all her ancestors, of her own father and mother!

"Come, Frederica," he pleaded, "let me show you that

Martin Luther taught what the Revelation of God teaches. It is an honor, and not a disgrace to do what one's Creator has commanded."

"I can't. O, Wilhelm, don't ask me!"

"But it is a question, not only of our happiness, but of the salvation of your soul. Think of that."

"No," she replied, suddenly raising her head with the feeling that she could bear the parting and the never seeing him again better than that suspense of suffering; "you will not return to the Church; then I can never marry you."

There fell another silence between them. At last he said, taking her hand, "Good-bye, then, Frederica," and he kissed her and then went out. And his face was almost as rigid and white in the moonlight as it will be at the last.

She dragged herself up to her room. Many a night since this trouble came on her had she knelt for hours before the image of the infant Christ, and before that of the Savior on the cross—images of a babe and a dead Savior—pleading with them—not that she might be shown her duty that she might do it—but that her lover might return to the Mother Church. She had found no help in them, nor in the image of the Virgin. She did not even look at them to-night. She dropped into a great arm chair and sat there far into the night, confused, benumbed by suffering.

As the days went by there came into her heart a desperate desire to escape from her childhood's home, so full, now, of painful associations, to escape from the pitying, loving eyes of her sister, from those unresponsive images of the infant and crucified Christ, and from that window overlooking the lake. Some distant relatives of theirs who knew nothing of the circumstances were just then about to start on a tour through Southern Europe. It was arranged that she should accompany them; her sister and brother-in-law believed that a change would be the best thing for her.

But little did any of them think, not even she herself, when she told them good-bye with tearless eyes, kissing them with burning lips, that the old castle would never be her home again.

Her relatives had been told that she was not well, and that **accounted to** them for her lack of **interest in all** they saw. **Sometimes** the thought occurred to her, as she looked on noble statues, glorious pictures or beautiful landscapes, that she should look at them and try to remember **them for the** sake **of** the years to come. But she found it impossible to arouse herself to interest. She did remember most of them, however, and some of them with startling distinctness, for in her morbid state of mind they were unnaturally **impressed on her.**

They extended **their** tour to countries which **they had not** at first **intended** to visit. But even in foreign cities **she** walked always **in** the shadow of the turrets and battlements **of** Charlemagne's castle; it always seemed **to** her that she had done right to refuse **to sacrifice the** respectability of her family by marrying **one of** another religion.

When they returned **home she** insisted **on** remaining in one **of the southern** cities of France, ostensibly to perfect **her** **knowledge of French.** Later, impelled by the desire **to have** **some occupation that** would allow her less **time** to think **of** the **past, she** became a teacher in a **girls'** school. Years passed and she still refused to return **home. Her** grief and **sense** of loss became milder. Only **now and** then these haunting recollections came back **with** such determination that **she could** not fight them off; and then for days she went about like **one in a** dream. But she was always a gentle and loving mother, **as well** as teacher, to the girls who were in her care. Her interest in life came back for their sake; there was only one thing that saddened her in connection with them: the yearly rending **of heart** strings as they passed out of the school forever.

Herr Gaussen had suffered, too, but his was a more health**ful** nature than hers. His religion had been a support and **consolation to him** in this as in all other trials. After two **years he had** married a sweet Christian woman. His early **love was dead** or latent.

After some years Frederica was persuaded to visit her home. During the **three** or **four** painful and happy weeks that she passed in **her sister's** home she wished with all her heart that some one would tell her something of Herr Gaussen. She had never heard anything but the bare fact that he was married. But she could not ask or intimate in any way that she wished to know. She would have prayed for it if she had had anything to pray to; but since that night when the images had failed her she had been poorer than the heathen themselves—she had not even had an idol. And reared as she had been she had no hope of approaching the invisible, spiritual God without the intercession of a saint.

But her wish was to be gratified. One day a lady was calling on her; in the course of the conversation she said, with all innocence:

"You knew Herr Gaussen. He is quite a wealthy and prominent merchant now. He has four bright, pretty children, and I think his is one of the loveliest and happiest families I ever saw."

Frederica started, and the album she was showing to the child at her side almost slipped from her lap, but she quickly recovered her composure, and the lady went on to speak of other matters.

But Frederica had come to feel that she could not bear the losing of the girls of her classes every year. She had a cousin in Mexico; she had resolved to go to her. Surely among scenes so new and strange she would not think much of the past. She was a welcome inmate in her cousin's home. But though she said, during these years that she was a Catholic, the crucifix that hung over her bed was no more to her than the parting gift of her sister.

She was contented and cheerful, living much for the happiness of others. Gretchen's dainty house girls were always Frederica's pupils. Now she taught needle work, painting or music to some poor girl who could not learn those favorite branches in the schools. She was always watching for some bright girl to teach. It must be said that often her high hopes of them were disappointed, owing to their circumstances or their lack of application, but she always recovered from the shock and was ready to adopt the next promising-looking pupil who presented herself.

CHAPTER VII.

"THE NEW WASHERWOMAN'S DAUGHTER."

FREDERICA sat this morning at the **piano,** carelessly running over some German airs. **Presently** she crossed the room to where her cousin sat, and **taking** up a book, said:

"**Well,** shall **we** finish the book this morning? I am disposed to read **if** you care to listen."

The lady glanced at the clock. "I think not, thank you. I must stop directly and prepare Oscar's favorite pudding for dinner. He looked worried about something this morning; I must **do** something to at least show him **that** I **am** sympathetic."

"O, **you practical** soul!" laughed Frederica, "the **idea of** comforting **the good** man with a pudding!"

"Well, it **isn't** the pudding exactly that comforts him, **but** the feeling for his vexations. I have known **pastry to prove** a pretty effectual comforter," **she** replied pleasantly.

She put aside her scarf and went out into the court. The next moment **she** opened the door and said:

"Frederica, **here** is your **new** washerwoman's daughter with the clothes."

Frederica **stepped out into the upper** corridor and asked the girl to **follow her to her room.** Mercedes, for it was she, followed her **into the** spacious, handsome room; with its pictures and pretty, graceful ornaments it looked like fairy land to her. The clothes were counted, the money was paid, and they passed out again into the corridor. Frederica had been talking kindly all the time to the girl. Now she plucked a geranium and gave it to her, saying, "You look tired, child." The next moment Mercedes' eyes fell on the book which Frederica had laid on a table **as** she passed to her room. It was Altamirano's "Cuentos **de** Invierno" (Winter Tales).

She had heard of it and had longed to read it. Eagerness flashed from her face; she made a step toward the table and put out her hand to grasp it, then remembering, she stopped.

"Do you like to read, dear?" asked Frederica.

"O, yes, Señora, very much."

"Have you ever been to school?"

"No, Señora, I only learned at home by myself."

"Did you ever read a book?" asked Frederica, wishing to continue the conversation.

"O yes, Señora, I have read Don Quixote three times, and some parts of it a great many times. And I have read the History of Mexico three times," replied Mercedes, feeling considerable pride in her achievements. "And besides them," she added, with a visible loss of interest, "I have read the mass book, but I didn't read it but once."

The lady repressed a smile. "Why do you not go to school?" she asked.

The girl's face clouded. "I can't go to school. I have to stay at home and work."

"But your mother ought to send you to school."

"My mother is dead. I live with my aunt, and she says the priests say it would be better for the common people not to know how to read," she said, summoning all her courage, but still feeling that she was guilty of high treason. "And besides that," she added in the hopeless tone of the poor, "my father can't afford to buy me suitable clothes to wear to school."

"Ask your father to let you come here and study with me, and we will see if we can't arrange it all."

The pretty court down below, with its roses and geraniums, became suddenly indistinct before the girl's eyes, and she laid her hand on the table to steady herself. Presently she said, in a choking voice

"I give you many thanks, Señora, but I don't think anything can be done," and if she had dared, she would have added to the quaint Spanish way of thanking her, the pretty Spanish act of kissing her hand.

"Well, ask your father about it, and never mind what your aunt says, and come and tell me to-morrow morning," said Frederica as Mercedes took up her basket to go home.

"I will, Señora. Many thanks. Adios."

"Adios, Mercedes."

And the girl went out into the hot and dusty street, dazed at the good fortune which had been offered her, but not at all hopeful. But it was certain that whatever came of it this Doña Frederica would be to her always almost an object of worship. "She is as beautiful as an angel," she said. "She looks like an angel, with her blue eyes and yellow hair; and her voice is sweet, as their's must be. How God must love her!"

I wonder if there is not in all noble souls a strong inclination to hero worship!

And Frederica, what of her? It was not a new experience to her, as I have said. But this girl's dark face and bright eyes, with the eager, hungry soul looking out of them, had attracted her more than any other had ever done.

But dinner came, and then visitors, so there was no time to think of her new protégé till she sat in her own room, after supper. She had to admit the truth of what Gretchen had laughingly said; she *was* the shabbiest specimen she had selected yet. But her face was bright, and then that look in her face when she saw the book! How she had wished for some girl to educate who had a real enthusiasm for learning! She would be to her like a daughter; perhaps God had sent her this girl. She, too, thought of God, and in a simple, natural way. Perhaps they would do each other good. Her lips quivered and her eyes were a little moist.

She arose quickly and went to a wardrobe. She took out two or three summer dresses of her own. Her womanly taste told her what dainty dresses could be made of them for Mercedes; and she would teach her to braid her black hair prettily and tie it with a bright ribbon. Think of the girl dressed so, and bending over her books! She would be almost pretty! And think of her turning that bright, olive face towards her's, flushed with love and gratitude!

"Such extravagant notions!" something said to her.   "She will soon lose all interest in the lessons, and go back of her own accord, as so many others have done, to the prospect of making tortillas and cigarettes all her life."

She had no idea of spoiling Mercedes by dressing her up very fine at first. A cheap, but neatly made dress, a new scarf and some shoes would be sufficient; and she would not waste those on her unless it really seemed that she was going to study.

At the same hour a storm of words raged fiercely between Mercedes' father and her aunt. The latter, of course, was violently opposed to her following a course which, she was sure, would only encourage her in "idleness" and indifference to the Church. The former had seen in the offer of the German lady a gleam of hope for his daughter and had determined that she should avail herself, if possible, of every advantage which should be offered her.

The girl sat meanwhile on a chair near the door, scarcely daring to breathe, her hands tightly clasped, her eyes big with terror, feeling sure she made more trouble in the world than she would ever be worth.

At last Atanacio, tired of the contest, sprang from the table, seized the whip with which he had all day been minding the cattle out of the cornfield and proceeded to chastize his step-sister. Such occurrences as this were not so uncommon either in his house or in those of his neighbors as they should have been.

After she was silenced he ordered them to go to bed. Her father has gained his point and Mercedes rejoiced; but with trembling. She would have to suffer from her aunt for all the instruction which she would receive from her benefactress, but any price seemed small to her.

The next morning her father told her with a determined air in the presence of her aunt, to go and tell Doña Frederica that he should be grateful for any instruction she would give her.

After an hour's talk with her new teacher the arrangement

was made that she should spend two hours each morning at
the house of the latter reciting and reading.   Then Mercedes
went home to the tasks of the day; and Frederica put on her
hat and gloves and went down the street to the little book
store and bought a small grammar and arithmetic.   She had
a geography in the house which would answer, and instead
of a reading book she would have her read selections from
Spanish authors, a good many of which she had bought for
her own use.

It happened that on her way home she passed a French
store and saw lying on the counter a pile of pretty dress goods
from the factory in the town; she passed resolutely; but
turned back and selected a dress and a neat, dark scarf and a
pair of shoes, reflecting, meanwhile on her own weakness and
on what Gretchen would say.

"But of course I can't have her coming to the house as my
pupil in that garb," she said to herself by way of justification.

Before the close of the next day the dress was finished.
Unlike most of the dresses for girls of her class the waist
and skirt were alike.   The universal scarf or shawl being so
convenient to cover defects, there is much carelessness in all
ranks on this point.

Frederica had put ruffles of red hamburg about the neck
and sleeves.

"I want it to look nice you know", she said, "for I intend
she shall leave off the scarf as soon as she enters the room."
She was very fastidious, this Doña Frederica!

. "O, I expect you will get her a hat before another week
passes, and then she won't need the scarf at all," replied
Gretchen with a smile.

"No, she shall never wear a hat if I can have my way about
it.   I very much admire the custom here of going with the
head uncovered, or covered only with the scarf or shawl or
mantilla when they are necessary.   In fact I have never seen
any covering for the head which is more graceful and beautiful
than the black lace mantillas; and then think of the expense and
worry that is saved by going without hats! Did I ever tell you

that I thought before I came here, that the Mexican ladies covered their faces all but their eyes with the mantillas?"

"You got that idea from stories of Spain, I suppose."

In a day or two Frederica gave the dress, shoes, scarf and other neat garments to Mercedes, telling her to wear them when she came for her lessons. She carried them home and displayed them timidly to her aunt and father. The former was silent and sullen, the latter, more pleased than he cared to show.

After the duties of the following morning were over she arrayed herself in the new clothing. She wondered how she looked, but with the sullen eyes of her aunt on her she could not even try to see herself in the tiny looking-glass. Her father had made excuses for lingering about the house much longer than usual that morning and Mercedes believed in the depths of her fluttering heart that his object was to see her in her new dress. At first he pretended not to hear her as she gathered up her books to start, but presently he looked around and there flashed into his eyes a look of tenderness which his daughter immediately added to her other precious recollections. Both he and she were embarrassed. He said nothing, but pretending that he had only turned to get his hat, took it up and left the house.

She put on her scarf and trembling with the dread of en-countering the neighbors' eyes passed through the court. There and in the street she heard from women and girls such comments as, "Look at Mercedes Gonzales!" "O, how fine!" "Isn't that Mercedes Gonzales? I hardly knew her!" There was no unkindness meant; but the remarks cut to the quick. To the day of her death she remembered that walk through the court of her home and the street on which she lived as one of the severest ordeals of her life.

Frederica, however, had little womanly ways, such as leaving her alone in the room now and then for a few minutes that she might become familiar with her surroundings, and with her own reflection in the mirror. As the weeks and months went by, besides coming to feel easy in that fairy land of a room and the neat clothing which her teacher provided her, her progress in her studies was gratifying.

She entered more and more into the meaning of her textbooks as she advanced from one to another. She felt the pleasure of learning, the delight of bringing order out of the chaos of her ideas, the joy of finding that things which had seemed complicated and difficult were simple, the happiness of feeling that in learning more and more of the works of the Creator, one is becoming better acquainted with that great Being himself.

As she imbibed more of the refined ideas of her teacher and of the household to which she belonged, the coarseness and hardness of the life in her own home became even more distasteful to her. Her newly acquired conceptions of liberty and justice, and her faint hope of escaping sometime from that miserable existence made her bear with less stoicism than formerly the continual annoyances with which her aunt harassed her. She occasionally, now, flashed up into fierce resistance and wrath.

Of course if I were telling you a story of an ideal girl I should have nothing but saintly virtues to describe; but I am telling you of a girl in whom all the passions of human nature were very strong. All I can say in her justification is that after each of these not very frequent fits of indignation, when she turned on her aunt with the feeling of a wild beast at bay, and answered her with hot words of reproach, she always suffered from attacks of repentance, made more torturing by the reflection that her greater advantages ought to make her more forbearing.

But when she had laid aside the shabby clothing, and arrayed in dainty garments, had turned her face toward the house of her teacher, her feelings might well have been expressed in the words which the young king of Israel wrote in the golden days of his youth: "The winter is past, the rain is over and gone; the flowers appear on the earth, the time of the singing of the birds is come." With Frederica she was gentle and gay, bright and talkative.

5

CHAPTER VIII

"THAT RELIGION OF RELIGIONS."

THERE was one person with whom Mercedes was happier than with her teacher. From the very day on which she received the first lesson there was a change in her father's manner toward her; and it became more marked as the months passed. He showed a gentleness and deference toward her that was touching. She became familiar with subjects of which he was ignorant. But he listened with the greatest interest as she told him with enthusiasm of the poems of Lope de Vega, and of Sor Juana Inez de la Cruz, of the musical sentences of Altamirano, the exquisite humor of Ochoa or the "eternal ideas" and "infinite sadnesses" of the "golden mouthed" Castelar.

On Sundays after the early mass, on great religious or national feast days he sometimes asked her to walk with him on the hills. Now they went to the little chapel for the view, now to the Secacion, a steep hill back of the town.

One afternoon, about three years after Mercedes' first acquaintance with Frederica, they stood together on this hill. She was much taller than she was that morning when she went to the house of her teacher to receive her first lesson; and her longer dresses, and her glossy black hair arranged in a knot at the back of her head, gave her the appearance of a young lady.

Looking up from the streets of the town one might have seen the two figures sharply outlined, standing like statues against the blue sky.

"Papa," said the daughter, after panting a little from the hard climbing to the top, and looking up fondly into the face which had grown rapidly older in the last three years, "are you tired? It seems to me you get tired much more quickly now than you used to do."

"Yes, daughter," he replied with affected indifference, and turning away his head, "I am growing older, you know."

"And very rapidly, from exposure and hard work," thought Mercedes, with a sharp pang. But she added aloud, "Doña Frederica says that I am getting along well with my studies. I do hope—I think of it all the time—that some day I can teach or do something of that kind and make money and pay those terrible debts. And then you shall rest and I will work for you. We will have our home, just you and I. Just think how nice it will be, with the floor swept clean and the chairs and tables shining with paint. And you shall have your *merienda* of chocolate every afternoon, and your [1]*desayuno* every morning, just like a Señor."

"Ah, child," he replied gloomily, "there is little hope of paying the debts. It is best not to build too fine air castles."

The girl knew it, but she was young and hopeful, and as her eyes wandered off to the hills the momentary sinking of heart was forgotten.

Her father aroused her from her reverie by saying abruptly, as if following a train of thought:

"Mercedes, I don't want you ever to confess to the priests. I don't want you ever even to speak to one of them if you can help it; for they are very wicked men. But you can go to mass if you want to; your mother always went."

She noticed that he never said whether her mother confessed, and she was always careful not to ask.

"Well, papa, I am a Catholic; of course, I'm that," she replied, her eyes feasting on the marvelous effects of light and shade on the opposite mountains, "you could not imagine me becoming a disciple of Martin Luther's, could you?" she added with a gay laugh.

"But I don't believe that images can work miracles, nor that the priests can forgive sins; that is, that they can forgive them as a great many people believe they can," she explained, a mystical look coming into her eyes.

"Of course, they can't forgive sins, Mercedes. Would God

---

[1] *Note.*—A light meal of chocolate and bread which gentlemen and ladies take before rising.

give such power as that to the worst of his creatures that ever walked the earth?"

"But you know, papa, that the Lord did say to St. Peter, the first pope of Rome, 'I will give unto thee the keys of the kingdom of heaven; and whatsoever thou shalt bind on earth shall be bound in heaven, and whatsoever thou shalt loose on earth shall be loosed in heaven.'"

"Yes, I know the priests say that, and I suppose they got it, as they say they did, from the Sacred Scriptures they sometimes mention. But they are such liars one never knows what to believe of what they say. And they take care that nobody else sees those Sacred Scriptures. Perhaps if we knew all that is said in them on the subject it would not mean what it appears to when they quote it to us."

"But I don't believe what they teach. I believe in 'that religion of religions which is Castelar's.'"

This is the form of Catholicism which, it seems, is professed by most of the educated men of the country who have not rejected religion altogether.

"And what does he teach about religion?" asked Atanacio, repressing a smile at this high-sounding announcement of his daughter's creed.

"He speaks with scorn of the wickedness and greed of the priesthood, and he compares Catholic Italy with Protestant Switzerland, and certainly not by way of complimenting the influence of Catholicism in Italy. But he does not like the Protestants, for all that. He says that 'the pagan religion will preserve the conscience more alive and its jurisdiction over one's life better than Protestant pietism.'

"He speaks with disdain of the doctrine of the sinlessness of the Virgin Mary, and with withering contempt of that of the infallibility of the pope. He says that in Rome 'paganism has been transformed and not destroyed,' and he goes on to show how a great many ceremonies and observances of the Catholic Church are only a continuation of those of the heathen Romans. He says that 'hell is a pagan creation, and the demons are the creation of magic, that 'the apotheo-

sis of the heroes has been replaced by the canonization of
the saints,' that revelations were not made to the Jews alone,
that the sybil of Cumas conceived the idea of the coming of
the Messiah in the very days in which Daniel was counting
on his fingers the weeks of years which must pass before the
fulfillment of that prophecy. He says that Virgil foretold the
coming of Christ as well as Isaiah, and that 'Athens with her
arts, Rome with her right, Alexandria with her science, have
contributed as much to Christian revelation as Jerusalem
with her God.' And he says that revelations have not ceased.
I don't understand it all, of course, but it is all very mystical
and beautiful, and all clothed in language as poetic and gorgeous as a sunset."

" Well, that may all be very fine, but it sounds to me more
like the talk of a heathen than of a Christian."

"O no, he is a Catholic, but not like these common Catholics, you know. I don't think he believes the priests can forgive sins as they believe it. At least he tells scornfully of a
priest whom he saw sitting in a church in Rome, forgiving
the sins of the people who knelt before him by 'giving each a
tap on the head with a staff, 'as if he were fishing on dry
land.' And he says, though he is a Catholic, that 'society,
science and life travel one road, and Catholicism another completely opposite.' I don't understand it all, as I said, but I love
to read his books for their eloquence. I have read some
parts of them a great many times. He writes very beautifully of the blessed Virgin, and his thoughts of her are connected with the most precious memories of his childhood and
with 'the sweet face of his mother.' You should read his
description of the singing of the *Miserere* in St. Peters. The
candles are all extinguished or hidden, and the white statues
seem in the fading daylight to start from their places, as the
music, solemn and penetrating, resounds under the great
dome and among the high arches. It must be sublime!" and
her voice trembled with emotion as she spoke. In her loneliness she was glad to find some one to whom she could talk
of her favorite books, some one whom she could trust not to

laugh at her, no matter how ridiculous her flights. Her
spirit was still going up and down, you see, seeking rest and
finding none.

It was a very fine religion which she had adopted, but
would it stand by her in the day of trial?

*   *   *   *   *   *   *   *   *

And the day of trial was at hand. A few days after this
walk on the hill Atanacio came home one night later than
usual, looking so weak and pale that his daughter sprang
toward him with the cry: "O, papa, what is the matter?"

"I'm very sick, daughter. Let me lie down as soon as
possible."

His pallet was quickly made and he lay down. He yielded
without resistance to Mercedes' proposition to send for a
doctor. Mordicai was absent, so she ran to ask the husband
of Cipriana to go for a physician.

Before he arrived the sufferer had told them, as his breath,
shortened by pain would allow, that he had become over-
heated, running after cattle which had gotten into the cornfield, and while he was in that condition a sudden rain had
come up and wet him thoroughly.

There are in Mexico no fences, and the cattle which are
allowed to run in the country are kept out by the laborers
whose business it is to stand guard around the fields. This
is a more economical arrangement than the building of
fences, as, notwithstanding the fact that the northern part of
Mexico is thinly settled, men are more numerous than trees.

The physician pronounced the disease pneumonia. He
returned every day only to find the patient worse and the
daughter nearer wild with distress. One evening she slipped
out after him and spoke to him in the court:

"Doctor, my father is very sick, isn't he?" she said, making a great effort to control her emotion.

"Yes, daughter," he replied, looking at her pityingly.

"Oh, Doctor, can't you do anything for him?"

"All that can be done now is to send for the priest. Poor child," he added, "he is all you have in the world."

Is there a nation in the world, I wonder, in which the physicians—these men who see so much of the awful suffering which sickness and death bring to human beings—have not tender hearts.

Mercedes gazed at him in agonized silence till she fully comprehended the terrible meaning of his words, then she gasped:

"Oh! Doctor, have you told him?"

"Yes," he said gently; and then casting about in his mind for some word of consolation, and lighting on a sentence which he had heard quoted by deathbeds, he said, "Remember that the Lord gave and the Lord takes away."

Mercedes looked at him blankly for a moment, and then turned and went into Cipriana's house. No one was there, and she dropped on her knees by a chair and sobbed:

"O blessed Virgin, spare him. O most holy Mother of God, only consolation of mankind, intercede for us!"

She arose, striving to calm herself, and went into the room where her father lay. More than a dozen sympathetic neighbors were gathered there. As she entered they made way for her to pass to the sick man's pallet. Maria de los Angeles was by his side, noisy and selfish in her grief.

"Oh! Atanacio, what shall I do," she was saying, "where shall we live when you are gone? And my poor Mordicai away from home! O, what shall I do! What shall I do! And your poor sool! your poor soul will be lost, for you never would have nothing to do with the Holy Mother Church. Oh! Atanacio, let me send for the priest, so he may prepare you to die. Well, let me put this scapulary on you, so the Father will send the holy angels to take you to heaven," she went on in a persuasive tone, as the patient shook his head at the mention of the priest.

Mercedes knelt by the pallet and gently pushed away her aunt's hand, in which she held the scapulary, some gray flannel scraps an inch square on which were some stitches in woolen thread, saying: "No, aunt, no, don't trouble him with them now."

The sick man's eyes had been wandering restlessly about the room till they had rested on his daughter. The awful agony of a soul that looks into the darkness beyond death had seized him, but still even in that supreme moment, he felt that it was necessary to speak of something else:

"Mercedes," he gasped hoarsely, and with many pauses, "when I'm go—when I'm not here any longer to take care of you, ask Doña Frederica to find you something to do. And tell her I blessed on my death-bed for her kindness to you."

Mercedes thanked God that he did not know that her aunt had said to her during these last terrible days that "if anything should happen to her father she would have to sell vegetables in the market for a living."

"And, daughter," he continued, tightening his grasp on her hand, "the debts, never mind the debts. Don't ever try to pay them. A young, helpless girl could never do it. And they have been paid over and over in the lives of your kindred."

His eyes closed and his face relaxed from exhaustion, or perhaps it was one of those sudden changes that we have all noticed on the faces of the dying, a sure presage of the approach of the last enemy. An awful anxiety weighed on the daughter's mind compared with which the thought of what was to become of her was of little importance. And the time was so short; she must speak, if he would only awake again from that stupor!

Presently he opened his eyes again. He was restless and fumbled with the covers and talked incoherently. But when his eyes found her he grew calm again.

"Oh! papa," she sobbed tremulously, "are you going alone? Have you no hope of salvation?"

"Do you believe there is a God, Mercedes?" he asked, his face twitching convulsively.

"Oh! yes, papa, I believe there is a God."

"But you don't believe there is a hell. You said so the other day."

"Oh! I don't know, papa, I don't know. There may be a hell. Oh! papa, ask the Blessed Virgin to plead with her Son for you. Look at the crucifix, papa, and plead for mercy." Maria had placed a crucifix on a table at the foot of the pallet, with two lighted candles before it. He turned his eyes toward the crucifix but no hope brightened them. Again he fumbled at the covers and talked incoherently. When he was calm again the daughter asked:

"Papa, may I send for the priest that he may give you absolution and the extreme unction?"

"There is no hope in that, daughter." But he added, as he noticed her agonized face, "if it will be any comfort to you you may send for him."

It was about an hour later when the priest arrived. The bystanders saw at a glance that he had been drinking and that he was in a bad humor. They made room for him to pass and he stalked to the foot of the pallet, and stood looking sullenly at the sick man.

"Papa," said Mercedes, bending over her father, who had been asleep or in a stupor for some time, "Papa, the Father is here."

He opened his eyes and looked at her intelligently a moment, then turned them on the figure in the long black robes. The sensual face was quite familiar to him.

"Yes," said the priest, in a taunting tone, "you managed to live without me but when you come to die you are not above sending for me."

The dying man was far out in the waters of the Jordan, with the terror in his soul of the "something" which awaited him on the other side, but the insulting words reached him. Something like his former spirit flashed into his eyes; he raised his head and glared at the insolent face before him as he replied in a hoarse voice: "You go home to your wine. I will confess to God."

He dropped back on his pallet exhausted. The Reverend Father strode out of the room well pleased to be relieved from the performance of a duty for which he was to receive no money.   He was followed by the muttered indignation of the men and the wails of the women.

Atanacio did confess to God as that can be done by a dying man racked with pain, delirious at times, and with the terror of death and of the judgment in his soul.   What a place is a death-bed to prepare to meet God!   Far be it from me to say that he found salvation.   It is doubtful whether he had ever known, even in his most rational moments, enough of the plan of salvation to save a soul.   To him Christ had always been represented as an angry judge; and he had always heard that it was only through the intercession of the Virgin Mary that any good could come to mankind.   As an object of honor and worship she was placed above the Trinity.   Every day in Mexico people are going into eternity hopeless, confused, lost forever, because of these teachings of the Church of Rome.

An hour after the departure of the priest he aroused from the stupor in which he had lain for a few minutes and tightening his grasp on his daughter's hand, called feebly: .

"Mercedes."

She bent over him and caught his words as his stiffening lips uttered them:

"Adios.   You must not grieve for me.   Doña Frederica will"—but he was gone.

CHAPTER IX.

"WE ALL HAVE A MOTHER—THE EARTH."—*Victor Hugo.*

PRESENTLY Cipriana led Mercedes gently away and the neighbors of the dead man prepared him for burial. When she returned after daylight to the room the lifeless body dressed in clean, coarse, white clothing had been extended on a rude bed or scaffold lent by one of the neighbors. The crucifix and some images had been placed on the bed and there were two lighted candles at the foot and two at the head.

No religious services were to be thought of, for a funeral would cost more than so poor a family could pay, and the Catholic priests of Mexico are not shepherds who administer consolation to the members of their flocks "without money and without price." The confession and the extreme unction

Note.—I attended the funeral of a boy whose mother, though well connected, was unable to pay the priest for his services. His presence, his mumbled incantations, so to speak, the holy water and other things of the kind, would have been a great consolation to her.

"Why is the Señor Cure (the cure or curate, the principal priest) not here?" I asked of a sister-in-law of the bereaved mother, the wife of a relative of the priest.

"O, poor Carolina could not pay him, you know."

They did the best they could without him. There was an abundance of crucifixes, images, candles, and flowers in vases large and small, and lying loose about the white bed on which lay the marble form. The president of the college, who was also the superintendent of the public school to which the dead child belonged, came, bringing all his pupils marching, and each carrying his flag of the national colors. They filed into the room and stood around the bier.

A pine coffin, unusually deep, and covered with cheap pale blue worsted, stood by the bier. It was not lined, and as I looked at the unpainted boards I shuddered at the thought that the form of my little English pupil was to be placed in that hard resting place. But I was mistaken. They filled a third of its depth with wheat bran, put a snowy are free, but that is because the priests expect to be paid for them when they are paid for the funeral and the masses which are to follow.

The lonely watcher on the Orilla del Agua sat by the humble bier, her black shawl falling over her statue like face, her eyes wide open and tearless, fixed on the lifeless features before her. Kind neighbors came and went but she knew little of it. Cipriana's husband notified the civil judge of Atanacio's death and made the arrangements for his burial. The only survivor, a young daughter, the judge was informed, was too poor to pay either the $.25 asked by the law of the poor for the registering of a death or the $.50 for the grave; so, according to the law, he had them for nothing.

At four o'clock in the afternoon they brought in the box in which they were to carry the body to the cemetery. It was not a coffin—it was the *andas*—a pine box with rods on each side by which to carry it. It was kept in the cemetery for the purpose of conveying in it to the grave the bodies of those whose friends were to poor to afford coffins.

Mercedes saw them lay him in the *andas* and then as she bent over him and laid her face against his cold face a wail

---

sheet over it and then laid the little body on the soft bed. They put in the banner which he had been accustomed to carry in the processions of his school fellows on the great national holidays, on the 5th of May and the 16th of September, and then filled up the coffin with white flowers, leaving visible only the little white face. A young man of the college made a speech composed for the occasion, telling in glowing terms of the superlative virtues of their young friend, and assuring his companions that because of his good conduct he was now enjoying indescribable happiness at the right hand of God; to which happiness they themselves would attain if they would follow in his footsteps.

After that was over and the relatives and friends had taken a last look, the coffin was placed in a hearse, two boys, one on either side of the vehicle, took each in his hand an end of the long, pale blue ribbon which was attached to the lid of the coffin, and the hearse moved slowly through the streets to the cemetery followed by the gentlemen and boys. Women do not often attend burials in this part of Mexico. Without further ceremony the coffin was placed in the grave, the earth was thrown in and heaped up and rounded into a mound like those which are so sadly familiar to us all.

of anguish broke from her lips which brought tears to the
eyes of all the bystanders.   She wondered vaguely if the separation would kill her, and perhaps wished that it might.
One of the women lifted her up and led her gently away, and
the men, closing the box slightly. lifted it on their shoulders
and bore it through the doorway, and through the court, and
through the great front entrance, and along the street to the
cemetery, to the department for the poor.

There a grave had been prepared, a grave which appeared
to be too short by a foot for the form of the man they bore.
But at the bottom there was an excavation to receive the
head so that the clods might not fall on the face.   They lifted
the body from the *andas*, lowered it, and placed the head in
this excavation.   This is not always done gently, but these
men did it so, remembering, each of them, that his turn was
coming, and that when it came he might be as poor as his
neighbor; thinking, too, that they would tell how it was done
to the young girl at home.   Then the clods fell.   There was
none of that fearful resounding of clods on the boards that
has torn so many hearts, but a dull, low sound that was more
terrible.   The daughter was at home, but her spirit had gone
every step of the way by the side of the *andas* and now it
stood by and heard with shrieks the falling of the clods.   At
length the task was done,—rudely done, but kindly; and they
took up the *andas* and laid it down in its place by the side of
the adobe wall of the Campo Santo.

In that grave Atanacio would be permitted to rest for five
years; then his bones could be digged up and thrown in a
pile with those of other people; and the grave could be used
for the interment of another body.

"That way of burying is not so common as it was a few
years ago," said a member of our church as he diligently made
cigarettes.   "It seldom happens now that even the very
poorest are buried without coffins.   My first wife died three
years ago, you know; I thought I should have to bury her
without a coffin as I had had to quit work for some time on
account of her sickness, but my cousin happened to come and

he lent me $4.00 to buy a coffin.   No," he continued quietly in answer to my question, "the excavations for the head are not always made; that is an act of special kindness."

"But don't they put boards or anything over the body? They don't—just throw the earth in—on the body?"

"Well, those who can afford it put a sheet over the body, or at least a handkerchief over the face.   But if they hav'nt those things what can they do?"

Let us talk of something else, dear friends.

CHAPTER X.

IN THE HOUSE OF HER FATHER'S MASTER.

THERE was no time for idle grief for Mercedes and her aunt; they sat down after the last scene of the tragedy to make cigarettes.   Could they save enough from the daily food of the family to pay for the rent of a house, little as it might be?

Her aunt's voice and all sounds seemed far off to Mercedes. We all know, I suppose, what these times are, when the spirit is benumbed or paralyzed with the sense of loss, when there is no plan in the mind, no hope in the soul, when the earth seems to stand still during that awful time of the involuntary and unconscious readjusting of our lives to sadly changed circumstances.

The young girl's imagination sometimes pictured to her the market where the coarse and poorly dressed women sat on low chairs or on the stone pavement sewing and gossiping with their vegetables spread out before them, the market with all its uproar of voices crying the goods in singsong tones; but she seemed to have lost the power of suffering on all but one subject.

The morning of the fourth day as they sat at their work there was a knock at the door and Mercedes as she arose to open it made the customary query, "Who is it?" and received the usual perspicuous answer, "I." Opening the door she found there Frederica and a servant girl   Forgetful of everything but the presence of sympathy she caught her hand exclaiming:

"Oh, Doña Frederica!"

"My poor child!" said the lady, putting her arms around her, "I only reached home yesterday and I did not know it till this morning." She had been out of town for two weeks.

She sat down and the girl knelt beside her and let the pent

up tears flow freely.   When she was calmer, Frederica would have talked with her but for the garrulity of Maria de los Angeles.   Finally she arose to go exacting a promise from Mercedes that she would go to her on the morrow.

"Something must be done," thought she as she returned home.   She thought of a plan which might possibly succeed, and waited impatiently for the end of the *siesta* that afternoon to try to put it into execution.

About four o'clock that afternoon she sat talking with Doña Flavia Salazar de Urbina, the lady whom we saw three years ago at the chapel of the Holy Wood.

They sat in a room of medium size.   The floor was made of smooth black stone, oiled and polished to shining.   The only thing that detracted in the least from its beauty was the irregular stripes of lighter-colored mortar with which they were joined.   Here and there were handsome, bright rugs. One of these, a large one, lay in front of a sofa made of polished cattle horns and upholstered with crimson rep.   On either end of the rug and facing each other sat a chair also made of horns and upholstered with the same material.   The inside blinds of the large and deep window were open showing the shutters wooden at the bottom for about a foot and a half and glass above.   The light fell subdued and rosy through shades of some gauzy, crimson stuff into which were woven or embroidered straw colored cranes and great bugs and flowers.   Beyond the blinds were the slender iron bars that protected the room from intruders from the street.   Near the window sat a round table with a rich brown cover.   On it was a large globe, a student's lamp and a newspaper or two.   Two or three well filled bookcases broke the monotony of the walls.   On the walls hung some maps and two portraits in oil, one of a lady, the other of a gentleman.   The latter showed a dark, handsome, Spanish face, and penetrating eyes.   The portrait of the lady was rosy and voluptuous. It reminded one of the portrait of Nina da Rienzi in Rome as it is described in "The Last of the Roman Tribunes." Subtracting some fifteen years from the age of the lady who was

talking with Frederica and we are sure we have the original of
this portrait; and the other is that of her husband.

It was here in this room that he sat in the evenings and
read his papers and letters, before he joined in the parlor his
wife and children and any guests that might drop in.

Doña Flavia was Don Francisco's second wife. He had
thought himself a very fortunate man when, a widower with
seven children, he had won the rich, beautiful and amiable
belle of Guadalajara, the Señorita Flavia Salazar. Six times
had he and his present wife given joyful welcome to the wee
guests whose tiny fingers knocked at the doors of their hearts.
Of the two daughters who had been born to him in the time
of his first marriage, one had died, the other was in a convent
in France.

Somewhere in the house was an old but carefully kept
daguerreotype showing two handsome, happy young faces
pressed close together; and Don Francisco was accustomed
to tell his friends, with a smile as he looked at it, how he set
his heart on having the picture made that way, and how Antonia (his first wife) refused because she was ashamed, and
only yielded after many entreaties from himself. The bitterness had gone out of his great loss and there remained only
pleasant memories.

The second wife was not less tenderly loved because he had
loved much the wife of his youth. But when her portrait,
which he had secretly had made, was presented to her on her
saint's day, the first after their marriage, he had hung beside
it, here in this room, a portrait of himself as he looked in the
days of his youth. It was with a pang as much for him as
for herself that Doña Flavia noticed that.

Very tender were the ties between husband and wife and
parents and children. Often Don Francisco and Doña Flavia,
sitting alone together, side by side talked of the good qualities in their children; often and with tender looks they com-
mended them, and sometimes even in the presence of
strangers, for their loving attentions.

In the midst of his own children and of his children's chil-

6

dren, beloved by all of them, **Don Francisco dwelt like a pa-**
triarch of old, like **the** head of a tribe, **like a king in** the army.

"Yes, **thank you,**" Doña Flavia **was saying,** "My sister
was better **when we last** heard from **her** than she was when
you saw her here as she went on to New York. The journey
was good for her, **and** especially the **voyage.** They **relieved**
our anxiety by telegraphing from New York and again **from**
Havre. The letter—we have received only **one yet**—was
written from Paris. My brother-in-law, Don Gregorio, wrote,
and he **said** that Emilia **was so** much **better** that they had **de-**
cided **to** leave the younger children **with some** nuns in a **con-**
vent while they went on **to** the Holy **Land.** Jose Maria **was**
going **to** spend some time **in a** university."

"**When** do they expect **to return?**" asked Frederica, **so**
busy **with other** thoughts and so **anxious to find an oppor-**
tunity **to speak** of the subject that filled **her mind that she**
was **very much** afraid she might betray a lack **of interest by**
making inopportune remarks.

"**I** think they **hav'nt** much **idea.** They **want** the girls to
study French **there a few months, and Emilia** and Gregorio
will probably **go to Baden-Baden to spend some** time after
they return from **Palestine.** Jose Maria **will not** return with
them as he wishes **to travel.**"

"**He impressed me as quite** an intelligent young gentleman.
He called to see us at your request, you remember, the last
time we were in Mexico. He **will** appreciate such advantages."

"**Our** family have always been fond of traveling," modestly
replied Doña Flavia. She not infrequently **spoke of** the tastes
and peculiarities **of** her family. "**We have not** seen Jose
Maria since he was a **child.** When **we visited** my sister in
Guadalajara **he was** always **off at** school, and when we were
in Mexico we **always** happened **to** miss him; he did not stop
to see us with **the rest of the family as they** went to Europe;
he went some months before them."

And so the conversation wandered **on** till at last Frederica,
despairing **of finding a graceful** opportunity to introduce the

subject she wished to speak of and yet dreaded, said humor-
ously, and, she was afraid, a little abruptly, after a pause in
the talk:

"Well, Flavia, I called to consult you about what disposition to make of one of my *proteges.*"

"I shall be glad to help you if I can," replied the lady,
laughing.

"You have heard me speak of a young girl whom I have
taught for about three years, and of the fine progress she
made, and of the pleasure she was to me in every way,"
answered Frederica, instinctively praying to the First Cause
or some other invisible Power, whatever it might be called,
to give her the right words, and to incline the heart of her
friend to hear her favorably.

"Yes," said the listener, "I remember."

"Well, her father, who by the way, was one of your husband's
peons, died the other day leaving her entirely alone, or worse,
for she is with his step-sister, a miserable old woman who
does not treat her well. She must, if I can possibly accomplish it, be separated from her and be put in the way of
making her own living. And I remembered," she continued
plunging along desperately, "that I had heard you say you
wanted a governess for your little fellows and I came around
to recommend this girl, Mercedes, as she is called. She is
quite young, it is true—only seventeen—but she is well qual-
ified, for she is bright and she has been quite studious. She
is a devoted Catholic, too. I assure you she is in every way
much above her class. It gives one a better opinion of the
common people to see one of them turn out so."

"Y-e-s," replied the hostess, "it is very gratifying, of
course. But think of employing the daughter of a peon for
a teacher for the children! Blood will tell, Frederica, no
matter what appearances may be for the time. I might now,"
she added, evidently anxious to accommodate her friend, "I
might find some plain sewing for her to do. But as to the
other, I should have to consult Francisco before I answered
you," and the look of perplexity slipped away from her face
at the thought.

"Well, here he is, ready to deliver his infallible judgment on any question," said a hearty voice at the door, and Don Francisco entered. He was a handsome, portly gentleman, bearing well his sixty years. He was dressed in broadcloth and held his silk hat in his hand.

"Ah, here is our friend Frederica! At your feet, Señorita," he continued, his face lighting pleasantly as he advanced to shake hands with her.

"I kiss my hand to you, Señor," replied the visitor with a gracious bow.

Don Francisco sat down in one of the chairs in front of the sofa. After a few general remarks were exchanged Frederica said:

"You did come in at just the right time. I was trying to persuade Flavia to take one of my *proteges* off my hands, and she, like a good wife, said she must refer so important a question to her husband." Then she briefly repeated what she had said to her hostess. When she had finished he said:

"The overseer was telling me to-day that one of the men had died, she must be his daughter. He was a good workman, too, he said; he was sorry to lose him. Atanacio Gonzales, was that her father's name?"

"That was it," replied Frederica.

"He was very much in his debt, the overseer said; though that is always the case with these peons; I suppose they can't very well help it, they are so poor."

"Frederica says that she is quite a capable girl," put in Doña Flavia.

"O, that is not to be doubted of a girl who was educated by Frederica. She is like that old king who turned everything he touched to gold." Don Francisco was not inferior to any of his countrymen in stately or graceful gallantries. But he spoke sincerely when he complimented the fair German.

The question was discussed at length and it was decided that in deference to the opinions of their friend they would employ Mercedes to teach the younger children and to do plain sewing. The salary, though small, would seem like a fortune to the girl. In fact the generous hearts of Don Francisco and Doña Flavia warmed no little toward the poor young creature of whom their guest spoke so affectionately.

Her love for learning touched a responsive chord in the heart of the former. · Shrewd and successful business man though he was, the making of money had never been a favorite occupation. Not even in the discharge of the duties of the high positions in political life to which his countrymen called him had he forgotten the pleasure he had formerly found in the reading of his favorite authors. So when his wife remarked, "Since she is bright it really will be a pleasure to help her, and especially as she is a daughter of one of our workmen," Don Francisco added:

"Yes, we will see what we can do," then continued. "his father and brothers served me, too, so the overseer told me, and he said that Atanacio was the last one of the stock; I suppose he did not take the daughter into account."

Don Francisco and his wife had early imbibed the idea that there was "a great gulf fixed" between themselves and the common people, and nothing had as yet occurred to convince them that as "face answers to face in the water brook" so the hearts of rich to poor.

They were very kind indeed to their servants treating them as good masters in the United States used to treat their slaves. They paid them well, seeing to the comfort of their bodies, gave them medicine in sickness, permitted them to exchange work now and then, so that the chambermaid of one month was the nurse of the following month and the nurse was the chambermaid; and the ladies of the family had always instructed them in the Catholic religion being duly attentive to an extract in their Catechism from a Bull of Pope Paul V. in which he promises an indulgence of a hundred days for each time they instruct their children and their servants in the said Catechism.

But that was a very different thing from believing that a peon could actually break away from his caste and become one of them; for he had the common blood in him, you know. Still, Don Francisco reflected, no patriotic Mexican could doubt that it was possible for some of the common people to become very noble and useful, for some of the greatest statesmen that Mexico had yet produced had belonged to the common people.

"Well, really I have made quite a visit," said Frederica as she at last arose to go. "I can't tell you how grateful I am to you both, nor how happy I shall be to tell the poor child this good news to-morrow."

"The gratitude is on our side Frederica. You have furnished us a governess, and besides that an opportunity to do good to a fellow being," replied Don Francisco as he and Doña Flavia arose to accompany her to the street door.

Two weeks later Frederica and Mercedes sat with Doña Flavia in a small room near the back of the first court in the home of the latter. The window opened on the court in which there were orange and lemon trees with golden fruit, shrubs, flowers and vines, and in the center a fountain whose slender jet of water fell back in sparkling showers. Over the glass shutters some inexpensive lace was tacked closely. In one corner sat a small iron bed, painted red. The flowers of the crocheted counterpane were clearly outlined against the red spread beneath. The pillows were long and narrow and through the open work of the pillow-cases shone the red covers. There was a wardrobe on one side, and there were two corner tables on which were some inexpensive ornaments.

"I hope you will like your room," said Doña Flavia kindly. "I have taken pleasure in arranging it. You see I had hung opposite your bed a picture of the Blessed Virgin and the Holy Child so you will see it the last thing at night and the first thing in the morning. I was very much pleased when Frederica told me that you were a devoted Catholic. It really is gratifying," she continued, turning to Frederica, "in these times when heresy is spreading among the common people, to find one who is truly devoted to the Holy Mother Church."

She was not without the hope that her remarks might influence her elegant German friend, who, she knew, did not observe the rites of the church as scrupulously as, in her opinion, it behooved a gentle-woman to do.

"And heresy is being introduced among the people is it?" Frederica replied quietly avoiding the word "common."

"O, yes indeed. Francisco has relatives living in the frontier along the Rio Grande and they write us that it is quite common to hear of gatherings of the ignorant people for the reading and explanation of the Sacred Scriptures. Just think of their defying the church in that way! There is no telling what pernicious ideas they will get. And they are even here in our own town teaching those dreadful heresies of Martin Luther."

The fair-haired lady winced. She never spoke of the doctrines of the teacher of Wittenberg. Her feelings had become more kind towards Protestants. If she had protested more herself against the rule of the mother church she would not now be a lonely stranger in a foreign land.

About two years before this she had seen in a newspaper an account of the death of the wife of Herr Gaussen. No hope had sprung up in her heart, he had long ago forgotten her, or his companionship with that lovely Christian woman had taught him that she was wholly unworthy of him. But he was in trouble now, a lonely man with motherless children about him. She found herself thinking of that almost every day. After all, wherein had he sinned in becoming a Lutheran? she asked herself. Was not he as capable of judging of the true meaning of the Sacred Scriptures as any Catholic priest?

But Doña Flavia was still talking "Those who are here in town call themselves—let me see what they do call themselves—Presbyterians; and they say the Baptists have established a mission here in the last few days; the Baptists, the very worst of all of them! There is no way to stop the spread of the disease now that the laws protect them. It is such a pity!"

"What do they teach?" asked the visitor.

"O, I don't know," replied the Señora Urbina.   "I don't
want to know.   It is dangerous to inquire into such things."
She had even tried to win back some of these Presbyterians.
She had had her coachman drive her elegant carriage to that
part of town, and alighting, had picked her way in delicate
shoes, with daintily uplifted skirts, into the poor house.
Her success was not flattering, and she had come to the conclusion that such obstinacy must be due to the influence of
Satan.

After supper Mercedes was sent for to go to the parlor.
It was with a timid heart that she entered the brightly lighted
room.   It was, as Mexican parlors generally are, a large,
long room.   The beams overhead were painted white with
gilded edges, and from them hung large lamps whose many
prisms sparkled in the light.   Two large windows opened on
the street, and over them were gracefully draped silken curtains.   A brussels carpet covered the floor.   At one end of
the room was the usual group consisting of sofa and two arm
chairs in front of it facing each other.   They were upholstered
in pinkish damask over which trailed vines and flowers.   In
front of one window sat a small stand with gilded legs on
which was a pot of exquisite artificial flowers.   There were
rugs and handsome tables with ornaments, a piano, and, on
the delicately tinted walls some portraits and other pictures.

There was the usual evening gathering of children, grandchildren and friends.   A group of girls and young gentlemen
at the piano were playing, and discussing the music.   Other
groups about the room were talking quietly.   Doña Flavia
beckoned Mercedes to come and sit near her.

In a few minutes Don Francisco entered and there was a
general movement at the end of the room to open the way
for him to the sofa, the seat of honor; but seeing a great arm
chair vacant by the side of his wife he sat down in that.
Mercedes noticed afterwards that he always sat by her, and
that his hand, unconsciously to himself, as it seemed, nearly
always rested on her shoulder.

Pretty, daintily dressed children flitted about the room now stopping a **moment** to kiss Don Francisco on the lips, then stooping as they passed to kiss **the** hand of an uncle or father as **it** lay on the arm of his chair, or slipping **an arm** about the **neck** of an aunt or mother to say something **in** a low tone.

Don Francisco was evidently a favorite with the young people. Now and then girls gathered about him in a circle and engaged in lively conversation. All appealed to him; one would not fail to see that he was the center of attraction in the room.

Presently Doña Flavia said, "Francisco, **this** is the **new** teacher."

"Ah," **he** said pleasantly, "Mercedes is your name isn't it."

"Yes, **Señor,** Mercedes Gonzales, at the orders of your Worship."

"Well Mercedes," he continued, smiling, "you will have a pretty good school. The boys and girls are like flies in my **house.**"

A little fellow who was lying on a **sofa** rolled over **and** laughed at his father's witticism.

"Would you like to begin to-morrow to see how little they know?"

"Whenever you please, Sir."

"Mercedes," said one of **the** little girls, coming up to her chair, "you didn't know there were ghosts in this house, did you?"

"No," **she replied,** trying to smile.

"Well, **there are, really,**" **she** averred, looking at her with very wide, would-be **solemn eyes,** "arn't there, papa?"

Don Francisco nodded and said abstractedly, "So they say."

Two or three more children gathered around to see the effect of the ghost story on the stranger. .

"O, it's a dreadful story," went on Carolina. "About three hundred years ago a wicked **old** Marquis from Spain lived here. One time when he was in another hacienda of his a great many miles from here he gave a ball, and when they were **all as** gay as could be singing and dancing and playing he told then that **he was** sick and that he was going to his

room, but they must go on enjoying themselves. But he
wasn't sick at all; he just wanted to come here to kill his
wife.   So he and a servant slipped out and they got on horses
and they rode and rode and rode till they came to one of his
ranches and there they changed horses and rode and rode till
they reached here. And the Marquis came in and murdered his
wife.   He wanted to murder his little baby girl too but the
nurse hid it so he could not find it.   And they went out and
jumped on their horses and rode and rode till they came to
his hacienda; and he went into his room; and it was nearly
day.   When it was time for breakfast he came out of his room
just as if he had slept there all night, and told them he felt
better.   But ever since he killed his wife a woman dressed
all in white cries at night in the orchard behind the house,
and sometimes away in the night a carriage with ghosts in it
and drawn by ghost horses drives out of this house and drives
all about through the streets of the town."

She ended breathless.   Little Lazaro put his elbow on Mercedes' knee and his chin on his hand and whispered, "Arn't
you scared, Mercedes?"

"Not very badly," she replied, slipping her arm about the
child.

Anita crept closer and in a frightened tone said to a young
gentleman who sat near the window, "Rafael, please close
the blind.   I am afraid of the dark out there."

A little while after the company broke up, those who had
dropped in coming up to say good night to Don Francisco
and Doña Flavia.   The grandchildren kissed their hands at
parting.

When Mercedes said good night to them Don Francisco
said, smiling:

"You must not dream of the wicked Marquis to-night."

She reached her room just in time, for all the evening the
knot in her throat had been growing larger.   She closed the
door and burst into tears.   But after a few minutes of violent
weeping she controlled herself sufficiently to say her prayers,
for in this time of affliction she had become more attentive to

religious duties. She knelt and repeated the prayer to the "Holy Guardian Angel" which is prescribed for the night in Father Ripalda's Catechism:

"O my holy Guardian Angel! Thou seest that delivering myself up now to sleep I am going to put myself in a state in which I cannot take care of myself; therefore I need now more of thy assistance and care. Do not permit, my Holy Angel, that the powers of darkness have dominion over me; deliver me from injurious, impure and troublesome dreams; and when I awake in the morning do not allow the devil to rob me of the first fruits of the day, but suggest to me some thought that may carry all my heart and affection to my Creator. Amen."

Then crossing herself many times as a protection against the evil influences that might linger in that room—for the murder might have taken place there, she reflected—she lay down. She cried herself to sleep; for the thought that all this good fortune had come to her through her father's death was a very bitter one.

She dreamed that the Marquis with the thin, dark face and the small, deep-set eyes bent over her ready to kill her. She struggled out of that nightmare, and after a long time slept again and dreamed that as she sat in her room she heard a carriage rolling through the court and the tread of horses, but it was not like the tread of living horses, though they went swiftly. She sprang up and opened the door, and there was the carriage, a very old fashioned one, such a one as Charles V. might have ridden in, it seemed to her, and it was all worm-eaten and dropping to pieces. She looked through the door, and there sat a ghostly lady "all in white." There were other ghosts in the carriage but she did not see them distinctly. As she looked the lady fixed her great dark eyes on her and cried out, "O save my baby! save my baby!" And then the phantom horses plunged forward with their phantom load, and away they went through the hall and past the parlor door, and through the great front door which opened to them of its own accord. And so they went on

through the streets of the town while the people slept.   Then
Mercedes awoke and was glad that this, too, was a dream.

After a long time she slept again and dreamed that she
heard the wild cries of a woman.   She went to the window
which, as it seemed to her looked on an orchard, and there
under a tree was the woman all in white wringing her hands
and crying; and as she looked at her suddenly it was not the
Marchioness but her father who was wringing his hands and
crying.   The red flames of purgatory arose around him.
When he saw her he stretched out his hands to her and cried,
"O, Mercedes, help me out, help me out!"   And in her struggle to break the spell that held her so she could go to him,
she awoke.   It seemed real to her; her father's own voice
had called her from the spirit world, and he had begged her
to help him.   She had wished he might come to her and he
had come—to beg for masses for the repose of his soul.

CHAPTER XI.

A FEW THINGS ABOUT SCHOOLS AND CONVENTS.

IN the first days of her life in Don Francisco's house Mercedes often wondered where was Magdalena, the pretty daughter of Doña Flavia whom she had seen at the **little** chapel on the hill. After a few days she asked. She was at school, Doña Flavia replied. She had been for three years in a College of the Sacred Heart of Jesus in a city in the southern part of Mexico. "We wanted her to be in the care of the holy nuns while she had to be away from us," she said, forgetting that Don Francisco had only consented, and very **reluctantly, to her plan.**

I **have been able to** get very little definite **information about Catholic schools in** Mexico. It is said that **all of them are under** the control of the Jesuits. That may strike you as strange since the followers of Ignacius de Loyola have been banished from the country. They are here, nevertheless.

Some people who have a great horror of the Jesuits are very complacent towards the Catholics in general. They do not know **that** Catholicism has become Jesuitism. The Jesuitical doctrines **which** authorize mental restrictions, lying, perjury, stealing, secret compensation and murder are now, so those who have studied the subject tell us, the doctrines of the whole **Roman** Catholic Church; and all the clergy and, in short, all **who** teach that religion are required to teach them. They are, then, taught in all the Catholic schools.

It is said that far more attention is given to the instruction of the pupils in the principles of Catholicism than in those of **the** text-books. A young lady who in her childhood attended a Catholic school in the city of Mexico told me that the principal thing she studied was the catechism.

As **to** the text-books, your attention has often been called to the Romanism in them. In the histories which they use there are gross violations of truth, for instance when they treat of such occurrences as the Massacre of St. Bartholomew's eve.

I was once betrayed by ignorance into buying some Roman Catholic text-books for the use of a class of young ladies to whom I was teaching English here in Mexico. Some of them had the books, spelling books and readers, having used them when they attended a Roman Catholic school in Texas, and they wished to continue to use them on account of the expense of buying new ones. I saw that they were prepared "By a Catholic Teacher," but I thought, "Of course they teach no denominationalism; no school books do that."

I found that they were full of Romanism; even the simple sentences in the spelling book which was intended for beginners in the United States were full of Catholicism. I refused of course to use them, and finally succeeded in selling them at a sacrifice to the principal of that school which the young ladies had attended.

You are familiar with the statement that there are no convents nor monasteries in Mexico.

In Bancroft's History of Mexico I find this paragraph which I translate: "Another notable act of Juarez was the decree of confiscation of the goods of the church on July 12, 1859, founded on the fact that the clergy had been the principal support of the royalists during the war of independence and since then the most powerful enemies of liberal ideas, promoting the present fratricidal war with the object of retaining supremacy in civil affairs as well as in religious affairs. This decree returned to the nation all the property which the regular and secular clergy possessed, separated the church and state and at the same time conceded to all the religious sects the right of public worship. Religious ministers were to receive for their services only voluntary contributions and they were not to hold real estate; at the same time it commanded the dissolution of all the religious societies, considering them dangerous to the public welfare. These measures aroused the malevolence of the clerical party who did not hesitate to oppose them in the confessional, in the pulpit, and by the worn out means of excommunication, making use of the timid consciences of the women and the fears of the people."

But the law stood firm and six months afterward the victorious army of Juarez, 25,000 in number, entered the capital, greeted by the acclamations of their friends, and proceeded to enforce it.

The monasteries and convents (they are all called convents in Mexico) were, many of them, in the heart of the city, and they had grown so large that they had crossed and closed streets. Juarez drew up his army in front of one after another where they closed the streets and commanded to batter them down with cannon balls. It was not a measure of war; it was only the easiest way to open the streets. Those of the monks and nuns who still lingered in defiance of the law fled when they saw that dark mass of men and the threatening cannon before the walls. After the buildings were opened thus the soldiers rushed in.

"We were so furious against the convents," said a gentleman who was a captain in that army, relating it many years afterward to a friend from whom, in turn, I heard the narrative, "that we rushed in and tore down the shrines and altars and broke the images and trampled them under foot, and threw the books into the streets."

Many of the books were picked up and preserved. Some of them are to be seen now in the halls of the National Library. Many of them were sold for trifles at the book stands. This old leather-covered, warped, yellow-leafed, worm-eaten copy of the Catechism of the Council of Trent in the book case at my elbow is one of them; in the last few weeks I have had occasion to consult others of them.

So numerous and so large were these convents that one wonders how there was room for houses of any other class.

When they were confiscated to the state and the inmates were expelled, they were given the choice of returning to their families or leaving the country. Many of them embarked for Italy where they took refuge in the convents of Milan; others laid aside the veil and the monastic habit and lived as other people; a few of the women continued to wear the habit, living as nuns in the houses of their relatives, and their faces never have, to this day, been seen in the streets. Prisoners they are, like His Holiness in the Vatican, and as worthy of sympathy as he.

There are not a few nuns in Mexico in charge of schools. I once traveled for some distance in company with two of them; it was on a train which at the end of its journey entered the City of Mexico. They were elegant looking women, in handsome but plainly made black dresses, bonnets and long veils. They conversed in low musical voices and in two or three languages. I could very well imagine that they were highborn and high-bred women. There was nothing about them but the nun's dress to indicate that they were tainted with the moral leprosy which is contracted from the use of the doctrines of Loyola and from other Roman Catholic influences and practices—nothing but the dress and a catalogue of a school in the shawl-strap of one of them, a catalogue of a College of the Sacred Heart of Jesus.

A great many kinds of very fine needlework are taught in the Catholic Schools here. When the young ladies become very proficient they are permitted to embroider with gold, silk and velvet robes for the Archbishops.

Magdalena's letter to her mother conveying the intelligence that this honor had been conferred on her gave great pleasure to that lady, not only because it was a proof of her daughter's proficiency in the art of embroidery, but because she was to be engaged in so high a religious work. All such good works would tend to shorten her prospective stay in purgatory.

When this letter was read to Mercedes she went off into day dreams about the elegance of the school and of the teachers, about the privilege or learning to make all those beautiful things, and especially about the religious training of which her mistress spoke with so much enthusiasm. Ah! the way to heaven must seem very plain to Magdalena, while she must go on all her life groping in the dark, a lost child!

If she could only become a nun, she thought, if she were only good enough to live among the holy nuns, spending her days and nights in meditations and prayers and good works, she might find peace of soul.

CHAPTER XII.

PURGATORY.

ONE afternoon, about a month after Mercedes began to teach in Don Francisco's house, she helped her restless, happy little charges, Jose Maria, or Pepe, as they generally called him, Lazaro and Alejandro into their riding suits, and watched them as each mounted on his own pony dashed off down the street with the servant for their usual afternoon ride. Then she went back into the house thinking how pretty and lovable they were. As she passed to her own room Don Francisco, who was sitting in the corridor with Doña Flavia, called her. She went up to them and at their invitation sat down near them on the bent wood sofa. After a little conversation about the children Don Francisco said pleasantly:

"Would you not like to have some money, Mercedes? You are unlike most young ladies if you would not."

"I thank you, Don Francisco," she replied with some confusion. "I owe you more than I can ever pay you; but I need some money—a good deal of what you promised to pay me, in fact—very much."

"What do you owe me for?" he asked, in surprise, straightening himself up in his chair.

"My father owed you, you know."

"O, that is it! Why, didn't you know that when a laborer died his debts were all forgiven?"

"Yes, Señor, I knew that. But if they are just debts," she continued, looking steadily at him, "if they are just debts they ought to be paid by the children."

Don Francisco winced a little and wondered if his shrewd overseer was not more exacting than he ought to be.

"Well, it is the custom to forgive all the debts, and if it were not I should not allow you to pay me anything."

"I thank you, Don Francisco. My father tried very hard to pay you. He killed himself trying to pay you; but no matter how hard he worked or how little he bought the debt grew larger and larger. It was the same way with my grandfather and my uncles. They all died trying to pay debts which grew larger and larger, they never knew how." And she gave way to her overwrought feelings by bursting into tears. The pent up indignation of three generations gave her the strength, now that she stood face to face with the oppressor of her people, to tell him of their wrongs.

"I know that the overseer did it," she went on as soon as she could control her voice. "And they say you never know much of what goes on in your haciendas. But none the less are your peons ground down year after year into deeper depths of poverty and anxiety."

"Well, child, I am afraid the overseers are not as good men as they might be; but it is all over now. So don't cry any more, and take your money."

"I thank you, Don Francisco," she replied as she took the money and then went to her room.

Don Francisco and his wife talked a little while and then he went out and walked a long time in the orchard. His reflections were not pleasant; he could not help feeling, notwithstanding what she had said about the overseer, that he was to blame to some extent, and that she thought so. There was something awful in the way that weak, helpless daughter of the people had turned on him like a wild beast at bay. What if there should come a great day of reckoning in which all these laborers of his should face him and accuse him! He had little belief in supernatural things, and things to come to pass after death, nevertheless he thought a good deal of the day of judgment that afternoon. They were strange thoughts to him, these of injustice and accusers, for he had always thought of himself as a generous and kind-hearted man; he had even been called a philanthropist, and the term had not sounded strange to him.

Two or three times he lighted a cigarette and then threw

it down and walked on with his head down and his hands behind him.

It was an evil, he admitted, the existence of these great
haciendas. But what could be done about it? Nothing till
he died and then his would be divided among his children.
Let time settle it! And with this reflection he went back to
the house and ate his *merienda* and went off to his office.

Mercedes had her cry out with a vague feeling that she
was responsible for all the sins of all the superintendents in
Mexico, and a great dread of the consequences to herself of
her outburst of indignation. She would have been willing to
sacrifice her own interests if there had been any hope of bene-
fitting those others of her class who were on Don Francisco's
haciendas; but she could not flatter herself with that hope.
However, as little trouble came of it for her as there was benefit in it for others.

She went on as usual with her teaching of text-book and
catechism. She put herself in the way of reaping whatever
of profit there is in the pope's promise of indulgences to
teachers, as she found it in the catechism which is in common use. It reads as follows:

"Indulgences. Seven years to school teachers each time
they, on Sundays or festive days, assemble the children to explain the Catechism to them; and one hundred days for each
time they do this in the classes on week days." Mercedes
had very indefinite ideas about it all; the teaching of the catechism was a good work, and as salvation was to be purchased
by good works it was well to be as diligent in the performance of them as possible. It is more difficult to introduce
the idea of the freedom of salvation into the mind of a Catholic than any other.

But there was another subject which troubled Mercedes far
more in these days than any thought of her own safety. Don
Francisco paid her regularly every month and with no less
regularity she paid to the priest all of her salary that she
could possibly spare to induce him to say masses for the repose of her father's soul. This money was not paid to the

priest who had visited her father on his death-bed; the sight of him was intolerable to Mercedes. It was paid to the cure. He was an aged man; by virtue of having been a priest for a great number of years he had at least one privilege of a bishop —that of saying High Mass (Misa Pontificial).

With the common people he indulged in coarse stories and jests; but as the spiritual adviser of the ladies of wealth and fashion he was supposed to adapt his conversation to their habits of thought.

The doctrine of purgatory is a rich mine of wealth for the Catholic Church. From McClintock and Strong's Cyclopedia we learn that the Jews received the idea of a purifying conflagration from the Persians. From the Jews it passed into the ethical speculations of the Christians. "But whatever the views of some church fathers on the subject as a doctrine, it was unknown in the Christian Church for the first 600 years, and it does not appear to have been made an article of faith until the tenth century when 'the clergy,' says Mosheim, 'finding these superstitious terrors admirably adapted to increase their authority and promote their interest, used every method to augment them; and by the most pathetic discourses, accompanied with monstrous fables and fictitious miracles, they labored to establish the doctrine of purgatory, and also to make it appear that they had a mighty influence in that formidable region."

"Purgatory, as a burning away of sins," said Dollinger at the Bonn Conference of Old Catholics in 1875, "was an idea unknown in the East as well as the West till Gregory the Great introduced it. He added the idea of a tormenting fire. This, the schoolmen gradually converted into doctrine which they associated with papal indulgence, till it came to apply to the dead generally, which of course made all seek for indulgence. It went on to have degrees; some could receive indulgence for a few of their sins, others for all, and so on; so that eventually the pope, having already the keeping of heaven and dominion on earth, obtained also sovereignty under the earth." (McClintock's Cyclopedia.)

Of the fees for masses for the dead the priest must pay a certain per cent. to the bishop, the bishop to the archbishop, the archbishop to the pope. No doubt, too, the pope is liberally paid to license such institutions as "purgatorial insurance companies, which for a certain premium paid annually insures the payor a certain number of masses for his soul in the event of his death." (Of the existence of such a company we learn in the Cyclopedia referred to above.)

It has been said that no matter how much money was paid for masses for the dead the priests seldom or never announced that the sufferer was released from torment. The reason for this is evident: as long as they could make the survivors believe that the relative was still in purgatory there was hope that they would pay for masses.

It often happens, however, that the money comes in too slowly to satisfy the avarice of the priest. Then he invents new methods to fill his purse. An additional advantage in these extra methods is that the money all belongs to the officiating priest.

Raffling is practiced in Mexico, not only for religious purposes, not only as a means of controlling the affairs of the unseen world, not only to obtain money for the building of churches and for the buying of the furniture for them; but it is practiced universally for private ends. Poor women will call at one's door to ask her to buy a number with the hope that she may be so fortunate as to win the prize—a pair of brass pendants for the ears; another displays to her admiring gaze a handkerchief, or a cushion, or a napkin, or an article of apparel, and solicits his dollar, half dollar or quarter, and his subscription on the dirty paper of names which she carries. If one has a horse to dispose of he is informed that an advantageous way would be to raffle him; if he wishes to select his intimate friends for the coming year—let him raffle for them.

If, therefore, he wishes his departed friends to escape from the torments of the condemned and enter into the "rest which remains for the people of God," let him raffle for it; the priest promises to say enough masses to insure the passage to heaven of the friends of those who draw the fortunate number.

One day several of the principal ladies of the church met with the Señor Cure in the parlor of the Señora de Urbina to arrange for a general raffle in favor of the souls in purgatory. The customary arrangements were made. A committee of ladies was appointed to go from house to house and solicit contributions. They were to ask for three cents from each person with the name of some sufferer in purgatory, if there was any in that place of torment who was dear to him.

Each name was to be numbered. As these zealous ladies would visit nearly every house in the town it would be a considerable sum which they would lay before the Señor Cure.

On a very few of the thousands of the slips of paper which he prepared he wrote, besides the number, the word "raffle," selecting the numbers carefully with respect to the names which accompanied them. For the person whose number was accompanied by this word sufficient masses were to be said to secure his exit from purgatory.

The raffle took place in the vestry of the church in the presence of a committee, the Señor Cure presiding. Afterwards the lucky numbers were announced to the congregation who waited kneeling on the stone floor of the church, the men with uncovered heads, the black-robed women with heads meekly bowed under black shawls or mantillas. They all waited, each in intensest expectation, their hearts full of tender memories, unusually fresh to-day, awed by the nearness of the unseen world and the mystery of the whole ceremony— hoping each to hear his chosen number called when the priest should enter.

Mercedes was one of those who knelt and waited, rapidly repeating Ave Marias and Pater Nosters, then forgetting them and slipping off into prayers for the dead, as she hoped and waited. But her number was not a lucky one. Neither was there a lucky number among those chosen by Doña Flavia for her mother who had been dead some fifteen years. The Señor Cure was too shrewd a business man to permit the escape of those whose relatives were able to pay for masses.

After the lucky numbers were announced the mass was

chanted with the usual accompaniment of burning candles, waving censers, smoking incense and the sighing and sobbing of music.   The priests in sacerdotal robes officiated, and the people were more and more impressed by the solemnity and mystery of the performance.

Filial love moved the Señora de Urbina to try again and again.   But the fates seemed to be against her.   Her mother, her pastor told her, must have committed some sin which was very hard to expiate.   But, he said, she should not be "weary in well doing, for in due season she should reap if she fainted not."

Among other methods which were used to accomplish the release of this good lady an all night meeting was held in the principal church by a society to which Doña Flavia belonged, and "His Divine Majesty, the Most Holy Sacrament" was exposed for their adoration.

At length the afflicted daughter resolved to have a raffle for her mother alone.   I cannot describe this proceeding better than in the words of a man who witnessed one of these private raffles in the house of a wealthy patron.   It was after he became a member of an evangelical church that he and his wife described it and acted part of it for my edification.

"All the rich ladies and gentlemen," he said, "were seated around the parlor"—

"All of them laughing and talking?" I asked, for I had seen so much levity in connection with these ceremonies that that seemed very probable.

"O, no! all of them very serious.   Crowds of servants and poor friends of the family stood around the doors and watched what was going on.   The cure stood by a table in the center of the room.   There were two goblets on the table and in each of them were the same number of slips of paper, all of them blank except one which bore the name of the person in purgatory for whom the trial was to be made.   Two little girls drew the papers from the goblets, drawing alternately, one from one goblet, the other from the other.   If the paper containing the name of the sufferer was the last to be drawn out, that indicated that it was not yet time for him to be delivered from torment, but if when that paper was drawn out there still remained papers in the goblets, then the cure was under obligations to say the masses for his deliverance."

"How much does each person pay the cure for the raffle?" I inquired.

"The prices differ. In this case they each paid $.25. "

"Did you believe in such things as that before you were converted?" I asked the man wonderingly, for he was a man of good sense.

"Why, of course. How could I help believing in it? All the Catholics do."

And I went off into wonder over the mysteries of the human mind, of the curious phases of thought and belief possible to minds which, according to all ordinary standards, are sane,— and into thankfulness that I had not been brought up in Roman Catholicism, that I too should believe such things.

But neither did the private raffle release the mother of Doña Flavia from the purifying fires.

There was not much hope in this raffle but there was evidently more hope of a successful end than in the general raffles. Mercedes resolved to try it.

She induced nine or ten women and girls, acquaintances of hers on the Orilla del Agua, to take part in the raffle, paying the money for some of them herself, though some of them, poor as they were, paid their own money. "Atanacio had a contempt for the Holy Church it is true," they said, "but that did not save him from purgatory, and of course it is right that his daughter should try to relieve him."

So it came to pass that one bright morning these women and girls knelt in the vestry of the church and watched the children draw out the papers. These children wore short calico dresses. Their stockings dropped down over their rusty shoes. The front part of their hair was tied on the tops of their heads, so that it made a topknot, that arrangement being convenient to keep it out of their eyes; the remaining hair was tightly braided. Now and then the performance

was interrupted for a few moments while the little fingers
clawed their heads vigorously.   But the heavenly innocence
was still in their faces, and there was not sufficient dirt on
the fat little hands that went fumbling in the goblets to obscure the baby grace.

The spectators scarcely breathed in their suspense; but
now and then there slipped through the red lips of the children a little rippling laugh as a hand missed the goblet or
dived into it with needless impetuosity.

Mercedes' mind was wrought to a high pitch by superstitious awe, and by another feeling; there was a dread, a
dark something that had shown itself among the shadows of
her mind now and then, during these months when she had
been trying to pay her father out of purgatory; it had never
before come so near, nor stared into her face with such men-
acing look as it did this morning.   It was the thought that
whatever her justifying reasons might be, it was a shameful
thing to disobey her father; it was a want of respect for him
on the part of his daughter, it was humiliating him among
his neighbors to permit that these priests, who, according to
his judgment, were the worst of men, should handle his name,
should make expiation for him.   She had a vague feeling that
this Something would some day come boldly out of the shadows and seize her and hold her in its horrible clutches while
it stared down into her eyes and read through them all the
disobedience and want of respect for her father.   The night
before as she sat thinking of this she had buried her burning
eyes and parched lips in her hands and had moaned: "O God,
I don't know what is right!   Have mercy on me!"

The papers fluttered and rustled as they were drawn out of
the goblets.   They were nearly all out.   The attention had
become intense.   The eyes of the women were on the little
white, fluttering things with which was so mysteriously connected more than life or death.   At last—they could not be
mistaken—they saw the name on a paper which one of the
little, fat hands grasped.   The priest would have given not
a little to snatch it from the child's hand and slip it back into
the goblet.

A sigh of relief broke from their lips as they arose to their feet. But there was no brightness of joy in Mercedes' face. Was this triumph? There was a mixture of feelings in her mind. Now that it was all over that dreaded Something had come out of the shadows and grasped her. She saw in his true light the man who stood before her with the forced smile in his eyes and the false words of congratulation on his lips. A horror of darkness had fallen on her in the midst of the bright day.

CHAPTER XIII

REVELATIONS.

AS the days passed this darkness was not lifted, neither was there any rift in the clouds. It seemed to her she must be contemptible in the eyes of God and man.

One day in the midst of this darkness she received a message from Frederica requesting her to come to her. She received her with a shining face, and there were roses in the girdle of her dainty summer dress, a phenomenon which Mercedes had never noticed before.

"I sent for you, dear," said Frederica when they were seated in her room, "to tell you that I am going off a long way; I am going back to Germany to live. I—in fact—I am going to be married in a few days," and the delicate color mounted to her cheeks and spread over the white column of her neck.

Mercedes only stared at her blankly and repeated "going off," "going to be married."

"Yes, dear, a friend whom I knew in Germany a long time ago has come, and we are to be married and go back to his home. I want you to be at my marriage. You can put off your black dress for that evening. You can get a pretty white dress; you will need it soon anyhow. Get Maria Goribar to make it for you; Doña Flavia will help you select it. You will come, won't you, daughter? It is very hard for me to leave you. you have been a great pleasure to me."

The girl, making an effort to repress a sob, and to connect in her mind such incongruities as her teacher, and priests and Romish ceremonies, replied: "Yes, I will·be at the marriage, of course. You will be married in the church?"

"No, we shall be married only by the civil officer here at home."

"And not in the church at all!" exclaimed Mercedes in amazement. "Shall you feel that you are married?" and then she feared that her unpremeditated words had given unpardonable offense.

"O yes, my friend is not a Catholic. He would not be married by the Church."

"Is he," stammered Mercedes, as Frederica paused, "is he a Free Mason?" She thought of the Protestants, but she could not insult her teacher by asking if she was to marry a Protestant. Still she knew it was scarcely less bad to ask if she was to marry a Mason.

A merry smile broke over Frederica's face. "O no, he is not a Mason—that is, at least—I don't know whether he is or not. But he is a Protestant, a Lutheran."

Mercedes felt as if she were slipping over successive precipices—a mason, a Protestant, a disciple of Martin Luther! She looked at the fair, womanly face before her as if she expected to discover in it the beginning of a transformation into something monstrous; then the recollection that she was to lose her only friend, her sweet, motherly teacher, swept away all other thoughts. She slipped down by Frederica's chair, and covering her face with her hands dropped her head on her shoulder and sobbed, as she had done after her father's death.

The lady's tears, too, fell on the dark, shining head. After some time the girl succeeded in calming herself. She looked up and said:

"But you are very happy, are you not, Doña Frederica?"

"Yes, dear, I am very happy. I shall be happy in my new home. I shall have a house full of boys and girls to care for. But I shall not forget my dear girl in Mexico."

They talked a little while longer, and then Mercedes went home, her mind full of confused thoughts. She must buy the dress and have it made. For a few days she had little time to think of her troubles, and in the meantime they were slipping away from her. The suffering was too intense to last, and besides that it was inevitable that a strong, healthful nature like hers should soon throw off gloomy thoughts. She was happy, too, for her benefactress, though the loss to her seemed an irreparable one.

The reader has guessed of course, to whom Frederica was to be married.

Three months before Herr Gaussen had been seized with a desire to see something of the United States of America. He came over, spent some time among the northern cities, visited the Great Lakes and the Niagara Falls, went to California, and while there decided to return by the southern route and visit some old friends in Texas.

He spent a few days with them and then started on his homeward journey. One day just before noon he stood in the waiting room of a railway station in San Antonio. He would find out what time the northern bound train went out, then leave his valise there and stroll about the town awhile. His intention was to go immediately to New York and thence to Hamburg. His thoughts had turned with new anxiety to his business and to his children whom he had left in the care of one of his sisters.

He stepped to the window to make some inquiries. The agent stood ready to serve him, when, in that instant, these words flashed through his mind, distinctly as if some one spoke to him: "Go to Salta, Mexico."

He hesitated and put his hand to his forehead. The agent inquired in a business-like way:

"What can I do for you, Sir?"

"Excuse me, nothing I think, thank you," he replied and walked away from the window and out on the platform.

"Go to Salta, Mexico!" he repeated. "What for?" Frederica lived there, as he happened to know; but he had not thought of seeing her on this journey, or of ever seeing her again. He had thought of her often since his wife's death; he could very easily have returned to all his old tenderness for her, but he had had no intimation of any change in her feelings with regard to the things which had separated them. In fact he had heard almost nothing about her since their parting so long ago. He knew, however, that she had never married. This mysterious injunction to go to Salta, Mexico, must have some connection with her; "it must mean —it could mean nothing else—" he caught his breath and grasped tightly the head of his umbrella.

He had not failed to learn in all these years of his Christian life that there sometimes come to men promptings from the invisible world, promptings which must be obeyed, or which, if they should be disobeyed, would be followed by leanness of soul. He had never disobeyed, he doubted if it were possible. Would he obey now? He could not do otherwise. Yet how strange it was!

There rushed into his soul a flood of tenderness for the woman whom he had loved in his youth,—a rushing, impetuous flood that swept away ever barrier that had lifted itself like granite between them. How distinctly he saw now the golden head and the innocent eyes that had been his joy and pride!

These thoughts flashed through his mind in a very few minutes. There was nothing unusual in the appearance of the gentleman who stood on the platform meditating in this way, his silk hat in one hand and his umbrella in the other. Those who happened to notice him probably thought of him as a quiet, well-dressed, distinguished looking German gentleman. A successful business man, he was, evidently; but a decided stamp of benevolence and culture in his face and manner convinced them that all his thoughts had not been devoted to money-getting. He spoke English with foreign constructions and a strong German accent. There was certainly nothing in his appearance to indicate that God had spoken to him; yet it was true.

He turned suddenly. He would obey the divine command; in fact he would have obeyed with almost equal promptness if all his feelings had urged him to do otherwise.

He walked briskly to the ticket window and rapped.

"I wish to go to Salta, Mexico," he said as the agent came up.   "Does the train pass this station?"

"No, you will have to cross the town."

"What time is the train due?"

"In a few minutes."

"Can I make it?" he asked with a start.

"You may, possibly," replied the agent indifferently, "but you will have to get a move on you if you do."

"Thank you," exclaimed Herr Gaussen, and seizing his valise he rushed out.   Fortunately a hack was near.

"Here, my man, what will you charge to carry me to the other station?"

"A dollar, sir," replied the driver, seeing an opportunity to make a few extra cents off a man in a hurry.

Herr Gaussen was already in the hack.   "I'll pay you a dollar and a half," he said, "if you will set me down there in time.   But you will have to get a move on you," he added, considering that phrase, which he had just learned, to be the correct one to describe rapid locomotion.

He reached the station, made a few rapid inquiries, bought a ticket to Eagle Pass, and gained the platform of the train just as it moved off.

When he had mechanically deposited his valise on the seat and settled himself comfortably with a black skullcap on his head, and a newspaper spread out before him as if he intended to read, he had time for thought.   And thoughts rushed and crowded and stumbled over each other in his mind.   But the prevaling feeling was one of awe, awe in which there was no fear.   It made him tremulous in every limb, but his heart was flooded with a soft, steady radiance.   A voice had come to him from the unseen world; the silent chimes of the universe had been condensed into sound which his soul could hear; God had spoken.   With moist eyes and quivering lips he exclaimed silently: "The Lord is so good! and to me, a sinful man."

Have revelations ceased?   The canon is closed, it is true; we can expect no more revelations which shall be addressed

to the whole human race. The vision of the prophet of
Patmos swept down to where the stream of time empties into the ocean of eternity, and farther out into eternity than
any other man can ever hope to see. No doubt God has
spoken to the Jews as a people for the last time before the
close of this dispensation. But has he not always spoken to
both Jews and Gentiles by special revelation? There was a
time, about 400 years, between Malachi and John the Baptist,
when no prophet raised a voice to rebuke or warn or console;
but in all that time did Jehovah give no sign to the sons of
men that he lived? Yes; there were answered prayers; there
was special guidance for individuals; there was that sweet
and wonderful thing which we call the Providence of God.

And so it has been since the Beloved John fell asleep. Do
they not—these divine messages—sometimes—at long intervals, it is true, but still *sometimes*—do they not ring out, or
speak in still, small voices in our souls, coming to us in the
midst of our commonplace surroundings and occupations, and
thoughts, filling us with joyful awe? Are not these among
the secrets of the Lord which many of us keep and ponder in
our hearts, holding them too sacred to be exposed to public
gaze?

Some such reflections as these occupied the mind of Herr
Gaussen as the hours of the day and night passed and the
train swept along through Southern Texas, across the Rio
Grande and down into Mexico.

Then he lived over all his acquaintance with Frederica, all
the love-making in their happy, youthful days. To him she
had been like "an apple tree among the trees of the wood,"
so fair and gracious and fragrant. Should he win her now?
Perhaps he was being sent to her for some other purpose.
But no· it was a part of his feeling about the going that he
should win her. Then, if he was to marry her, "*as* he was
to marry her," he said, correcting himself—her religious
opinions must have changed; for if they had not she would
not marry him, neither would he desire to marry her, for
there could be no congeniality between them, and worst of

8

all, she would not be a suitable mother for his children.   She had changed; he should win her at last; it had been revealed to him.

What a loving mother she would make for his children! his ambitious, manly boys, his fair, gentle, little daughters!— his daughters, so like the lovely and loved wife whom he had lost.   She could never lose a place in his heart, he felt sure of that, whatever new ties he might form.

He stood on the platform of the car and looked about him. It seemed to him the Sahara Desert could scarcely be more barren than this part of Northern Mexico through which he was passing.   The paths ran off through the dust in all directions till the horizon came down and cut them off or they ended at the base of picturesque mountains whose outlines were unsoftened by the presence of vegetation.   The whole landscape was glaring and parching in the relentless sunshine.

Herr Gaussen was never given to puerile impatience, and especially at this time when he was being led by an unseen Guide he felt that it behooved him to bide His time; but it seemed to him that he had never seen a train move so slowly.

And yet it was not one of those "accommodation" trains that stop for wood, that stop for water, that stop for other trains to pass, that stop in the depths of the woods apparently to allow the passengers to gather ferns and wild flowers, that stop—for no reason that the passengers can divine, that get loose from the engine and run backward as if they were going on an unwilling errand.

He was on a train that swept on steadily, rapidly, majestically, with a journey before it to be made on time to Durango, which was as far as the road had then gone on its journey to the Pacific.

He was at the station at last.   As he descended from the train he saw a plain little American house, that had evidently been built by the railroad company, and a few Mexican houses.

A great lumbering diligence, such as we see in the pictures in the history of France, stood ready to convey the passengers to Salta. They bestowed themselves inside and on the top. ·The trunks and valises were strapped on the top and at the back, the driver on his **high perch drew over his** head a **sort** of white buggy **top to protect** himself from the sun, made his long whip vibrate **and crack** over the backs of the eight mules and the journey **began.** On and on they ploughed their way over the dusty, barren **plain.** The cloud of dust arose and covered and almost stifled them. The man who assisted the driver was sometimes on **the** top, sometimes climbing over the sides of the diligence like an immense monkey. Two gentlemen discussed with animation the amusement of fencing and the rules of dueling. The uncouth-looking man with the two large pistols and a knife in his belt **fell** into a very unbelligerent slumber.

The mountains **were sometimes** near, sometimes far off. Now and then they **passed** *arroyos*, great ditches with **perpendicular** sides, **cut by the** swift, strong currents of water which pour **down from** the mountains in **the** rainy season. In the midst **of** some of these *arroyos* stood pillars **of** earth, perpendicular and with their tops on a level with the land around them. The capricious current had **cut about** in an unaccountable way leaving them standing while **it** swept everything else before it. **A** white-washed shrine stood on the top of **a very** steep hill. They who went **up** to worship the saint **within,** suffered enough labor and fatigue to expiate not **a few sins, according to** their **ideas.**

Now they **came to an hacienda, the one** from whose little chapel the Virgin **of St. John was** brought to secure rain. It was like an oasis in the **desert.** There were great green trees, and a yard about the handsome stone house full of many colored flowers; there were vineyards, and cactuses as large **as** trees, and sparkling streams of water.

Then they came in sight of the town nestled among the mountains, and the little chapel of the Holy **Wood** perched on the **top of** its lonely rock. When they entered the town **the** whip poised itself over the backs of the mules and aimed and struck like **a** serpent at one and another till they picked up

their feet and flew, and the heavy diligence bounded and
thundered after them over the cobble stones of the streets.
The women in the outskirts of the town who sat on the ground
at their doors looking each other's heads, suspended their
occupation to watch the flying vehicle, the many dogs barked,
the passers-by stopped to look, the inmates of the houses
came to the doors and windows; it was the Passing of the
Diligence.

They paused once to deliver the mail bag at the post-office,
and then rushed on again. They dashed up to the hotel and
dismounted with a great deal of hurrying and loud talking on
the part of the driver, his assistants and the servants of the
hotel.

Herr Gaussen was conducted into the parlor to wait till his
room was ready for him. It was a long room; there was an
ixtly carpet on the floor. There were two center tables, on
one of which was a wine service, and on the other a chess-
board. On the walls were mirrors and pictures of the Virgin
and other saints, among which was conspicuous, that of the
half-mad St. Francis of Assizi, with his thin face, white hair,
penetrating eyes, and bony hands. Herr Gaussen sat down
in one of the Vienna rocking chairs. Presently the landlady
came in. She spoke English; and that was a mercy for Herr
Gaussen.

"Good evening, Señor."

"Good evening, Mam," replied he, rising and feeling less
helpless as he heard her English salutation.

"O, seat yourself, *caballero*, have the goodness to seat yourself."

"Thank you," he said, and sat down.

"Wish you a room, Señor?"

"I do," said Herr Gaussen.

"Pardon, *Usted*; a million of pardons. The room is not *ar-
reglado* yet. It is ready in a few minutes. *Usted* will have
to wait a few minutes. Am sorry, sorry," said the hostess
effusively.

"That makes nothing, nothing at all, Mam," replied the
guest.

After this display of their proficiency in the language of DeFoe and Shakespeare, her ladyship with a "with permission," passed into the court and went to the room which was being prepared for the guest.

When Herr Gaussen entered it a quarter of an hour afterwards he saw a bare floor of black stone which was still damp from the wiping up with a cloth, a table which was too tall for any one to write on it unless it were the giant of Gath, a rocking chair, and a narrow brass bed covered with a fringed purple and white counterpane. At the head lay a round cotton bolster whose pink calico cover shone through the open work of the case.

A wash stand containing a bottle of drinking water and a metal pan and pitcher completed the furniture of the room. There was no window, the only light, when the folding doors were closed, being admitted through the narrow transom which was guarded by iron bars.

After supper he wished to learn, if possible, something of the residence of Frederica. But he could find neither host nor hostess. He went out into the street and presently reached the plaza. It happened to be the 16th of September—the national Independence Day. The platform where the speeches had been read that morning by the Director of the college, the Señor Cure and other prominent men of the town was still there and adorned with the national colors.

The band was playing in the center of the plaza and the young gentlemen were promenading in one direction while the young ladies walked in the other so that they might meet and exchange glances. They were waiting for the hour appointed for the beginning of the ball in the *casino* across the street. There were plenty of firecrackers, sky-rockets, Roman-candles, and other simple fireworks to attest the patriotism of the Mexican youth.

Herr Gaussen strolled about awhile in the plaza, and at the same time Frederica and others of the family sat in the balcony of their house and looked down on the animated scene, and neither dreamed that he was almost in the presence of the other.

After a while Herr Gaussen went back to the hotel and made an effort to sleep on that uninviting bed till the morning. Then he again attempted to learn something of the Señorita Van Ness; he did not know the name of the relatives with whom she lived. But the Señor and the Señora had attended the ball the evening before; it was long past noon when they came out of their rooms. Then the landlord, who also spoke English, assured him that he knew quite well where the lady lived. Herr Gaussen put a letter into his hand and asked him to have it sent to her. He had simply written her that he had run down to Salta to spend a few days and that he should be glad to call to see her that evening if it would be agreeable to her.

Within a half hour he received her reply. She should be glad to see him, she assured him in an equally simple and direct way.

The afternoon seemed almost interminable to him. He went out and walked about in the streets. As he turned a corner his attention was arrested by some wild shouting. He stood still. Was it an insurrection, he wondered. The next moment he saw coming down the street a long line of uncouth men, ragged and dirty, many of them with their pantaloons rolled above their knees and the sleeves of their shirts above their elbows; on their feet they wore sandals. There were perhaps fifty of them walking in a line at regular distances from each other. Each of them carried on his head a basket which would contain nearly a bushel. The purple grapes were piled high up in them and hanging over the edges. Over the tops of most of these heaped up baskets nodded roses and bunches of yellow wild flowers. They advanced with a regular step, some of them holding up their baskets with both hands to rest their heads. But not once did they fail to respond boisterously to the shout of the leader. "Long live the Holy Mary of Refuge," "Long live the Holy Christ of the Chapel," he shouted, and they responded, "viva! viva!" They were the grape-carriers, the "basket-carriers," as they are called. In the months of August and September many processions of these basket-carriers go about the streets, as in those months the laborers of every landlord in this grape-growing district are bringing the grapes from his hacienda to the wine cellars of his town house where the wine is to be made. Their shouting at the bringing in of the vintage was not agreeable to many of the citizens of Salta, and even the president of the town had mildy remonstrated with them, but the sturdy basket-carriers had reminded him that it was a very old custom, and that at this season and in this occupation they were privileged characters.

Herr Gaussen stood still and watched them. A daintily dressed child of less than two years had escaped from its nurse and stood just outside the street door of the house opposite. It extended its dimpled hand to salute the workman nearest it. He stooped under his heavy load, gently shook the little hand, and then passed on. Every carrier who followed him did the same as the tiny hand was extended to each one.

The house of their employer was only a little farther up the street. As they approached the wide front entrance the leader shouted repeatedly, according to long established custom: "Long live Our Lady of Guadalupe!" the others responding each time with gusto: "Viva! viva!" The Virgin of Guadalupe is the patron saint of Mexico.

They passed in, traversed the first court, and entered the wine cellar which opened on the second court. Herr Gaussen followed them knowing that it would be understood that he, as a foreigner, wished to see this strange phase of the country's life.

There were several large stone vats in the cellar; in all of them barefooted men were tramping the grapes to the sound of music. They waded deep in the juice of the vine, the perspiration pouring from their slightly clad bodies; often they slipped and fell and lay in the red liquid, having only strength left from that fatiguing exercise to keep their heads above the surface.

The foreign gentleman wondered how much of the fine flavor of the celebrated wine which issued from those wine presses was due to the manner of its preparation. It also occurred to him that whatever of pastoral poetry there was in the vintage and in the treading of the wine press it must be for the lookers on and not for those engaged in those occupations. It often happens so.

At length Herr Gaussen, who stood talking in French with the overseer, looked at his watch and found that it was six o'clock. He excused himself and hastened back to the hotel.

He did not remember ever having in his life given so much attention to his toilette as he did this evening. The supper was late, but it was over at last. At another time he would have been amused to see the gentlemen embracing as friend encountered friend in the dining room, to see the elaborate bowing and waving of hands, the courteous and long-drawn-out contests as to which should pass through the door first, as to which should be served first. But now he ate as quickly as possible and hastened away.

At last he and Frederica stood face to face. There was nothing extraordinary about their meeting, for though, when Frederica had read his note she had hastily closed her door and knelt by her bed, trembling and burying her face in the snowy cover, and had with the greatest difficulty controlled her thoughts and her hand to reply in a matter-of-fact way she had schooled herself through the succeeding hours to permit no heightened color nor trembling of the hands to betray her.

They shook hands and sat down; they made the usual inquiries and replies; they talked of his tour through the United States, of his impressions of the town, of mutual friends in Germany.

But when they first looked each into the face of the other a great heart ache had seized each of them for the lost youth of the other. It would come to each of them after awhile that whatever there was of lines in the face of the other or of silver in the hair, were indications of a riper and richer character wrought out for him by the experiences of joy and sorrow through the revolving years. But that must be an after knowledge; in the first moments they could only be to them signs of the years that to them were in a certain sense lost years.

Gretchen and her husband came in and were presented to their cousin's friend. They talked awhile pleasantly and then went out. No indication was given that either of them thought of their former acquaintance till he held her hand at parting and said: "I should like to call to see you to-morrow evening, Frederica," then there was something in his tone and in the way he looked at her that sent the hot blood to her cheeks.

But she answered indifferently enough:

"We shall be glad to see you whenever it is convenient for you to visit us."

The next evening she and Herr Gaussen sat talking as the evening before. She sat on the sofa and he in an arm chair about two yards from her. He was thinking, "What is the use of delay? She must know what has brought me to Salta." He would speak his mind to-night if he could only bring it about to do so naturally. If he could only annihilate that two yards of space between them! He remembered that if Marshal Ney's division could have reached the summit of Mont-Saint-Jean, Napoleon would have gained the battle of Waterloo. But there were difficulties in the way. Once he arose and walked to the window, making some remark about the plaza, intending to sit down on the sofa by her side. But he returned to his chair. He was becoming desperate; he was little accustomed to cowardice or embarrassment in the presence of men or women. Presently he bethought him of a railroad map which he had in his pocket. He took it out saying:

"I was trying to-day to get a correct idea of the railroad system of Mexico. Perhaps you will assist me." It was only natural, then, as well as necessary that he should go and sit down by her that she might explain to him that interesting subject.

"The two longest lines," she said, "connect points on the

Texas boundary line with the City of Mexico. They are,
this one from Laredo through Monterey, Saltillo and San
Luis Potosi to the City. It is a narrow guage road· It is
called the National, you see. The other great line is the
Central, from El Paso, away up here in the North-west corner of Texas, to the City. Then this one, the International,
from Eagle Pass on the Texas line to the Pacific. You see it
has only reached Torrion as yet, but it will be built on through
Durango to the ocean. There is a road from Mexico City to
Vera Cruz; and besides these great trunk lines there are several branches."

Now Herr Gaussen was not feeling the least interest in all
this; he could scarcely be said to hear it; but it was a matter
of no little consequence to him that his hand sometimes
touched hers as they glided about over the map. However
he folded it up so soon and changed the conversation that it
occurred to her that he had not felt so much interest in the
development of the country as she had at first thought.

Presently he said, "Frederica, I suppose you have guessed
why I came to Salta; were you glad to see me?" then he
thought that "Glad to see me," was the most unbecoming
thing he could have said, and her reply proved it to him.

"Yes, I suppose you had business in Salta; and of course
I am always glad to see old friends."

Then followed a long and awkward pause. She had, as if
carelessly, moved farther away from him. He looked at her
curiously; should he have to win her by some long process?
Perhaps he had been to hasty. But almost without resolving
to do so he made another effort.

"Are you still a Catholic?" he asked. He would not again
call her "Frederica," but he could not address her as a mere
acquaintance.

She felt the color coming into her face under his gaze but
she replied quietly:

"No, I am not a Catholic now. I—I began to read the
Bible months ago. I could not read it and remain a Roman-
ist." She looked up at him and met his eyes. The tenderness and solemn joy in them thrilled her.

"**Frederica**," he said, "Frederica, if you had said such words as those to me fifteen years ago our lives would have **been** very different."

He saw her lips tremble and her **bright** head was **bowed.** "It is not too late yet. Will you marry me now?"

We know how she answered him. Some time that evening she told **him** how the Señora Urbina's contemptuous words about **the** congregations of ignorant people who gathered for the study of the Sacred Scriptures, had reminded her of **the** little **New** Testament which **had** been sent her by **some one** soon **after their** parting. "I knew you sent it, but **I** would **not** read it then. But I **could** not throw it away. I carried it everywhere I went. **I took** it out of **my** trunk at last,—it **has** been six months ago—and read it, **and it** was after that that the great change came. You know how that is."

"Yes," he said gently, "I know."

"I have **been very wicked** and **rebellious. I** have **not de-**served **that God should be so kind to** me now."

Then **he told** her about the strange command to come to Salta, **and she** held her breath as she listened. But just before **he left** she said with a little laugh and a blush: "And so you knew all the time that I would marry **you** at last, **not-**withstanding **my** pretended indifference."

"**Yes**," he replied with **a smile**, "I knew it."

CHAPTER XIV.

A CIVIL MARRIAGE.

A day or two afterward while Herr Gaussen was dining with the family, Herr Bunnsen said to him:

"By the way; I had forgotten to tell you that you have to notify the civil judge and have the bans published. I will go with you this afternoon to his office."

"How is a marriage published here?"

"A written notice of it is pasted on the public buildings where it will attract attention two weeks before the marriage is to take place. Come to think of it," he continued abruptly, "your marriage will have to be published two months beforehand."

"Why is that?" asked Herr Gaussen, laying down his orange suddenly.

"Because you don't live in this country. The object of the law is to prevent imposition. When both the parties live in the same town or state fifteen days is thought to be long enough for any imposition to be exposed. But if one of them lives in a foreign country a notice of his approaching marriage must be sent to his home and published there so that if there is any impediment to the marriage the civil judge may be notified of it."

"And is there no help for it? I am extremely anxious to get back to my business and my family,—and especially as I shall have the pleasure of carrying your cousin with me," he added with a pleasant glance at Frederica.

"It is too bad that you should be detained so long," she said.

"But after all you will have an opportunity to see something of the land of the Montezumas," said Gretchen by way of consolation.

"Yes," said Herr Bunnsen. "there are some things that are really worth seeing. I will see if I can find time to run about with you a little;—unless you think the time would pass more quickly and pleasantly here in Salta," he added with a mischievous glance at Frederica.

"Perhaps we might all go south and visit the most interesting cities, and to Yucatan, too, and to Central America to see those wonderful ruins I studied about at school. O let's do, papa!" said Helena getting up and going round to her father's side to put her arm about his neck. She made a very pretty picture.

"I wonder if you wouldn't like to go on to Peru and Paraguay," said he, pinching her cheek. "But couldn't we, mother, arrange to run down to Mexico and Pueblo for a few weeks? My business will take me in that direction."

"Why, yes, I should think we might if it is agreeable to Herr Gaussen and Frederica. We promised Helena a little trip during her vacation."

"I assure you I am very much obliged to you for your kindness, but I must be getting back to Germany as soon as possible. And Miss Helena will think there are no ruins here worth looking at after she has seen a few ruined castles on the Rhine."

It had been decided that Helena should accompany Frederica to Germany to finish her education.

"But you know I should see those afterwards anyhow, the one you used to live in, Aunt, and others besides. But after all I'm not so sure they are more interesting than those here. O I could explain the ruins here to you Herr Gaussen. I have read about them till I feel quite learned on that subject." And she went back to her place, for her mother had frowned a little at her, the most serious form of rebuke she ever administered to her rose-bud-faced daughter.

"But really it is a good law, that about the publication of the bans," said Herr Bunnsen, returning to the original subject of conversation. "It is one of the best laws made by the Constituent Congress. Juarez was one of the ruling spirits in that Congress. He was a fine man, a wonderful man, I might say. He was wise and far seeing and moderate. He was an Indian of pure blood. One who is acquainted with his public career can scarcely believe that when he was twelve years old he could not read and did not know a word of Spanish. It makes one smile to think he was educated for the church; for the Catholic Church has never had a more powerful and inveterate enemy in Mexico. The reasons for the laws made by this Congress are very forcibly stated; this is especially the case when they speak of the introduction of civil marriage instead of religious marriage. Helena, if you will bring me that thin red book on the third shelf of my book case I will read Herr Gaussen a little of it. While he is spending these two months with us we must teach him something about our national history," he added with a smile. They speak thus of marriage:

"The restoration" (to the officers of the civil law of the right to preform the marriage ceremony,) "was not only just and logical, but to the last degree necessary on account of the enormous abuses which the spirit of faction and other causes not less worthy of condemnation had introduced in the administration of matrimony by the clergy. What right, what plausible reason could recommend that the foundation of society and of the most interesting relations in the life of a man should be left to the mercy and arbitrary power of bishops sworn against liberty and the laws of the nation? Ought it to be tolerated longer that matrimony should be in their hands a weapon of sedition, and that men whose only crime has been to obey the laws of their country should not be able like all other men to make legitimate the election of the companion of their lot and of their life? Should it be longer permitted that in many cases money should be one of the accepted means for dispensing with the impediments to marriage? And should it be allowed that in a democracy poverty should often be a positive impediment to marriage irreproachable so far as morality and justice are concerned?"[1]

---

[1] *Note.*—It is said that before the laws took marriage out of the hands of the Church matrimony was impossible for about two-thirds of the

"Now how does that strike you?" asked Herr Bunnsen.

"That is very good. I do not doubt I should admire it very much if the author did not interfere with my plans just at this time. But what does he mean—exactly—by civil marriage?"

"That means that in this country no priest nor minister of the gospel of any denomination can unite persons in matrimony. It is declared by the laws of Mexico to be a union of Church and State, and they will have none of it. You will have to be married by the civil judge or go up to the United States where they have union of Church and State to that extent, to be married by a minister of the gospel."

"So they consider that a religious marriage indicates union between Church and State?"

"You see how it is. In the United States a minister of the gospel, for the simple reason that he is such, is entitled to the privilege of performing the marriage ceremony. The civil marriage is not objectionable when one becomes accustomed to the idea," he added after a pause. "A minister of one's own faith can be invited to be present and to pray. The Catholics go through the whole ceremony of marriage in their churches after the civil marriage, and the priests assure the parties that the religious marriage alone is valid, while the law, at the same time that it permits the religious marriage by a wise toleration, declares that it amounts to nothing. The ministers of some of the Protestant denominations also perform the marriage ceremony after the civil marriage, declaring at the same time with charming naivete that it is a mere farce. I was present once at one of these mock marriages. It was in a Protestant chapel. The bride was in white dress, veil and orange blossoms. The pastor,

inhabitants of Mexico, because they could not afford to pay a priest to perform the ceremony. Even since the adoption of the law which makes marriage a civil contract a large proportion of the ignorant people, if they can possibly save the money, are married by the Church alone, being taught by the priests that the civil marriage is not valid. Few besides the well-to-do are married both ways; and fewer still, except those whom the Church calls heretics, will risk their souls and sacrifice their respectability by being married by the civil law alone.

after telling them that they were already married, went through the whole ceremony as if he were uniting them in marriage."

"Well," said Herr Gaussen, taking out his watch, "do you suppose the civil judge has finished his *siesta* by this time and opened his office? I am anxious to see if he can on any grounds give me a dispensation that will make it possible for us to go home in less than two months."

"Ah, my dear sir," said Herr Bunnsen as he took down the hats, "you ought to have brought with you in your pockets, some papers duly signed by the civil officers of your town testifying that you were a proper subject for matrimony. A marriageable man should never leave home to travel in a foreign country without such papers, for though he may have no intention when he starts of looking for a companion, there is no telling what may happen before he returns to his fatherland!"

"Oscar!" said the Señora de Bunnsen, in a shocked tone.

Herr Gaussen only smiled as he said good evening to the ladies and bowed himself out.

They found the judge in his office. When they informed him of their business he seated himself on a very high stool at a very high desk, supporting his feet on a box and did the necessary writing in a large book. When he was consulted about the time it was necessary for the bans to be published he said:

"If the Señor knows any reliable person in Mexico who can testify that he is eligible for matrimony it will not be necessary to wait longer than two weeks if his testimony can be received in that time."

"Ah, I have it!" exclaimed Herr Gaussen. "I am acquainted with the German Consul in the City of Mexico."

So he had his "dispensation" and the marriage was to take place in two weeks after all.

The evening of the marriage came. Most of the invited guests were present. Curiosity had been sufficient to bring them, though they were all more or less scandalized that the

German lady whom they had known as a Catholic, should marry a Protestant.

Mercedes was there in her dainty white dress, broken-hearted over the coming loss of her friend, and uncertain whether she should rejoice or be sad at her happiness, since she was to marry a Protestant. But she could not help thinking when Frederica introduced her to him that he seemed to be in every way worthy of even her beloved teacher, unless it were in that mysterious, indefinable moral lack which prevented his being a Catholic.

The ceremony was performed by the civil judge. He was accompanied by the *alcalde* (another civil officer), and by two witnesses. Besides these two witnesses, there were two chosen by the bride and two by the groom. Herr Gaussen and Frederica stood before the Judge.

"Señor Gaussen," said the judge, pronouncing the name as well as he could, but certain that no one would have known under other circumstances whom he addressed, "Do you receive for a wife the Señorita Van Ness who is present?"

"Yes, Señor."

"Señorita Van Ness, do you receive for a husband the Señor Gaussen who is present?"

"Yes, Señor."

Then at his request they joined hands. While they stood thus he read them some articles of the law framed by the Constituent Congress:

1st, That matrimony was a civil contract; 2nd, that those who were married were entitled to all the rights and prerogatives which the civil laws conceded to the married; 3rd, that bigamy and polygamy were prohibited; 4th, that a divorce could be obtained for certain grave causes mentioned in another article, but that this legal separation did not leave the divorced free to marry another person.

The judge then said:

"I, as judge of the civil register of this municipality, solemnly declare that I have concluded this civil contract be-

9

fore the witnesses who, with me, sign the deed, and that you are legally married for all lawful purposes."

He then read them more of the law to the effect "that the man whose especial gifts are courage and strength ought to give and will give to the woman protection, encouragement and direction, treating her always as the more delicate, fine and sensitive part of himself, and with the magnanimity and generous benevolence that the strong owes to the weak, especially when this weak one has delivered herself to him, and when she has been confided to him by society. That the woman, the principal endowments of whose sex are self-denial, beauty, compassion, perspicacity and tenderness ought to give and will give to the husband, obedience, affability, assistance, consolation and counsel, treating him always with the veneration which is due to the person who supports and defends, and with the delicacy of one who would not wish to exasperate the ruder, more irritable and sterner part of herself. That each should treat the other with respect, defference, fidelity, confidence and tenderness; and that it should be the aim of both that what the one expects from the other when he enters into this contract should not be disappointed in their union. That each should try to moderate and to lessen his faults, etc."

Then followed various quaint and wholesome counsels relative to the future years. After this, the deed was signed by the witnesses and by Herr Gaussen and Frederica.

Then followed the congratulations, much conversation, an elegant supper, and more conversation, during all of which Herr Gaussen, though unable to talk except with one or two German guests and two or three gentlemen and ladies who spoke a little English, conducted himself with so much dignity and grace that all of the ladies thought it "a great pity that such a nice gentleman should be a Protestant."

To himself and to Frederica it was a circumstance to be regretted that there could be no religious exercises in connection with their marriage. "I like the civil marriage," he said, "but I should be glad if we could have a prayer by a minister of the gospel." But in the few minutes that he and Frederica were left alone before they entered the parlor to be . married he drew her hand into his arm and they bowed their heads while he prayed that their union might be for the glory of God, for their own spiritual good, and for the good of all with whom they should be associated.

The next morning they, accompanied by Helena, started for Germany. Herr Bunnsen and Gretchen were left alone. They soon decided to join their boys and girl.

After they were gone the house "remained awhile silent and tenantless, then went to strangers;" and Mercedes could never again enter the room where she had spent so many happy hours as a student.

CHAPTER XV.

FROM SAINT IGNACIUS DE LOYOLO.

I HAVE said that in the days of preparation for Frederica's marriage that Something that had grasped the conscience of Mercedes gradually relaxed its hold. She could not determine what was right nor what was wrong in her conduct with regard to the masses for her father, and it seemed to her at last that the only thing for her to do was to let it slip out of her mind as she felt that it was doing.

Her father was becoming to her a sad, sweet memory. She clutched desperately at her grief for him as she felt it escaping from her; but she could not reverse the order of a kind Providence. There are sickly natures which bereavement blights forever, but Mercedes was too young and strong and healthful both in body and mind not to recover from this grief.

There were doubts in her mind in these days about the existence of purgatory, but she was sometimes troubled with doubts about the existence of all unseen things. Now and then, and more frequently than formerly there flashed through her mind like lightning, the thought, "Is there a God?" It always frightened her.

In the conversation of the gentlemen who frequented the house she detected a tone which indicated no great respect for the Church, though they were always, she noticed, on their guard in the presence of Doña Flavia. She was convinced, though she had been slow to come to that conclusion, that Don Francisco was no admirer of the Church. When Doña Flavia had expressed disgust that Frederica should marry a Protestant he had said some mild words of defence. Everything tended to produce confusion of ideas with respect to religion.

One morning she and Doña Flavia and the children sat at the breakfast table. A servant brought in some little papers which had been thrown at the door. They contained the day of the month, an advertisement and the date of the declaration of the infallibility of the Pope. Mercedes read it and then that same longing to know the truth which had prompted her to make startling inquiries before, made her look up wistfully at Doña Flavia and ask:

"Doña Flavia, do you really believe in the infallibility of the Pope?"

That lady instantly assumed a more reserved air as she looked at the girl curiously. "Yes, in matters pertaining to the Church I believe he is infallible," she replied. "But," she exclaimed after a pause, turning her beautiful face toward Mercedes and looking at her with wide open defiant eyes as if she represented the Papacy, "if I should do anything that he did not approve of and he should excommunicate me and should declare that I never could be saved but must be forever lost, do you suppose I should believe him? By no means. He is only a human being like myself."

Ah, Doña Flavia, would not your excommunication by the Pope be a matter pertaining to the Church? It is marvelous how Catholics can contradict themselves. Mercedes was more puzzled than ever, but then both sides were true "somehow" she ought to believe, and she did—of course.

"The priests teach that to the common people but they never try to make us, the enlightened class, believe it. They know, of course, that it is not the truth," continued the lady.

"Then do you mean to say that—that the priests teach what they know to be false?"

"Why, yes, of course they teach falsehoods constantly to the common people. It is necessary in order to keep them in subjection to the Church. They are so ignorant that the priests can't appeal to their reason and therefore they must be controlled by these stories. But they never teach them to *us*," she reaffirmed proudly.

Ah, Doña Flavia, are you quite sure?

"But is it right to tell lies?" asked Mercedes. The doctrine was by no means new to her; she was only trying to understand it now that she sat at the feet of one who was so capable of solving her difficulties.

"O yes, when any good is to come of it. They invent and tell these stories, you know, to keep them in the fold of the Church. Their ignorance makes such a measure necessary. It is also because of their ignorance that they are not permitted to read the New Testament. It is written in so elevated a style that they could not understand it. They would get all sorts of perverted ideas from it; and therefore it is best for them to know only what the priests think proper to teach them about it."

Mercedes wondered if there was danger that the enlightened class might get perverted ideas from the New Testament, for she knew that they, too, were forbidden to read it. She persisted, though she knew that she was treading on dangerous ground:

'Then it is right to tell lies under certain circumstances?"

'O yes, it is right to tell them when it is done for the good of the Church," replied the Catholic lady with the air of one who was giving some useful and important information

Just then Don Francisco passed through the room. He had been "giving a turn" as he would have said, in the orchard. His wife appealed to him:

"O, Francisco, am I not right? Is it not right to tell falsehoods when any good is to come of telling them?

"Certainly, certainly," replied the gentleman, with a superior air and very emphatically, "it is right to tell falsehoods or to do anything else from which good is to result." And he passed out of the room.

"I suppose, then, it is right to steal under certain circumstances, as we have always heard that it was?" asked Mercedes glancing a little uneasily at the children who had lingered about the room listening at the conversation.

"Certainly," replied the lady without hesitation, "under the circumstances designated by the Church stealing is right.

FROM SAINT IGNACIUS DE LOYOLO. 135

The Fathers established degrees with **regard to** all kinds of theft. One may steal a great many **small sums from** different persons and not commit a great sin, because he does **not injure** any person very much; but if he steals the amount **of those** small sums from **one** person he **does** commit a grave sin. But there are cases in which stealing is not a sin at all," continued the good lady with **the air of a** theologian.

"For example, secret compensation is right. If some one owed me a debt and would not pay it I might take secretly the property of the debtor to the value of the debt. If one should be condemned by judgment to pay a debt which he had **not** contracted, **or** which he had already paid, he could have recourse to secret compensation. A servant, if he is not paid enough, **or** if he is overworked, may pay himself secretly from the property of **his master.** But you **are** familiar with all this."

"I suppose **you accept the** teachings of the Church with **regard** to all **the** other great sins?"

"Yes, it has been decided by the high authorities that under certain circumstances it is not wrong to commit even the greatest sins—murder, for instance. But these things **are** above our comprehension. **It** is our duty merely to submit **our**selves to those who are over us **in** authority and ask no questions. By **the** way, Mercedes," she said with **her** low, musical **laugh** as she arose from **the** table, "are you overworked, or do I **owe you anything?**"

"No, **Señora,**" **said** the girl, lifting **her head** proudly and looking **her full in the** face **as the** blood swept over her forehead and cheeks. "**But** if I were or if you did, I would not steal."

"She looks on **me** as one of the common people to whom the priests must teach lies. As common as I may be I would not be so priest-ridden as to believe such doctrines as she has just stated in the presence of her children!" she thought as she **stepped** out into the court and glanced up into the blue sky.

"**O that I** did know right from wrong," **she** said in her heart, "**but I'll** do **the best I can.**"

CHAPTER XVI.

ST. FRANCISCO'S DAY.

THERE were in those days some circumstances connected with the home life in Don Francisco's handsome house which had the effect of driving serious thoughts from Mercedes' mind. In the last days of September and the first of October there was much preparation and secrecy in the great house. The 4th of October was Don Francisco's "Saint's day," and every member of the family was busy preparing a present for him. Doña Flavia was making a handkerchief case, Mercedes a pair of slippers, one of the little girls was embroidering his name on a handkerchief, the others were making other pretty and useful things; and if the work of the plump little hands was not perfect, it still showed much youthful skill, and the little maidens knew as they sat working with pursed-up mouths that their loving efforts would be appreciated by "Papa." The boys had bought presents with their own spending money, after much consultation with Mama and Mercedes, and much talking around Papa to see what he would probably like.

You must know that in this country "saint's days," and not birth days, are kept. The child is generally named for the saint on whose day it is born, but if another name is preferred it is given and the day of the saint who bears that name is kept with festivities instead of the birth day. It was so in this case; Don Francisco was born in June, but his mother was so impressed with the Roman Catholic virtues of St. Francis of Assizi that she conferred his name on her baby. Don Francisco had made up his mind long ago that his distinguished namesake was a thief, a liar and a madman, but it did not seem to him desirable on that account to set himself against what seemed to him a delightful custom in connection with his home life. If any one in Protestant America is inclined to blame him, let him remember that he keeps Christmas, another Roman Catholic institution, with the giving of gifts and much joyfulness of heart. As to Saint Francis, I don't suppose he was thought of on that day unless Doña Flavia, in her morning devotions, implored his continued protection and grace for her husband.

The presents were given after breakfast, and they were received with much appreciation. There were many little reminders of love and esteem from relatives and friends outside the family. Don Francisco was never so happy as on his "saint's day," unless it was on the day of Doña Flavia's saint; and he remembered this one afterward as the happiest he had ever had, perhaps because it contrasted so sharply with the days which followed. Sad changes come sometimes near the close of long and prosperous lives. But there was no cloud over this day; if Don Francisco felt any apprehensions they were only such as he had long been accustomed to.

A large company of relatives was invited to dinner. The grown people ate at a long table in the dining room, the children under fifteen years old at tables in the adjoining rooms. The Señor Cure, though a distant relative of the family, did not grace this feast with his presence, perhaps because such innocent domestic pleasures were too tame for his tastes. Don Francisco reflected that his absence, like every thing else, contributed to his happiness to-day.

"I am always," said a sister-in-law of Don Francisco to Mercedes, speaking from the fullness of her heart as she passed her in the corridor on her way to the dining-room, "I am always very contented when Francisco is happy with his friends." And Mercedes thought a minute later as she glanced at the faces around that hospitable board that they were all very contented. And she thought, too, how well her master deserved it all. If there was any lingering resentment for the wrongs done to her people she said to herself heartily that he was not to blame for them; he was noble and good; he was a victim of a system just as she was. It was very pleasant to her to feel in unison with them all on that day.

In this gathering of intimate friends there was not much of that ceremony which attracts the attention of foreigners in the hotels and on the streets. Now and then, notwithstanding the attendance of numerous servants a gentleman arose from his seat, and went to the other end of the table and brought a dish to help the lady by his side. Don Francisco, himself, in the excess of his hospitality and pleasure went around the table with one or two dishes, stopping now and then to join in a gay conversation or start one. There were thirteen courses before the dessert, that is, four or five more than they had every day. According to invariable custom the first was soup and the last was *frijoles* or dried beans, a dish handed down to them from Aztec ancestors. The latter were brought in soup plates and eaten with spoons. Some of the dishes were so red and some so green that the American lady who sat at one end of the table reflected as she ate them that if they would not hurt Mexicans they would not poison Americans either. There were roast and turkey in dishes of gravy that was not only fiery in color but fiery in taste, too, from the abundant accompaniment of the national *chile* or red pepper. There was "coffee with milk," as they would have said, not meaning to indicate by that expression that the sugar was wanting. There was an abundance and a variety of wines. For dessert a small glass dish of very sweet preserves was set before each person. This he ate without bread or cake. Then followed fruit, and at last the wine glasses were lifted all at the same time and while they were held thus one of the gentlemen addressed to the host a speech of congratulation, to which he replied with a bow, a smile and a graceful wave of the hand; each couple then clinked their glasses together and the wine was drunk. This ceremony was repeated several times. But there was no intemperate drinking in the dining-room.

The children in one of the adjoining rooms gaily followed

the example of a handsome but naughty nephew of Doña Flavia's and drank the glasses of wine which they found by their plates, and before touching their soup sent a servant to the dining room asking for more wine.

This was very amusing to the company. One benevolent-looking old gentleman who occupied a seat of honor near Don Francisco's chair, the grandfather of several of the children, was especially amused; he called the attention of all those near him to the fact that "before those children had begun to eat they had drunk all their wine and had sent for more."

A nurse passed through the dining room with a baby, a baby as rosy and dimpled and divine-looking as any a Madonna ever clasped. A wine glass was pressed to his laughing, rose-bud lips. Mrs. Peek, the American lady whose husband had recently been employed by Don Francisco as overseer of his vineyards, and who was stopping with the family until her husband could rent a house, thought she understood now why it was that one of the little girls of the family sometimes slipped into the pantry and drank wine until she had to sleep off the effects of it.

Mercedes sat by a gentleman of middle age, a lawyer from a neighboring city. He had found that he had by his side a bright girl, an interested listener, and he was taking a kindly pleasure in talking to her. He told her something of his college days in the City of Mexico and afterwards with the Jesuits in California.

"I was in college in the City of Mexico," he said, "during the reign of Maximilian and Carlotta. The Grand Duke"—true patriot that he was, he would not say "the Emperor"—"The Grand Duke was very handsome, handsomer than the Grand Duchess, but both of them were kind and were liked by the Mexicans. Maximilian's state carriage is in the National Museum now. It is very fine, all gilt and crimson velvet, with little gilt cupids flying about it. It was drawn by six white horses. There were little silver bells on the harness, and when the people heard the bells they all ran out to the street or to the doors and windows to see the royal carriage

pass.   When you go to Mexico you will see the carriage and
many other interesting things in the Museum."

Mercedes gave a little start and said quickly, "O, I don't
expect to ever go to Mexico; I'd as soon think of a trip to the
moon."

"It can't be so impossible as that," he replied, smiling.
"No communication has as yet been established between the
earth and the moon, you know."   Then after a little pause
he continued, "French was the language of the court, so all
of us young fellows thought it would be the greatest of
accomplishments to speak French.   We were not thinking
so much about our rights and liberties as about the splendor
of the court."

"Were there any titled people in the court except the sov-
ereigns?" asked Mercedes, unable to imagine a court without
them, and yet equally unable to imagine nobility in plain,
republican Mexico.

"O yes, the emperor, as they called him, made dukes and
duchesses of the wealthy Mexicans who were about him."

"And what did they do with their titles when he was
dethroned?" asked Mercedes, laughing.

"They had to put them into their pockets then," replied
the gentleman with evident enjoyment.

"Napoleon III. was very unkind and unjust to Mexico in
trying to establish a monarchy here, wasn't he?" asked Mercedes by way of continuing so interesting a conversation.

"Yes, and it was a just punishment of Providence that he
should be dethroned and banished from his kingdom."

Just then they noticed that there was a lull in the conversation around the table.   They had all ceased talking out of
respect for the benevolent-looking old gentleman who had
been so much amused at the request of the children for more
wine.   He was beginning a story in his slow, measured tones.
Perhaps he thought there was too much discussing of history
and literature and social events; the claims of religion should
not be so long forgotten.   He was saying:

"The other day I read in a newspaper that a poor woman

in whose family there had been a death went to a priest and asked him for money to defray the burial expenses, requesting him at the same time to come to her house and see the need for charity. He went; and while he was there he noticed on a table a pile of books. He picked up some of them and found among them a poisonous reptile. He took it up by the tail and it was turned to stone in his hand. He gave it to the poor woman and told her to sell it as a curiosity for the money which she needed. It was evidently a miracle," he added in conclusion, "to supply the need of the poor woman."

"Evidently," fervently repeated his pretty daughter-in-law, who sat by his side.

Mercedes did not mean to see anybody after this narrative; she felt instinctively that Don Francisco would be ashamed of it and she pitied him; but it was a vital question to her—the truth or falsehood of this, the only religion which she knew. She would give not a little to know what these intelligent, cultured men thought of the Church and her miracles. One swift, involuntary glance around the table before she fixed her eyes on her plate showed her that some of the gentlemen were steadily contemplating the contents of their plates while others were watching Mrs. Peek. That lady was a Protestant. She and her husband attended the meetings in the humble hall over whose door was the inscription, "Culto Evangelico," and tried to understand the sermon of the humble Mexican preacher. Her boys went there to Sunday-school, and neither she nor her husband cared who knew it. It was probable that her husband would lose his position on account of it, unless he could make his services so invaluable to his employer that a wife's influence would have little weight in comparison with that consideration, but that worthy pair, prompted either by their natural independence, or by higher motives, persisted in their course.

Mrs. Peek had listened respectfully to the story, and when a brief glance had shown her that she was an object of attention, she thought, during the awkward silence which followed:

"They needn't be looking at 'the Protestant;' she is not so incredulous as they may suppose, for it seems very natural to her that the touch of a Roman Catholic priest should turn even a poisonous reptile to stone." But the next moment she said to herself, reproachfully, "Now that is mean of me. The gentlemen looked at me because they were so ashamed of the story. The women all believe it, I suppose. They do believe such things."   ·

Some excuse was found just then to adjourn to the parlor. The afternoon was passed pleasantly with conversation, music, walks in the orchard, and promenading in the broad corridor around the court. With the evening many other invited guests arrived. The young gentlemen dropped in alone, that is without ladies, unless, as it sometimes happened, one brought his mother; fathers and mothers arrived with their daughters. An elegant supper was spread in the dining room. A large room had been arranged for dancing.

The parlor presented an animated appearance; there were groups of young ladies and young gentlemen, the former not far from their "mamas," though apparently quite easy under the maternal surveillance. There were also groups of older ladies and gentlemen sitting near the walls, and conversing pleasantly.

Mercedes' attention was attracted by a conversation between Mrs. Peek and three or four ladies who had been present at dinner. They had evidently observed that the eyes of the gentlemen had been directed toward the Protestant lady after the unfortunate narrative of the benevolent old gentleman, and they were taking their feminine revenge.

"Is it customary, Mrs. Peek," said a plump, handsome young matron in black velvet, "for American gentlemen to push back their chairs after dinner, and put their feet on the dining table to smoke?"

"No," replied Mrs. Peek, with slightly heightened color, "I never knew of an American gentleman's doing so. Why do you ask?"

"Well, I didn't know," said the lady sweetly. "You know

the **customs in** different countries are so different; and I've heard **that** gentlemen from the United States do that in the **hotels** here."

Then after a little more indifferent talking a tall, slender, graceful young lady with lustrous brown eyes and soft, abundant brown hair, whose brunette beauty was heightened by a dress **of** some soft cream and pink material, said pleasantly:

"Mrs. Peek, you attend the services of the Presbyterians in the street of Ramos Arispe, don't you?"

"Yes, I frequently go. I am a Presbyterian."

"Is it true—excuse me, I only ask for information—does the minister give money to those who **attend** the services?"

"No, he could not afford **to** do so. The minister is a very **poor** man."

"But he might be **supplied** with money by the missionaries. I don't know, **of course**," she said apologetically, "but I have heard **that** when he goes around shaking hands with **them all** after the services he leaves a piece **of** money in the hand of each one."

"It is a mistake. I have never heard of **any** one's being paid to attend the Protestant meetings."

Mercedes was wondering who would **give her** the next cut when she heard one lady say to another, evidently intending that the Presbyterian lady should hear her remark:

"What **enormous feet** American ladies have! And they do wear such horrid **shoes, with** such broad toes and low, broad heels!"

Mrs. Peek slipped **her** shapely **foot,** in a fine American shoe, a little farther from under **her** dress, and continued to ply her fan with much composure.

Then another, affecting to believe that Mrs. Peek was not well enough acquainted with Spanish to understand her, said **in a low** tone:

"**What** amazes me most is the behavior of the American **girls.** I was shocked last Sunday night at the ball in the *casino* at **the** way that girl who is visiting the Robledos conducted herself. **Did you notice** it?"

"No, I was not there."

"She didn't stay near Margarita Robledo at all. She was all the time talking with young gentlemen, and she actually stood out on the balcony and talked with one for awhile. And they tell me that the young men call on her, and she receives them alone in the parlor; and they say she even takes rides with them. I can very well believe it, for I know that last Sunday evening was a week ago she went alone to the theater with a young gentleman, and after it was over he took her home alone; she went right out into the dark with him alone. After the play was over I saw him myself take up her wrap and put it around her. I'd rather my daughter were a nun in a convent than that she should come to conduct herself in that way."

"Perhaps," said the listener, kindly, "the young lady doesn't know the customs of this country. Those things, I think, are customary in the United States."

"Well," replied the other with a little laugh, "when I go to the United States I may follow the customs of the United States, but here I prefer those of my own country."

Just then Don Francisco came up and said, pleasantly:

"Mrs. Peek, I have been telling those gentlemen and ladies over yonder about your singing, and they would like to hear you sing some English songs. Will you let me take you to the piano? With your permission, Señoras," he said, bowing to the other ladies as Mrs. Peek arose to go. When she had finished playing Mrs. Peek retired to her room.

Soon after the dancing began, and as the first couples of girls and young gentlemen glided gracefully over the floor Mercedes excused herself to Doña Flavia and slipped out. The scene would have been fascinating to her but for her bereavement. Far into the night in her own room she heard the music, the dancing in the ballroom, and the merry voices of the children in the corridor.

CHAPTER XVII.

"AN AWFUL DAY."

IT was the day on which the Señora Doña Flavia Salizar de Urbina learned that her husband was a Mason. As she remarked afterward, and as she will remember till the day of her death with great distinctness, it was a beautiful day; the sun shone as brightly as she had ever seen it, the birds sang as sweetly, and the flowers in the court were just as gay. There was no sign given her of coming trouble.

She went to mass, accompanied by Mercedes, and as they returned a friend joined her. As she manifested a desire to talk privately with Doña Flavia, Mercedes dropped behind, but she could not help hearing, for the neighbor was excited and talked louder than she intended.

"Flavia, did you know there was a Masonic lodge in town?"

"Yes, Concepcion, I know it. Doesn't it seem that everything conspires against the interests of the Holy Mother Church in these wicked times?"

"Yes," said her companion, too full of the communication that was struggling for utterance to notice Doña Flavia's pious reflection, "there is a lodge. They have fitted up a room for their meetings at the back of the old college. Think of their holding their meetings in a house that was built by the Holy Fathers! And more people belong to it than some of us have any idea. Yes, there are men in this town who have been Masons for a long time, and their wives have no idea of it! There are a good many women in this town who would leave their husbands if they knew they were Masons, but the trouble is they don't know it."

Doña Flavia looked at her curiously.

"But I've found it out now," went on the neighbor with

10

great satisfaction. "They can't keep their wicked secret forever. I can tell you who the Masons are."

Doña Flavia looked at her a little apprehensively.

"You wouldn't suspect, now, that Juan Guerrero was a Mason, would you? Well, he is, and his poor wife knows nothing about it. It would kill her, poor child! if she knew it. But she ought to know about it, and she shall know it to-day. Ah, Flavia," she said, stopping short and laying her hand on that lady's arm, "you love your husband and you have been very happy all these years, but it would all be over if you knew that he had been deceiving you, and had been seeking to destroy his own soul by acting in defiance of the Holy Church."

The missal slipped from Doña Flavia's hand, and the rosary almost fell. She was very pale. She began to say, "I don't believe it," then checked herself. She did say, "I think you must be mistaken," but the other was ready with proofs. When they reached Doña Flavia's door she paused. She was convinced. A greater trouble than she had ever had before in the whole course of her easy life had fallen on her.

"Adios, Concepcion," she said. "I cannot go in now; I have something to attend to. Mercedes, I do not need company; you can go on to school."

The gossiping neighbor would gladly have accompanied her to see her "die," but something in Doña Flavia's face forbade it.

The Señora de Urbina went back to the church which was now almost deserted, and kneeling before the image of the Virgin she repeated the "Ave Maria," the "Pater Noster," and the "Apostles' Creed" an almost incredible number of times. One who has not heard a Roman Catholic going through that exercise can have no idea with what rapidity they can be repeated.

There are those who exhort us to be specific in prayer. The two last of these formulas are familiar to you. The "Ave Maria" runs thus:

"God save thee, Mary; thou art full of grace; the Lord is

with **thee;** blessed art thou among women and blessed is thy **Son, Jesus.** Holy Mary, Mother of **God, pray for us** sinners, **now, and** in the hour of our death. **Amen."**

As she felt no relief of spirit from these exercises she went on to repeat other prayers "to the most Holy Mary," prayers which she had learned from her missal. If her memory failed her she opened the book and read.

"I adore thee, oh thou who art full of grace! the Lord **is** with thee. I adore thee, oh, instrument of our joy, through which in thy Son the sentence of our condemnation was rent and changed into judgment of blessing. I adore thee, **oh.** temple of the glory of God! holy house of the king of heaven. Thou art **in** Jesus Christ the reconciliation of God with men. I adore thee, oh mother **of** our joy! in truth thou art blessed, because thou alone **among** all women wast worthy to be mother of our Creator: all nations call thee blessed; oh Mary! if I put my confidence **in thee I** shall obtain the means of salvation. If I am under thy protection **I** will fear nothing, because to **be** thy true worshipper is a shield inpenetrable to the assaults of my enemies."

Then with the hope of further propitiating her and gaining her intercession in this trial her rapid voice slipped on into a confession of the Immaculate Conception of the Virgin whom she confessed as "my queen, my refuge, my life, my succor, my defence, my joy, my fortress and my hope." On and on went the swift, **low** voice in the silent church and now and then the words **were borne on** sobs:

"Oh, Queen **of** Heaven, **of** thee it was said: Who is this that looketh forth **as** the morning, fair **as** the moon, chosen as the sun. Thou didst come to the world as the resplendent morning, anticipating with the light of thy holiness the coming of the Sun of righteousness. Oh day in which thou didst appear in the world! Well may it be called day of salvation and grace. Thou art beautiful as the moon," etc.

Then again:

"Oh, Mother of Mercy, propitiate thy Son. All the world recognizes thee, who art in the highest heaven, as the com-

mon propitiation for all peoples. I beseech thee, oh most
holy Virgin! to concede to me the succor of thy supplications
before God; supplications which are more estimable and more
precious than all the treasures of the earth; supplications
which oblige God to pardon our sins, and secure for us a
great abundance of grace; supplications which put to flight
our enemies, confound their designs, and triumph over their
ardent efforts."

Two little girls who had been sent in with an offering of
flowers for the image of St. Felipe de Jesus told their mothers that "Flavia Salizar was on her knees much time before
the image of the Blessed Virgin, and that she wept much."
And it was true.

At last she went home with her head bowed and her thin
black silk shawl drawn closely about her face. She shut
herself in her room and went into a fit of hysterical weeping.

Just after the tragic close of the reign of the Emperor
Iturbide, in the first days of republican Mexico, that is during the year 1825, "certain political clubs were organized
under the name and with the formulas of Masonic lodges of
the Yorkine rite, their founder being the priest of the parish
of Tobasco, and the senator for that State. In opposition to
these were the lodges of the Scotch rite, which were organized between 1813 and 1836 and which counted among their
members Negrete, Echavarri, Guerrero, and many prominent
leaders whose party favored the restoration of the monarchy."

The *Yorkinos* were the republican party, the *Escoseses*, or
those who belonged to the lodges of the Scotch rite, were the
royalist party, and to that party the clergy belonged as a
matter of course. The republic continued, but the Yorkine
party, through the faults of ambitious and unscrupulous
members, was destroyed. The lodges of the Scotch rite lost
their political power. They revived, but never since then
have they had a distinctive political character, though it is
probable that the many prominent men who belong to them
seek to use their connection with them for political ends.

When the royalist party was crushed out and Mexico became thoroughly republican, the clergy, finding that the Masonic lodges would no longer further their political designs, withdrew from them. They found, moreover, that, as they might express it, in introducing and fostering Free Masonry they had warmed and nourished in their bosom a serpent which was to turn and sting them, for the numerous lodges were diffusing a spirit of inquiry and of religious liberty among all ranks of the people.

When Don Francisco went home to dinner that day, he looked into his study and not finding Doña Flavia there he started into their bedroom which opened into the study. The door was locked. He was a little surprised; he went back through the study and stepped into the corridor. A servant saw him and came up to say that the "Señora" had a severe headache and had told her to tell him that she preferred not to see any one. She had never before refused to see him no matter how sick she was.

He was too much accustomed to dread that she should discover that he was connected with a Masonic lodge not to have his apprehensions aroused.

When a school was to be selected for the sons of his first marriage she had set her heart on their being placed in one of the Catholic schools of the country, pleading that she had a right to have something to say in the decision of that question because she had been a good stepmother. He willingly acknowledged that, but refused to place his sons in these schools because, as he explained to her, they were all under the influence of Jesuit priests. That argument had no weight for her; and naturally when the question had to be decided for her own sons the discussion led to worse feeling on her part, for, knowing that he was in the right the father had had his own way and had sent them first to secular schools in the City of Mexico and afterward to a college of the same character in California.

As was to be expected, when Magdalena was to be sent away from home to complete her education all of Don Francisco's pleading and explaining was of no avail. He saw that if he persisted he would be rushing into breakers worse than he had ever anticipated. Sick at heart, he, the statesman, who knew the teachings and influence of the Jesuits, the philanthropist, who knew the character of convents, gave his lovely and tenderly loved daughter into the care of the nuns who had charge of one of the "Colleges of the Sacred Heart of Jesus." Did he do right? He often asked himself that, and generally answered his question by exclaiming, desperately: "What else could I do?"

There were other things, too, for which he might well anticipate trouble if a report of them should reach his wife's ears. Perhaps she had seen a copy of a speech which he had made during the last session of Congress, in which he had spoken of Juarez as the "Savior of his Country," extolled the law granting religious toleration, and made some observations which no one could consider complimentary to the influence of the priests on the political affairs of Mexico, concluding by reminding his hearers of the shameful words of a Mexican prelate, uttered in a speech to the pope, that "He hoped the day would come when the Mexican eagle would drag itself in the dust before the papal throne."

He remembered with satisfaction that this speech had been much applauded in the Chamber, and—there being no line in the course of the years over which vanity may not accompany us—he had thought that "if Flavia could have heard that speech, and the applause with which it was received, she would have been proud that she was his wife—if she were not such a Catholic." Had that speech brought him trouble?

His was an open and sincere nature; he would have been glad to confide to his wife all his thoughts about politics, religion and everything else, but her fanaticism had made it necessary for him to conceal, as far as possible, his liberal, patriotic, and philanthropic course in relation to the former. With respect to the latter he said very little in her presence, but persistently and earnestly he attempted to uproot from the minds of his boys all belief in the superstitions of the Catholic Church.

In this course he was attempting to counteract the equally persistent and earnest instructions of their mother; and the result was that the young people's minds were in a sad state of confusion. "Was father right? or was mother right? or were they both right in some way that they could not understand?" What are children to do when two infallible teachers differ? What was Don Francisco to say when the bright eyes of his boys dilated with surprise, and they replied: "But, papa, mama says that the priests are good men, and that we ought to confess to them, and do everything they tell us to do"?

One by one, as they crept up into their teens, they learned to listen in silence to both father and mother, and to ponder in their own hearts, or discuss timidly among themselves these contradictory instructions; and both father and mother had been saddened over the growing silence on the part of their sons. Each of them thought he was right and felt aggrieved by the other.

Don Francisco had to give up his daughters almost entirely to the influence of their mother; he could never get *them* into his office down town and talk with them as he could with his sons.

It was true, he had nothing to offer his boys in the place of Roman Catholicism; but they had better have nothing than that collection of degrading superstitions, he thought. "I can give them nothing in the place of it—nothing but Free Masonry"—he said to himself drearily that afternoon, sitting, with his elbows on his desk and his head on his hands, pondering over these things as he was in the habit of doing.

Free Masonry was not a religion. He was by no means sure that compliance with the rules of that order was all that a man needed to make him feel comfortable about that going out into the dark alone after death. He knew from travel and observation that the Protestant nations were characterized by prosperity and a spirit of progress, such as were to be found in no Catholic nation. He liked the principles taught by these Protestant creeds, the "liberty, equality, and fraternity;" they were what he liked best in Free Masonry, too. He was glad for the Protestants to come to Mexico, inasmuch as they diffused these principles. But as to the Protestants themselves, he was not sure that they were so much better than the Catholics. If the pagans had persecuted the Catholics, and the Catholics had persecuted the pagans and the Protestants, the Protestants had also persecuted the Catholics and each other.

If Don Francisco had ever had a hint in his reading that they were not all Protestants that were called Protestants, it was a very vague one and it had made no impression on him. How could he go feeling his way blindly up and down the centuries, searching for "a little flock in the wilderness," who had never persecuted, but who had always been persecuted; a people who had always taught and really practiced those grand principles of Free Masonry, "Self-denial, liberty, equality, and fraternity?"

"Pietists—that is what all these Protestants are," he said to himself, "with their strict observance of Sunday, their refusing to go to balls and theaters on that day—on the day which should be given to harmless recreation!"

No, he did not want his children to be Protestants. The traditions of some generations of aristocratic ancestors forbade that. He preferred that they should retain the name of "Catholics," but have little or nothing to do with the Church except to be baptized, married and buried by it; and he would not grieve if they omitted those expressions of deference for her.

"As for this matter of a preparation for a future life," he said, getting up uneasily and beginning to walk the floor, "if there is a future state of existence, nothing can be known about it with certainty anyhow. One can only hope that by being a good citizen, a good son, husband and father it will turn out all right."

If this statement of Don Francisco's religious opinions is

confused, it is at least no more confused than his opinions
were.

Two hours later he stood before the door of his wife's room.
His fears were probably ill founded, he was wrong to borrow
trouble, he had said to himself, trying to recall an easy and
cheerful feeling about his domestic affairs, to entertain which,
it had long seemed to him, would be the climax of human
happiness. He knocked, but as there was no answer he
opened the door softly and entered. The room was in perfect order; the crucifix stood in its place on the bureau
and the mass book and rosary lay by its side, as usual.
There was no smelling bottle nor any other attendant of a
headache among the books and ornaments of the center table
nor on the tiny marble table by the bed. The great, beautiful, shining brass bed, with the picture of the Virgin in the
head piece held by the slender coils of yellow metal, looked
as if its snowy surface under the lace curtains which hung
down from the "likeness of a kingly crown" above and were
looped back with ribbons, had never been disturbed.

Carefully dressed, with her shining, wavy brown hair arranged in its usual simple and elegant style, Doña Flavia sat
in a wicker rocking chair near the window. She was evidently better of the headache.

She did not look up as he approached; perhaps she had not
heard him, he thought.

"Your head is better, I hope," he said, speaking pleasantly and smiling.

"I have not had the headache," she replied in a cutting yet
musical voice.

"Maria told me at dinner time that you said you had the
headache and did not want to be disturbed."

"I told her to tell you so because I did not want to see any
one then. I have been quite well all day."

"Then what was the matter!" he asked with a sinking
heart, but going straight to the point. If trouble was coming it would be better to meet it bravely.

She arose from her seat that her face might be more nearly

on a level with his as she replied.   He thought of the gla-
ciers as he had seen them among the Alps with the sunlight
on their cold, beautiful surfaces.   She had tried to remove
all traces of weeping from her face and had dressed carefully
for this interview.   "She wished to show him," as she told
her sister some months afterward, "that it was Flavia Salizar he had trifled with."   She looked him full in the face as
she answered:

"I have learned to-day that you are a Mason."

He returned her look without flinching.   He would have
told her a falsehood if it would have deceived her.   "Why
should he not?" he would have reasoned if any reasoning
had been necessary to his mind.   "Would it not be better to
tell one lie than that a whole family should be plunged into
unhappiness by the truth.   Was it not taught in the laws of
Spain that deception was right under certain circumstances?
Did not Victor Hugo's saintly 'Sister Simplicia' tell a lie to
save a good man from trouble, and did not the author say
that it was set down in Paradise as one of the whitest deeds
she ever did?   Juan Valjean would not tell a falsehood for
his own sake, perhaps, but he told them without scruples for
the sake of others."

There are special reasons why the author of "Les Miserables" should be a favorite among the Mexicans.   Was it not
he who called Napoleon III. "Napoleon the Little"?   And
was he not banished by that monarch for twenty years from
France?   And did he not return to France and enter Paris
the day after the republic was proclaimed?

Don Francisco was well acquainted with the teachings of
the Roman Catholic Church on the subject of lying, but he
was not so well aware that he himself was indebted to her
for is belief in the usefulness and harmlessness of lying on
some occasions.   He preferred, as we have seen, to cite Victor
Hugo's teachings as a reason for the faith that was in him.
But even if he had received his "liberal" ideas about falsehood from that author, it is still probable that he would have
been indebted to the Church for them, for Victor Hugo grew

up in an atmosphere of Roman Catholicism, so that whether he would or not the principles of that religion had become a part of every nerve and fiber of his spiritual being, if I may be permitted to express it so.

"Yes," said Don Francisco quietly, "I have been a Mason for six years."

"How can you speak so quietly of having deceived your wife for such a length of time?"

"I would gladly have told you, but I knew you would oppose it. My duty to my country required me to become a Mason. If you will examine the teachings of the Masons, Flavia, you will see that there is nothing wrong in them."

"I don't care to discuss the subject or to hear it explained. I have borne enough. For years you have acted in direct opposition to my wishes; you have done all you could against the church of your forefathers and of your wife; you have spared no pains to drag your children and mine into infidelity and heresy. I demand a separation."

Don Francisco was astonished. He had never thought of her going so far. He was indignant, but he controlled himself, and said quietly:

"You are excited, Flavia. Wait till you are calmer, and we will talk of this."

"No, it would better to settle it now; I don't want to have to refer to it again. I desire a separation. I want to have the privilege of bringing up my children in the fold of the Church."

Just then there was heard outside a rush of little feet toward "mama's room," and a confusion of merry voices and childish laughter. They sounded like the clear, happy songs of birds under a black sky in the lull of a tempest. Don Francisco stepped quickly to the door and turned the key, with the bitter thought that it was the first time that his children were ever locked out from the presence of their parents. Then he said quietly:

"They are my children, too. I have as much right as you to say what they shall be taught. But if you will persist in

talking of such absurdities I will have to remind you that
even if the law would grant you a divorce it would give you
only your daughters, whom you have completely under your
influence anyhow, and it would leave our sons to me.   But as
you have no just cause for a divorce the law would not give
it to you.   And if you leave me without one I will keep all
the children."

"The Church would give me a divorce under such circumstances."

"I don't doubt it," he replied scornfully, "there is no iniquity that the Roman Catholic Church can't be counted on
to sanction.   But you forget that the Church, in Mexico, no
longer has the power to make or sever marriages."

She gazed at him a few moments, slowly realizing her helplessness.   Then she sank into her chair and covered her face
with her hands.   Pity seized him, and regret for his em-
phatic words.   Could he not have told her the truth more
gently?   He drew a chair to her side, and sat down.   It was
the priests who were to blame for all this, and not his sweet,
fair wife, he thought.

"Flavia," he said gently, laying his hand on her shoulder,
"don't cry.   I spoke too emphatically.   I did wrong.   We
will forget it all."

"Please go away and leave me alone," she moaned.

"No," he said, "I can't leave you so, dear.   Forgive me;
you know I love you.   There, don't cry, and let me open the
door for the children."

"I wish you would leave me alone," she repeated impatiently.   And after a few moments he went out softly, and
shut the door.

CHAPTER XVIII.

THE LORD'S DAY.

NEARLY two weeks after the events of the last chapter, one Sunday afternoon, Doña Flavia and Mercedes sat together in the parlor sewing. The members of that well-ordered household did not usually work much on Sunday, because that was a day of *fiesta*—a day of rest and recreation. I should make an exception of the servants; they usually worked more on that day than on others, for there was generally company for dinner on Sundays.

There was no company to-day; nevertheless it had been a very busy day. Doña Flavia and Mercedes had gone to early mass, then the latter and the housekeeper had superintended the cleaning of the parlor, study, and dining room. After the carpets and curtains were shaken and put down and hung up, and the furniture was all in its place again, Doña Flavia and Mercedes had daintily re-arranged the delicate ornaments, fastidiously draped the curtains and discussed and had changed some of the pictures. So the morning and part of the afternoon had passed, and now, as I have said, though tired, they sat together, sewing.

The cause of all this unusual exertion was the expected visit of a bishop, or perhaps I should say, the Bishop, for he was the favorite bishop of Doña Flavia and of most of the "honorable women" of the city. His visit had been expected for some time, as for some weeks he had been writing and sending messages to the wealthy ladies of the city to the effect that as soon as other imperative duties would permit he would visit Salta.

He was to come this week, and though there had been plenty of other days on which the house cleaning could have been done, all had agreed that it would be better to do it on Sunday, as they could have more assistance on that day.

The cleaning would not have been necessary for any other visit, but, as Doña Flavia remarked, "She always liked to have everything as elegant as possible when the Señor Bishop came, because he was so elegant himself."

When he had last visited them he had affectionately urged the ladies of the Church Society to build a chapel for the image of St. Felipe de Jesus, a young Mexican priest who was crucified in Japan and afterwards canonized by the Church, the only Mexican on whom that honor has as yet been conferred. The chapel was to be a small room, or large alcove, opening by one whole side into the church.

Great efforts had been made to complete this chapel before the bishop's return. Subscriptions had been solicited, the contributors being assured that their names would be deposited in a glass urn that would be kept on the altar, and that three masses a month would be said for them, whether living or dead.[1]

An opera troupe which had visited the town had, at the solicitation of the ladies, given a performance one Sunday night for the building of the chapel. During the vacation of the schools they had given balls on Sunday nights in the girls' public school building, and from the sale of the refreshments they had realized some money; a lottery, which was owned by the Society, and was run in the interest of the Church and for general benevolence, had also proved a source of profit. More than one Sunday afternoon had been enlivened by bull-fights, the proceeds of which had been devoted to this pious purpose. After each of these entertainments a very gratifying sum had been paid into the hands of the treasurer of the Society, for, notwithstanding the fact that the *torreros* (bullfighters) who took part on all but one of these occasions were men of but little renown in their profession, all the élite of the town, gentlemen, ladies and children, attended, "because it was for the Church." The com-

---

[1] *Note.*—El Tiempo, a Catholic daily paper, published in the City of Mexico.

mon people went because they always did so if they could save money enough.

I insert here a description of this diversion that you may have an idea of the way in which the Lord's Day is kept holy in Mexico, as well as of the manner in which the Holy Apostolic Roman Catholic Church is at least partially supported. This description was written for me by one who had witnessed the fights. He is now, however, a minister of the gospel. That fact, by the way, may account for his having divided his description into "firstly," "secondly," "thirdly," as if he were writing a sermon:

"1st. The amphitheater. A wall is constructed which incloses a circular space of about forty yards in diameter. Running around the inside of this wall are the seats, arranged like steps, which are for the spectators. Some seats cost more than others. . There are several exits and entrances. On the outside of the amphitheater, but joined to it, is a lot in which the animals are shut up. It has two doors leading into the amphitheater, one through which the animal enters, and one through which he is taken out.

"2nd. Selection of animals. Those who have the management of the amphitheater wish to obtain the wildest and fattest animals that can be found. Having made a contract with the owner of a herd they employ experienced men to select the animals. They go into the inclosure where the herd is collected, mounted on horseback, and by the use of the experience and practice of years, and with great danger to their own lives and to those of their horses, they effect the separation of the chosen animals from the rest of the herd. It nearly always happens that one or two horses are left dead in the inclosure. The separation being accomplished they drive the animals to the town and shut them up in the lot adjoining the amphitheater. And with that the adventure of these men is finished.

"3rd. The Corrida (the fight). Generally the animals are tortured in the afternoon. The next morning a clown, dressed in gay colors and with his face painted, followed by the company of *torreros* in the red, green and blue costumes, in which they fight, and accompanied by a multitude of common people and a band of music, go through the streets to announce the *Corrida*.

"When the hour has arrived in which the spectators are to assemble the band station themselves in a convenient place and pour out their melodies on the air for the purpose of attracting all who have the taurine taste (*el gusto taurino*). Very soon crowds of persons are seen to pour in, filling the amphitheater in a few instants till not another one can find a place on the seats before alluded to.

"The judge of the *Corrida* notifies the corneteer, who is by his side, when the time to begin has arrived. He gives the signal and a furious bull, which has been pricked and tortured for the purpose of exciting to the highest degree all his fierce instincts, rushes through the door into the arena.

"The sight of so many people about him further arouses his fury, and with the velocity of a cannon ball he hurls himself upon his opponents, who are waiting for him. For a few minutes the *arrastradores* play with him, deceiving him with their *capotes*. The arrastrador is a man who carries a red sheet or *capote* stretched on rods. He infuriates the animal by running toward him with the *capote* extended before him. The animal plunges his horns through the *capote*, but the *arrastrador* has nimbly sprung from behind it so that only the *capote* is gored. There are usually two arrastradores.

"The two *cazadores* on spirited horses display their skill in throwing the lasso, in which art figure more than one hundred ways of catching the animal. The *topador*, mounted on a very poor horse, so that his ability may be the more conspicuous, has an opportunity to show his herculean strength by arresting the attacks of the brute with the point of his spear.

"In the meantime the *bandarilleros* arm themselves with their *bandarillas* to await their turn. The *bandarillas* are sticks tipped with sharp iron and ornamented with bright paper; one of them is in the shape of a large flower; this one they nail into his forehead. There are generally three of these men, including the captain. Their turn arrives, and at the order of the judge they enter the **arena**. **Each one** in his turn tantalizes the furious **wild** beast, and then **one** after another they spring on his horns and drive a pair of sharp irons into his back. When they have tortured him **to** their own satisfaction, and that of the spectators, the order **is** given to kill him. This act nearly always devolves on **the** captain. He takes his sword, and **in the** manner **which is** prescribed by his art **plunges it** behind **his shoulder into his** heart.

"The **play** with **one animal** being thus **ended** they continue with another and another till three are killed, that being the number employed in each *Corrida*."

Often horses are **killed, and** not seldom a *torrero*. In one of the *Corridas* given for the building of the chapel I have mentioned **a man was** killed, **and it was** characteristic of a people so educated **that** they expressed themselves as "well pleased **that he was** killed **because he** went into the arena drunk."

The gentlemen and the feminine portion **of the best society** did not attend *corridas de toros* regularly, just **as they did not** go to **all** the theatrical performances **that came along; they** only **went** when there was some unusual attraction, or when it was **for** the church or **some** other benevolent object. The fresh, young faces **of the** boys **of** the best families were seldom missing from **the** amphitheater. **It was** Don Francisco's habit to inquire of **his boys,** in his pleasant way, every Sunday evening, after they **had attended a** *Corrida,* "if the *toros* and the horses **were** well **killed."**

Good fortune had brought the greatest *torrero* of Mexico to Salta during the building of this chapel. This *torrero,* Ponciano Diaz—who, I beg leave to state, is not a relative of Señor Don Porfirio Diaz, the president of the republic—had **come** bringing with him several other *torreros* who fought **under his** direction. The bands of music, accompanied by a **large crowd of people,** among whom were some of the prin-

11

cipal men of the town, friends of the celebrated *torrero*, had met him some way from the town as he came from the railway station.   He was conducted to the best hotel of the town where he was received as a distinguished man.   His visit to this comparatively insignificant place was a favor which the town could not have reasonably expected, for he had recently returned from Europe loaded with honors and riches.   He had been received in the City of Mexico with no little applause and with no little flattering notice by the newspapers.

[1]The church society of Salta appointed a meeting and consulted with tremulous enthusiasm.   They went in a body to request "Don" Ponciano Diaz to give one of his entertainments for the benefit of the chapel.   The president of the society, Doña Flavia Salizar de Urbina, was to present the petition; and never was there a president of a society of ladies who could present a petition to a distinguished personage with more impressive elegance.

The great man received the ladies with all the grace and dignity of a bull-fighter.   With many gracious compliments, circumlocutions and smiles, with much dwelling on the good cause to which he would be lending a helping-hand, and perhaps with some delicate hints that it might be for the good of his own soul, since we are all sinners, or at least that it might be a work of supererogation that would be set down to the credit of some poor soul, the request was presented.

With the delicacy and tact that would naturally be conspicuous in the character of a gentleman of his profession Don Ponciano gave the ladies to understand that he was now worth thirty thousand dollars, fruits of his toils in Europe; why should he still risk his life?   Why should he not retire from business and live like other gentlemen on his income?   However, as the ladies were importunate he condescended to ride through the town in the procession accompanied by some of the principal men of the city; and they should of course have the proceeds of a *corrida*.   And their point being

[1] *Note.*—A young lady belonging to the best society of the town related to me this call on "Don" Ponciano. She was, perhaps, herself one of the society.

at least partially gained the ladies retired with many thanks to their benefactor.

The chapel had been finished at last, and the girl-faced "saint" in his long robes had been placed on a pedestal, his feet at a convenient distance from the floor to be kissed by the children. It was nearly all paid for, too; they owed now only a small sum for the new robes in which they had dressed the saint. They hoped to pay for these with the proceeds which were accruing from the raffling of various fancy articles.

Doña Flavia and Mercedes were busy this afternoon finishing, the former, an exquisite sofa cushion, the latter, a linen handkerchief which she was ornamenting with drawn work. On the morrow Maria would carry both of these articles, wrapped in a snowy towel, from house to house together with the paper on which were to be written the amounts paid for the chance of drawing the lucky numbers.

Both Doña Flavia and Mercedes were sad and the conversation between them was not animated. Doña Flavia had at first felt humiliated by the failure to rule her husband or leave him. Then her better feelings had waked up and she had reflected that he was good and kind notwithstanding the errors of his creed and practice. She felt that she had stood on the brink of a precipice, and she rejoiced that she had been kept from bringing herself and her family into notoriety by taking the fatal step. Silent martyrdom would be better than that.

These feelings had lasted a few days till she had confessed to the Señor Cure and he had strengthened her faltering resolutions "to give her husband no rest nor peace till he should consent to do what would be for the good of his own soul and those of his children—abandon Free Masonry and return to the bosom of the Holy Mother Church out of which there was no salvation." These resolutions were further strengthened by the announcement of the bishop's visit. Her troubled soul rejoiced that she was to have advice and consolation from so eminent an authority in the Church; it would be almost as if the Holy Father in Rome should speak to her!

Mercedes had been troubled ever since the day of the conversation between Doña Flavia and Doña Concepcion. She had noticed since that day that Doña Flavia had spent more time than usual in the church praying to one or another "saint"; that often Don Francisco and she did not appear in the dining room at the same hour, the one complaining of headache, the other of unusual business in his office; that they were seldom both in the parlor in the evenings at the same time, and that both of them were always preoccupied and not cheerful. Two or three evenings when she and other girls had left the parlor to promenade in front of the house, and look at the moon and stars and "talk," she had watched him through the study window sitting at the center table on which the student's lamp burned, his head resting on one or both hands, and the "Monitor Republicano" spread out before him. And she saw that for an hour at a time the paper was not moved.

The night before, as she lay awake because of a vague dread that some great trouble was coming, she had heard steps in the court and slipping across the room and peeping through the curtain she had seen Don Francisco standing under an orange tree. He was looking at the stars, and now and then he rubbed his hand across his forehead. As she watched him he stepped to the fountain and, lifting the water in his hand, he bathed his forehead as if he were feverish. He had evidently not retired, though she knew from the striking of the town clock it was two.

It was sad, she reflected, that so noble and talented a man should be a Mason. She knew nothing about Masonry except that it was a secret order which was opposed to "religion"; and according to report they did dreadful things in their secret meetings. It was even said that they kept a pot of poison in their hall which they made use of when their secrets were revealed. But would the genial, dignified, honorable Don Francisco do dreadful things? She could not believe it, and yet—. The evil, she had heard (it was astonishing how much she had heard in the last two weeks), was wide spread. The very president of the republic was a Mason—he was the Grand Master of the Grand Symbolical Diet, they said; and Mercedes thought he must have advanced very far in wickedness to have such a title as that. She had been told that most, if not all, his Cabinet and nearly all of the most prominent men of the nation were Masons.

.Would they all—all of these men who were trying so earnestly to lift up the republic and make it equal to the greatest nations—would they all do dreadful things? And yet, poor Doña Flavia! And she knew from chance remarks that she had heard that there were many other wives who were greatly troubled, and some of them had even threatened to leave their husbands.

At last the cushion was finished and Doña Flavia clasped her white, jeweled hands over its bright colors. Mercedes had already put the last stitch into the handkerchief and was patting it as it lay folded on her knee.

"Well," said Doña Flavia with a sigh of relief, "this time to-morrow, if God wills it, the Señor Bishop will be here."

"Yes, Señora."

"I have been thinking, my daughter, that this would be a good opportunity for you to be confirmed. I shall have Anita and Pancho confirmed while he is here. My other children were confirmed in infancy, only a day or two after they were baptized, but owing to some circumstances the confirmation of these two children has been neglected until now," and a shadow flitted across her face. The "some circumstances" were Don Francisco's indifference about it. She thought of this and a good many other little things with new bitterness, now.

"I don't know, Señora, I should have to confess first, and I would rather not confess," replied Mercedes quickly, remembering her father's commands about it, and the terrible —not exactly remorse nor repentance—but "feelings" she had had about the masses.

"Why, dear," said Doña Flavia, smiling insinuatingly, "you have not done something that you object to confessing, I hope."

Mercedes' face flushed with indignation. She saw the cunning of the remark—but dimly, for like most persons of innocent and sincere natures she was slow to believe evil of others. Later, in her own room, she said to herself fiercely, "She wanted to force me in that contemptible way to confess. I despise her!" and her feelings were all the more strong because she felt that her rage was impotent. She was correct in her inference; Doña Flavia had not been under Jesuit influence all the days of her life for nothing.

Mercedes was always helpless when she received an underhand thrust, even when it was given by one of her own age to whom she might have replied. It was so both because she was slow to believe in the evil intention of the other, and because she felt that if she should reply in the same manner she should be as despicable as the one who had given the first thrust. She always let such things pass without notice, and therefore she was considered by some "a poor-spirited" girl. She replied now with some confusion, and making an effort to tell the truth:

"No—yes—I can't bear to think of being questioned about my inmost thoughts by any person."

"O, it isn't so bad. You have an exaggerated idea of the difficulties of the confession. And besides the priests who will come with the Señor Bishop to confess the people are elegant gentlemen; you cannot fail to admire them. You would look so well in the confirmation dress. Come into my room and let me show you Anita's."

Mercedes followed her as she led the way to her room. She spread out the dainty little dress and gauzy veil on the bed.

"And here," she said, taking something off the shelf of the wardrobe, "here is a beautiful white dress which I have just had made for Magdalena; I dare say it would fit you quite well. You could be confirmed in it, and you could wear my wedding veil; I have it yet. Think about it, dear. You should be willing to do anything that would be for the good of your soul."

"I will think about it, Señora. But it is not likely that I shall change my mind." After a little more conversation she said, "I will go to my room now, Doña Flavia, with your permission."

"Go with God," said the lady kindly, using an ordinary, but a tender adieu. She had never been so affectionate with Mercedes before.

CHAPTER XIX.

THE SEÑOR BISHOP.

THE next Tuesday morning Doña Flavia and the Bishop sat together in the parlor. The afternoon before the whole town had been moved to receive him. Not even the coming of "Don" Ponciano Diaz had stirred them more. Several of the most prominent men of the city had, according to established custom, met him at the station, though at least one of them had observed, with a smile: "This is a great ado over a mere man like myself. The other day when I arrived from Paris there was no such stir as this."

A few miles from town a multitude of people had met Don Francisco's handsome carriage, in which the Señor Bishop and three inferior priests were seated. While the gentlemen of the town were saluting him and kissing his hand the men unhitched the horses from the carriage and tied two long ropes to the tongue. When the salutations were over the women seized the ropes and drew the carriage along the dusty road. The Señor Bishop was in his black, sacerdotal robes, and as they passed along his hand on which flashed the pastoral ring showered apostolic blessings on the kneeling people. When the women were overcome with fatigue the men took the ropes and completed the journey, drawing the carriage through the streets adorned with arches, ornamented with colored paper, banners and images, till they stopped in front of Don Francisco's house. There Doña Flavia, her children, and by special request, Mercedes, stood to give him and the others a cordial welcome.

Don Francisco was not there, neither did he see him till he came to supper; the business in his office was very pressing, indeed, this week. Though when he could not avoid being with the Señor Bishop he omitted no stately courtesy, his prevailing feeling toward him was the wish that he could open his massive, carved front doors, and call his servants to kick the elegant bishop into the street. It was of that he was thinking when Mercedes had seen him under the orange tree a few nights before. Well he knew that every incident of his domestic life would be exposed to the gaze of that man. All the forty years of his married life he had writhed under the thought that some priest or other knew, or could know if he wished, every thought of his that he had ever confided to his wife.

On this Tuesday morning the Señor Bishop was standing by the piano admiring a vase of flowers. He lifted the vase and held it now near to enjoy the perfume, now at a little distance to admire their beauty. "How exquisite!" he exclaimed. "What delicate perfume, and what a wonderful blending of colors! When I was in college Botany was one of my favorite studies."

"I think a love for flowers is a characteristic of all great souls," replied Doña Flavia.

He was a very handsome man; he was tall and finely proportioned, elegant in dress and irreproachable in manner. He had a liberal education, and to this were added a rich, melodious voice, and a poetical way of expressing his thoughts. His fine, clean-shaven face wore an expression that was generally considered benevolent. He was about forty-five years of age. As he held up the vase his magnificent figure showed to full advantage in the dress of a private gentleman.

Doña Flavia sat in a wicker rocker, as handsome in her way as the Señor Bishop. Her face was a little flushed. These observations about the flowers and his "great soul" were only a parenthesis in the conversation. She had been telling him her domestic troubles.

"Yes, Señora," said the Señor Bishop, suddenly setting down the vase of flowers, "Free Masonry is the deification of Satan. It deceives and mocks the people with promises which it never fulfills. But only in nations, such as Italy

and France, where it enjoys unbridled liberty, have they
made public the fact that they adore Lucifer as God, and that
they are working everywhere to substitute his worship for
the Christian worship. Satanism or Masonry! this is the
real obstacle which prevents the nations from going forward
in the road of progress and true civilization!"

Doña Flavia's eyes dilated with horror. If he had told her
her husband was a cannibal she would not have been much
more impressed.

"Yes, Señora; but happily this declaration, made only by
Catholics a few years ago, is to-day on the lips of all those
who contemplate the shameful backwardness of the nations
which are governed by Masonry. Protestants, Rationalists,
and even Atheists who do not belong to this community of
the devil abominate it, considering it the most formidable
enemy of happiness both of individuals and of nations!

"Why should we conceal the fact?" went on the Señor
Bishop warmly. "Evil triumphs, and perhaps in the next
century there will be built public basilicas and altars where
in the midst of heinous abominations the highest worship
will be rendered to the Enemy of our nature. The great
periods of history always terminate with the preponderance
of evil over good, with the empire of Satan over man." The
Señor Bishop paused to allow these fearful truths to take
effect on the mind of his hearer; then he continued in another
tone:

"At last the truth will prevail. But God has wished to
reserve those supreme triumphs for himself. When the time
is fulfilled he will hurl the lightning of his omnipotent justice
which will reduce to powder, as if they were frail vessels of
clay, the nations which proudly rise up against Him and his
Christ."[1]

This rose-colored view of the end of Free Masonry gave
little comfort to the spirit of Doña Flavia, since it was probable that her husband and sons would be involved in the
catastrophe. As dreadful as it had seemed to her before she

___
[1] *Note.*—All of this interesting and important information about Free
Masonry is translated *verbatim et liberatim* from El Tiempo.

had not thought it was so bad as this. She listened with a lacerated heart to the instructions which the Señor Bishop gave her as to the manner of winning back her husband to the Church. They were similar to those which she had before received from the Señor Cure.

Just then the folding doors opened, and Mercedes, who had been requested to come in after school hours, entered. Doña Flavia had found time to tell him something of her. His face lighted with pleasure as he went to meet her.

"My daughter, you have come in to sit with us awhile. We shall be very glad to have your company."

"Thank you, Señor," replied Mercedes, as she kissed his hand. He led her to a seat and then sat down in an armchair not far from her.

"The Señora Urbina has been telling me of your love for books. I think we must be kindred spirits," he remarked, smiling kindly at her.

"Yes, Señor, I am fond of reading," she said, simply.

"Will you tell me who is your favorite author?"

"I—think the Biografies of Distinguished Mexicans is a very interesting book."

"Ah, yes; with what appreciation the author writes of the authors, sculptors, artists, and warriors of Mexico!"

"Yes, I read the biography of St. Felipe de Jesus in that book. It was very interesting. It was a grand day when the news that the Holy Father, Urban VIII., had canonized him was received in Mexico. What grand *fiestas* they had in honor of it! And his mother went out in the solemn procession by the side of the viceroy; and the government gave her and his four sisters a pension because her son had been canonized. Those were the days in which the Church was respected in Mexico. Ah me!" observed Doña Flavia. She seldom read anything but the mass book, the catechism, and other Catholic books of devotion, and she was glad of this opportunity to display some knowledge of general literature.

The Bishop made some appropriate reply and then went on talking about the artists and literary men of Mexico,

many of whom he knew personally. Mercedes thought she
had never had the privilege of listening to so charming a
conversationalist. "How condescending, how fatherly, how
delightful he is!" she said to herself. "If my father could
have known such priests as he, he would not have disliked
them so."

At last he gracefully introduced the subject of religion.
After some preliminary remarks, he said:

"By the way, my daughter, have you been confirmed?"

"No, Señor."

His look of interest changed into one of fatherly solicitude
as he said:

"My dear daughter, you should not longer neglect that
duty and privilege. You can not hope to enjoy the presence
of the Holy Spirit until you have been confirmed. Will you
not allow me the pleasure and honor of confirming you while
I am here?"

Mercedes felt her face growing very hot.

The Bishop continued, adopting the tender and beautiful
"thou" form of the Spanish:

"Tell me, dost thou walk far from God? How many years
hast thou had no peace in thy soul? As many at least as thou
hast been wanting in compliance with the requirements of
the Church. Dost thou long for peace? Resolve, then, at
once, think a few minutes, cast one glance over thy conscience, give one step more and thou hast done it all. Never
let fall from thy lips, my daughter, that excuse, as foolish as
impious: 'I confess only to God!' Those who so proudly
blaspheme of confessing only to God, it is certain that they
never remember that God exists. It is as ridiculous as if a
criminal invited to present himself before the authorities to
receive pardon, should say, 'I will not present myself to any
one except the king.' But suppose the king should not wish
you to appear before him, but before those whom he has
elected to represent him? 'No,' he replies, 'I will have
nothing to do with any one but his Majesty!' Dost thou
know, my dear daughter, what would happen to one who

should act **thus?** Putting off presenting himself **before** the authorities? **The** civil authority would **seize him and** he would pay dearly for his nonsense. **Now, make the** application. God has declared that **he does not wish** to have anything to do with thee except through the intervention of his priests. Thou hast the offer **of** pardon. Who knows **if** while thou refusest to accept it under the conditions with which it is offered death will **seize** thee, for he has a great liking for pouncing on the unprepared. Believe **me, my** beloved daughter! Come in time! What detains **thee? Is it** shame? **That is a great sin!"**

Mercedes could **make** no reply to these arguments. **She** sat with bowed head **and** crimson face, listening.

"The Señora Urbina has told me that **you** dread the confessional. But the only gate to heaven is through confession to the **priest.** Christ showed us this when **he** delivered the keys of the **kingdom of heaven to** St. Peter. He made him the porter to open and shut the gate. He would not then admit souls **to** eternal life in **any** other way; that would be an inconsistency of which we could **not** imagine our Lord guilty, **could** we?"[1]

"Is confirmation necessary **to salvation?"** asked Mercedes timidly.

"No," he replied gently, "you were regenerated and therefore saved by your baptism, **you** know."

"Regeneration. That means a great change **in** one's character, does it not?"

"Yes."

"It has always **seemed a pity to** me that it should take place in infancy, so that no one ever feels the change, or has any idea how it **is."[2]**

---

[1]*Note.*—These arguments for confirmation and confession are translated from El Tiempo.

[2]*Note.*—Mercedes, of course, looked at baptism from the Catholic **standpoint.** I read **or** heard of a very extraordinary occurrence which, **it was said,** happened here in Mexico: A **girl** of about thirteen years of **age was** baptized. She had been brought up far out in the mountains, **and either** through the neglect or **purpose** of her parents she had been

"But it is proper that baptism should be conferred on infants, and it should be done as soon as possible, without danger to them." And he proceeded to prove this to her by quotations from the Decrees of the Council of Trent, the Fathers, and the Sacred Scriptures.

"But it is wonderful that such great and far-reaching changes should follow so simple a ceremony."

"Yes. But all great things are simple," said the Señor Bishop.

"I thank you for the explanation, Father. But I think," she added, with a light laugh, "there must have been something wrong with my baptism. Perhaps the Father omitted a word or two in the ceremony and the charm was broken. I am not conscious of having any title to the privileges which it confers."

"You cannot expect to have peace of mind until you have availed yourself of all the privileges of the Church." And then he quoted the Fathers to prove to her that "the sacrament of confirmation" was instituted by the Lord, and that through it the "love of God is shed abroad in our hearts by

---

deprived of the "holy sacrament of baptism." She had heard of it, however, and of its wonderful virtues, and she finally effected her escape from her home, reached a town, and asked in the streets for "holy baptism." The wealthy ladies came to hear of it and they were mightily moved. They dressed her as a bride and conducted her to the font. But neither the priest nor they could understand how baptism was to be conferred on a person who was standing; they may have had doubts as to its validity. The girl was too large to be held in arms, so they laid her on a table and the priest performed the ceremony.

I heard of a case in which a gentleman from the United States, desiring to marry a wealthy Mexican young lady, was suddenly converted to Catholicism. He stood up in front of the altar and declared to the congregation that he had never before known the true faith; then he laid himself on a table and was "baptized." And after all that the young lady broke the engagement.

Another reason which is given for their being laid on a table is that it is done in obedience to that passage which says: "We are buried with Him by baptism;" "for," they say, "you know people are always buried in a horizontal position."

the Holy Spirit, which is given unto us"; and that by neglect-ing it one might grieve the Holy Spirit.

And at the end of it all Mercedes said, "You are very kind, Father, I will think of it."

When Mercedes had gone out the Señor Bishop and his hostess talked of other matters pertaining to the Church. They spoke sadly of the loss of the temporal power, and the Señor Bishop again warmed into eloquence:

"Think," he exclaimed, "of the lonely prisoner in the Vatican! Robbed of his dominions, and his rights trampled on, he lives on the contributions which the Catholics and a few generous souls are accustomed to send him; and in his august poverty he divides with the needy and with the regions chastised by penury and by scarcity, the bread which is sent to him. Nobody is ignorant of the excellent qualities of the pope, and nobody withholds from him the praise which is his due, and nevertheless he continues to be a captive, aban-doned by the potentates of the earth, on whom rests the obligation of going to his assistance, and the responsibility of all that he bears and suffers—of his lot so full of privations and bitter trials."[1]

The Señora Urbina was affected almost to tears by this pathetic picture.

Two days later Mercedes, dressed as "a soul in grace," that is, in a white dress, a veil, and a wreath of orange blos-soms, glided across the church, and knelt by a confessional. These, the confessionals, are small black structures, scarcely tall enough for a man to stand erect in them, and just large enough to contain one chair. The penitent kneels outside and puts his lips to the small wire-covered window and whispers his confession into the ear of the priest, which rests against the other side of the wire. Both the priest and

---

[1] *Note.*—From a sermon by the Cardinal Archbishop of Toledo, Spain, published in El Tiempo. At the time that this sermon was published nearly every copy of this paper and others contained descriptions of the princely presents which were being received by the Pope during his Jubilee.

penitent are in full view of those who may be worshipping or passing about the church.

After the confession Mercedes went to a table at which one of the priests was standing and, laying down twenty-five cents, took up a ticket which she was to show on the day of confirmation to prove that she had complied with the preliminary requirements.

The next Sunday afternoon, when the sun was setting, a multitude of people were gathered in front of the church. Infants, children, and even a few grown people were waiting to be confirmed. Among the latter was Mercedes, again in a white dress, veil, and orange blossoms; and by her side stood Cipriana, her god-mother, whom Doña Flavia had been at the pains to dress in respectable black for the occasion.

As the Señor Bishop approached in miter and surplice, resplendent in jewels and gold and silver embroidery, she knelt, and lifted to him, as to a true embassador from Christ, who possessed mysterious, God-given powers, her pure, trusting face, with its tremulous lips and eager, expectant eyes; for now, at last, God was to confirm in her the work which was begun in her baptism, and peace from on high was to be given her.

The Bishop made with the "holy oil" the sign of the cross on her forehead, and said, with a solemn voice: "I seal thee with the sign of the cross, and I confirm thee with the Chrism of salvation in the name of the Father and of the Son and of the Holy Spirit." He then gave her a gentle blow on the cheek to remind her that she was to bear bravely all adversities in the name of Christ; and with a low, "Peace be with thee," he passed on. A priest followed with a snowy towel and wiped the oil from her forehead, and the Confirmation was over.

The next morning the Señor Bishop left, not going with pomp as he had entered the town, for, as the people declared, he had gotten so much money in the town he knew it was prudent to go as secretly as possible. One face that bent down at Don Francisco's door to kiss his hand with its flashing pastoral ring was **weary and worn.** His **"Peace with thee"** had brought no peace **to the owner** of that face.

Why had she confessed and been confirmed? Because she **had** thought through feverish days and nights of the solemn, tender words of the Bishop: "We ought to obey God rather than man." It must not hereafter be her fault if she had no peace of mind.

CHAPTER XX.

SOME NEW FACES.

"YES, and as good of heart as he was talented; he took the poor to eat at his own table."

The speaker was an elderly gentleman with a kindly face. He addressed two young ladies. The elder of the two was tall and slender, with gray eyes and brown hair, drawn smoothly back and gathered into a Grecian knot. The expression of her face was intelligent and pleasing. She wore a dress of some dark material. The other young lady was also tall and slender. There was no color about her if we except the clear brunette complexion, the bright red of her lips, and the fainter red of her cheeks. She wore a black dress and long, graceful black scarf. Her hand, in a smooth black kid glove, rested on the handle of a plain black silk parasol. Her black hair was straightly parted, combed smoothly back and the braids were coiled into a knot just above the nape of her neck. Young as she was, for she was evidently not more than eighteen, there was about her something of matronly grace and quiet dignity of manner. And yet there lurked in her dark eyes an expression which indicated a keen appreciation of humor. Altogether one felt that behind that dark face there was an eager, enthusiastic soul.

They were in the Academia de San Carlos, the Academy of Fine Arts, in the City of Mexico.

When they had come up into the galleries of paintings the elder young lady, who had often visited the Academia, and, indeed, was quite familiar with everything of interest in the city, had modestly approached a gentleman, who was without a hat and at leisure, and seemingly in charge of the place, and had requested him to lend her a catalogue of the pictures. He replied that a catalogue was being prepared, but that it was not yet finished. He courteously offered to take them through the galleries and tell them about the pictures.

They had gone first through the galleries of old Mexican paintings belonging to the time of the viceroys, galleries rich in paintings of Saints and Madonnas with the Holy Child and other Scripture subjects—pictures which grow on the beholder the longer he looks at them; then they had seen in the European gallery the two pictures by Murillo, "San Juan de Dios," and "John the Baptist in the Desert," the tiny picture of "Adam and Eve in Paradise, and their Expulsion," by Michael Angelo, and many other interesting and beautiful paintings; and lastly they had lingered long before the glory of the gallery, Cogette's "Deluge."

They had been through the gallery of landscapes, by modern Mexican artists, and had noticed with patriotic pride that the most beautiful represented the Valley of Mexico, the beautiful "Valley of Anahuac."

Their guide, who added much to their pleasure by his evident enjoyment of the part he was performing, had then taken them back across the European gallery to the other two galleries of modern Mexican paintings. There he showed them the picture of Bartolomé de las Casas, the Protector of the Indians,—a picture so large that it had the whole end of one gallery to itself—and told them of the young artist who painted it; and another by the same artist, representing Galileo demonstrating to a priest that the world moves. The pale, thin face of the priest was full of contempt for the words of the philosopher.

"He doesn't believe a word that Galileo says," remarked the young lady with the grey eyes.

"Nevertheless the world does move," replied the gentleman with a smile, quoting the words which the philosopher murmured as he arose from before the pope, where he had, under pain of death, retracted his declaration that the world moved. And so they had gone from one picture to another, and as they had feasted their eyes on the rich and delicate colors, and their souls on the noble sentiments which the pictures inspired, the guide delighted them with reminiscences of the artists.

At last they stood before a large painting which represented Christ and the two disciples about to enter the castle of Emmaus. They had "constrained him, saying, Abide with us, for the day is far spent." The red light of the setting sun was over the castle and the three figures; that of the Savior was full of majesty and grace; there was an expression of reverence on the faces of the two disciples, and of wondering curiosity at the gracious words which the Stranger had spoken.

Mercedes—for the girl in the black dress and scarf was she—looked at it for some time with breathless admiration.

"It was painted by Ramon Sagredo. He is dead now," said the gentleman.

"How talented he was!" exclaimed Mercedes, wishing she could know exactly the artist's thoughts as he put the colors on the canvas.

"Yes," he replied, "and as good of heart as he was talented. He took the poor to eat at his own table."

How simple and beautiful and Christlike the expression! What a fitting qualification in an artist who would paint the God-man, him who preached the gospel to the poor, who was poor himself.

With unsteady lips, and eyes a little moist, Mercedes turned and saw for an instant the tender abstracted look on the face of the man who spoke thus of his dead friend; but a slight movement caused her to look beyond him, and full into the face of another person who stood a little behind him. He was a tall young man of about one and twenty. He wore very shabby clothing; in one hand he held a much-worn hat and a book on which Mercedes read the name, "Luis de Granada." His features were characterized by strength rather than by regularity; his complexion was dark and his face was slightly marked by the smallpox. His eyes were bright and penetrating.

At the moment that Mercedes turned intense feeling gleamed in his eyes and flashed from every line of his face. But he was watching her, and all of that feeling, gratitude, or whatever it was, was poured into her eyes rather than into those of the gentleman who had uttered the touching words. She involuntarily looked into his eyes for a moment, and the look in hers fully answered that in his. They returned to him sympathy for his poverty, for he was evidently one of "the poor;" enthusiam for his love of that book[1] into which the "friar" has poured so much of his poetical soul, and (her mind flying from one conclusion to another) a fellow feeling with him in his love for all good and noble things in books and out of them.

It was only for an instant, then she remembered what she was doing, and turned away with heightened color. Her two companions, occupied as they were with the picture, had not noticed her.

"We meet," says an Arabian proverb, "in the desert in the dark, and lift our lanterns and look into each other's faces and then pass on." But ever afterward, through whatever of darkness or of light our paths may lie, though we may never meet again, we remembered those persons whose souls have answered ours and hope that life goes well with them. These are moments of soul recognition. I am not speaking now of "love at first sight," by any means; this soul recognition may occur between persons of the same sex and of the most unequal ages.

The next moment a party of young people passed them and a girl remarked in a whisper that was distinctly audible:

"What a grotesque object to be in an art gallery! I wonder that it is permitted." And with a flash of pain in his face the young man moved away.

Mercedes and her companion looked at a few more of the pictures, and after cordially thanking their guide left the Academia.

---

[1] *Note.*—It is said that the author was threatened by the Inquisition because of the evangelical sentiments of this book, and that he occasionally introduced the name of Mary to escape condemnation.

The way Mercedes came to be in the City of Mexico was easy and natural enough, though she had thought it was as improbable that it should ever happen as that she should go on a trip to the moon.

Don Francisco had conceived the plan of bringing his family to the capital to spend the winter in the hope that new scenes might divert his wife's mind from the dangerous channel in which it was running. She had willingly agreed to the plan, because as Magdalena had now completed her school life she could enjoy the society of the capital.

So it came to pass that a few days after the Bishop's visit they went first to Monterey to attend the wedding of a nephew. Then leaving that city behind, sleeping among its picturesque mountains, they passed Saltillo just after daylight, and perhaps a half hour later the battlefield of Buena Vista. There were few stations along the road, none which contained more than a few houses, till they reached San Luis Potosi. It kept Mercedes thinking that the government ought to bore some artesian wells and then form a colonization society. There were towns, as she learned afterward, but they were hidden behind hills a mile or two from the road.

The station of San Luis Potosi was built in the American style. And what a crowd of people! What rushing hither and thither! But back of the handsome, new, modern buildings about the station were weather-beaten Mexican dwellings and quaint old churches that looked like they might belong to the time of the Conquest.

Then night had come and a new day, and they opened their eyes on another world. The country had been transformed, as if by magic, in the night. Now there greeted their eyes green, dewy meadows, with starlike flowers, widespreading trees, creeks and little rivers and lakes, and grazing herds. The southern part of Mexico is fair and fertile as the land of promise.

But still there were few towns along the way; neither were there any country houses.

Once down below them a thousand or fifteen hundred feet or more they saw a town the name of which they had been seeing on stereoscopic views. They could have tossed biscuits on the tops of some of the houses. Just before they reached the City of Mexico the train passed over the mountains. There were ravines, cool, shady, green, and lovely with flowers; there were trees, and clear mountain rivulets, over which old moss-covered trunks of trees had fallen, forming foot-logs, and little, dashing, foaming cataracts.

The train ascended majestically, winding gracefully, as a serpent, in semicircles up the mountain side; not slowly, not laboring and panting and stopping to rest like a tired animal, as I have been told the trains ascend the Rocky Mountains; but easily, continuously, rapidly, like one who is conscious of his strength and glories in it.

As they entered Mexico they saw the Castle of Chapultepec, which stands on the site of a summer palace of Montezuma, and is now the summer residence of the President of the Republic.

They did not rush into a great car shed among many other trains. They stopped at an unpretentious station; then a rapid drive through the paved streets, full of people, of wagons, of carriages, of street cars, past stone and brick houses of two, three or four stories, past beautiful plazas and old churches, through the principal drive of the city, broad and straight and level, and adorned with splendid bronze statues of Gautemozin and Colombus, and an equestrian statue of Charles IV. of Spain—the Little Trojan Horse, as the Mexicans call it—the largest equestrian statue in the world, except, perhaps, that of Hadrian of Rome; past all this and much more till they stopped before the handsome house in San Cosme street which Don Francisco had taken for his winter residence.

Mercedes and her friend, when they left the Academia, went down the street a little way, turned a corner and went up the street toward the Cathedral. As they passed the National Museum Mercedes' friend remarked:

"How that Aztec calendar does stare at one?"

"Yes; what a study it is though! They tell me there is a great deal of Free Masonry in it. It seems to me nowadays there is more or less Free Masonry in everything," replied Mercedes with a grim smile.

"By the way, you said you had visited the Museum. What interested you most there?"

"O, I don't know. There are so many interesting things: the Cross of Palenque, the hideous God of War, the Goddess of Water, and the Stone of Sacrifice. I think I like best the things up-stairs that are not so ugly: all those beautiful things from the sea, and the birds, the Quetzal and the Bird of Paradise, especially, and, well, the mastodon and the teeth of the prehistoric man."

"Yes, for beauty, give me the last, certainly," said Maximiliana, who was in fine spirits. She was generally in a gay humor when she was with Mercedes. She had been delighted to meet her in the Portales on the Plaza de Armas only a week or two after the arrival of Don Francisco's family in Mexico. She had lived in Salta and had known Mercedes in the latter's less fortunate days, and now was glad to see the improvement in her. She herself had married a printer three or four years before and come to Mexico to live. She had no children, and as she lived with her mother-in-law she was free from household cares. Her frequent visits with Mercedes, after the latter's lessons were over, to interesting places in the city made a pleasant variety in her life.

"You saw the State carriage of the Grand Duke Maximilian? That and some large vases in the Academia, which he brought from Austria, and some other little curiosities are about all the royalty we have left us," she continued, scornfully, for, notwithstanding her royal name, Maximiliana Valle was a staunch Republican.

"Well, that is enough," replied Mercedes, who was not a whit behind her friend in Republican sentiments. "We don't mind those things. They make a place more interesting;

MAGDALENA.

and one can bear royalty very well when it is shut up in a
museum."

"Let's go into the Cathedral a little while," said Maximiliana as they approached that fine old building. "I want
to show you the 'black saint.' He is the special patron of
discontented wives. If a wife wants her husband to die she
measures him carefully with a ribbon while he is asleep, and
then she takes the ribbon and hangs it on the arms of the
saint, and presently the husband dies. That is some of the
doings of this precious Roman Catholic Church you are so
devoted to, Mercedes."

"You don't mean to say there are women who do that?"

"You shall see. The saint's arms are extended this way,
and they are full of ribbons."

They passed the statue at one of the side entrances of the
cathedral yard, and went up the walk between the beds of
flowers till they were in front of the door of the chapel of the
black saint. They would have entered, but Mercedes turned
a ghastly face to her friend and, grasping her arm, detained
her. She had taken in the whole scene at a glance. There
at the side of the room on a pedestal was the black image.
It was a very good representation of a negro boy of about
twelve years of age. On his extended arms the long, slender
ribbons were heaped up.

But this was not what had driven the color from her face.
In front of the image knelt a lady in a plain but elegant black
dress, with a black lace *mantilla* pinned over her waving
brown hair. Her eyes were uplifted to the face of the saint,
and her hands were clasped in supplication. It was Doña
Flavia. In the doorway leading into the nave of the cathedral stood Don Francisco with staring eyes and pallid face.
The pallor of his countenance was in strange contrast with
the exquisite colors of the costly flowers he held in his hand.
Mercedes' eyes met his for an instant, and then recovering
herself she hastily drew her companion from the door and
they left the cathedral yard.

"Why, what is the matter?" exclaimed Maximiliana, who

had not expected Mercedes to be so much effected. "Did
you know that lady? What makes you look so?"

"O, I can't talk about it. It is so dreadful, so dreadful! It
seems like murder!"

"Well, I should think it did! But such things have the
approbation of the Holy Apostolic Roman Catholic Church,"
replied Maximiliana, forgetting the kneeling lady, but settling it in her mind that her friend from Salta was a very
susceptible girl indeed, and not very well acquainted with
the character of the Church. She was the more determined
to enlighten her, for Mercedes' devotion to the Church was
a great defect in her eyes.

But for the present, as they went on down the street, she
set herself to divert her friend's mind by calling her attention
to the handsome things in the show windows.

"Look what pretty hats, Mercedes. The merchants say
they can scarcely sell any parasols now since the Mexican
ladies have taken to wearing hats. Look! here in this window are Ponciano Diaz's costumes and the *banderillas.* I
wonder if he is going to fight. Those things are always displayed in the windows before he fights. There is a female
torrera in Spain who they say has promised to visit Mexico.
She will a create a sensation when she comes." Then with
more energy than ever, and almost in a whisper:

"Look! look! do look, in that carriage! That is the archbishop's niece who lives with him in his palace. Isn't she
magnificent! Let everybody bow down!!"

"The Archbishop's niece!" exclaimed Mercedes, aroused at
last, and letting her mind slip back into its former habits of
thought, as she grasped the idea of a woman's living in the
presence of so much holiness.

"Yes; she astonishes everybody with her splendor when
she goes out."

"The Archbishop is a good man, isn't he?" asked Mercedes,
thinking of the charities of Bartolomé de las Casas.

"Well, I should think not," was the reply, in a tone of disdain. "He **was a** traitor to his country; how could he be a good man?"

"How was he a traitor to his country?" **asked** Mercedes in a faint voice, seized by her habitual feeling when she had to listen to things against the Church that the ground was slipping from under her **feet.**

"He invited the French to invade Mexico."

"Is that true?"

"It is **a** historical fact," replied her companion, **greatly** enjoying the situation. "O Mercedes, you would give up all belief **in** the superstitions of the Church if **you** had a husband **to tell** you what its character really was."

"I am not at all sure that I should. I know a good many ladies who have husbands, and yet they have not lost respect for the Church. I am astonished that you have so little reverence, Maximiliana. I should think you would be afraid to talk so," replied Mercedes, with warmth.

"I ought **to** have reverence for these things as the priests have, **I** suppose. Like Father Sultano, for instance. He is a priest in one of the finest churches in the city. He became disgusted because the ladies went **to** early mass with their bangs on crimping pins, and he resolved to teach them **a** lesson; so he took the Blessed Virgin and rolled **up** her hair in the **same** way, and when the ladies came he called their attention **to** her, and asked **them** how they thought she looked in **the** church with her **hair** on crimping pins. They were horrified, **but he** told them that they desecrated the church in the same **way. He** liked female beauty himself, you know. But," and **her** tone changed into one of pure amusement, "General Fulano de **Tal** happened to go into the church and he saw the image; and **he** took that priest aside and he told him if he didn't take down the Virgin's hair and fix her up in a style suitable for the church he would report him, and the priest made haste **to** obey his orders. Now what do you think of that?"

"That shows that the **priest did** have—did have—"

"That shows that he did have respect for the church, doesn't it? and apparently more for the temple than for the idol."

"Maximiliana, one would think you were a Protestant!" burst out Mercedes, conscious that she was getting the worst of the argument.

"No, Señora," replied her companion, a little nettled, "I'm not a Protestant; neither am I a Catholic. I'm a Freethinker. Tomas is a Freethinker, and he knows what is right, for he has read a great many books. He says that Roman Catholicism is a collection of degrading lies and superstitions; and he says that we ought to be willing to examine all religions without prejudice. That is what a Freethinker believes. But I don't believe I should be a Catholic if I didn't have Tomas to tell me things, for I know some things by myself. But," she added after a long silence, "I don't mean to hurt your feelings by telling you all this, Mercedes."

"No, of course I know that, Maximiliana. We are too good friends to quarrel. I get so mixed up in my mind about these things that I don't know what is right nor what is wrong. I feel like I can't do without some religion, but, of course, we don't want to be Protestants. It's awful to think of it!"

"If they were right I suppose we should want to be with them, shouldn't we? Of course, though, I don't say they are right."

Mercedes made no reply. She could not say she should want to be with those "pietists," even if she knew they were right. And there was the aperture through which the "strong delusion" might enter.

A few minutes later they entered a street car, and soon they stood before Mercedes' home. She waited a few minutes till Maximiliana took a passing car to return home; then she entered the house.

As Mercedes went up the stairway Magdalena swept down it in an evening dress. When she saw Mercedes she exclaimed, "Mercedes, where is mama? Why, are you sick,

Mercedes, or just tired? You must have walked too much. See how pretty my dress is! I have been trying on new dresses all the afternoon, and looking at them in my glass, and I thought I'd go down and see myself in the glass in the parlor. Won't this be lovely with my new opera cloak. Papa promised to take me to a concert this evening," and away she went down the steps and into the parlor, a very vision of loveliness; and Mercedes escaped into her own room.

CHAPTER XXI.

THE GROTESQUE OBJECT.

H E grasped his hat and book more tightly and left the galleries. The thoughtless words of the girl had cut to the quick, for though he was little accustomed to gentle speech, he had never become insensible to cutting expressions; and it was very hard to be spoken of as a ridiculous object in the presence of that other girl who had just looked at him as if there might be some fellowship of soul, at least, between them. But fortunately he had seen the look of indignation which Mercedes had flashed at the girl. After all there was more of sweetness than of bitterness in the occurrence. He lifted his old hat and slipped his hand, drawn somewhat by the constant handling of rough and heavy things, over his forehead and said, almost aloud: "The Lord is very good to me. He has always given me so much encouragement."

Every one who has been in the City of Mexico has noticed in the streets certain living creatures, which indeed he will have no trouble in recognizing as women, notwithstanding their disguises. The heads, arms and feet are bare. A piece of straight, dark, woolen cloth with horizontal stripes extends a little below their knees, and is bound about the waist with a string, all the superfluous fullness being gathered in front, because of the superior facility in the art of dressing themselves which this arrangement affords. Another straight piece of woolen cloth, about a foot in width and reaching to the waist before and behind, covers the body, the head being passed through a slit in the middle of it.

The coarse black hair hangs in tags; the skin is brown, the features of the Indian type. Notwithstanding the conspicuous poverty of a woman of this class she often displays on her fingers and in her ears not a little copper or brass jewelry, the touching reminder that there still exists in the degraded body a woman's soul.

She goes about the streets often bowed double under an immense load. Often an infant is strapped to her back, but if she needs to carry a load of another kind on her back this small burden is shifted to the front. If she has another child who can bear the weight of the baby it is, of course, strapped to his back.

The men of the same class are not so curious looking. They wear pantaloons, shirts and sandals; and as they go they make the air hideous with the crying of their goods, as they seek purchasers for their fruits, toys, earthenware or kitchen utensils; or they go bowed under heavy jars of water, which are held on their backs by a strap or bandage of cloth, which passes across the forehead.

Those of whom I write you are the native Mexicans, or as they are called, the Indians, to distinguish them from the mixed race—those of Indian and Spanish blood who are known as Mexicans. The former class are also called Aztecs, though it is probable that many of them are descendants of the more cultivated Toltecs, and of other tribes and nations.

It is estimated that more than one-half of the population of the Republic are pure Indians. They speak Spanish as well as their native tongues, except in remote districts where they have not come into frequent contact with the ruling class, that is the mixed race, and the comparatively few foreigners who take part in the government.

Some of these Indians of pure blood have risen to distinction. Benito Juarez, so often referred to in this story, a statesman of whom, no doubt, any nation would be proud, was an Indian of pure blood. So was the great scholar, Ramirez, and the distinguished savant, statesman and orator, Altamirano, was an Indian of full blood, or as he would have said, a Mexican. He was a gifted writer.

The nationality of those who win renown, as well as of all others, is disguised now under Spanish names. When the

Spanish priests were converting and baptizing the Mexican Indians at the rate of hundreds a day they gave them what they called Christian names, that is, Spanish surnames coupled with "given" names generally taken from the Bible or from the list of "saints."

Did you ever think how strange it would be if a foreign enemy from—you knew not where—appearing suddenly as if they had dropped from the sky—should disembark on your shores, and sweep over your land like a besom of destruction; should make of your merchant princes and of your great men beasts of burden to carry mortar and stones to build again the cities they had destroyed; should send off ship lòads of you and sell you as slaves; and at the same time should baptize you by the hundreds in the name of a God of peace and good will, calling the Smiths, Cuitlahua; the Jones, Maxixcatzin; the Browns, Nezahualpilli; and should require you to speak a language in which there was not a word of Saxon or Latin? That would be like what the Spaniards did in Mexico.

Because of these changes of the names there is danger of attributing all there is worthy of notice to the Spaniards, or at least to those in whose veins there is a good deal of Spanish blood, overlooking the fact that history proves that Indian intellect and courage and prudence have been the principal factors in making Mexico what she is; for was not Juarez an Indian?

The fate of the Indians in Mexico was not similar to that of the Indians in the United States. There they retreated through the shadows of the forest toward the far West, melting away before the white man. Here they remained, and they and the mixed race, which has sprung from them and the Spaniards, are the people whom you call "the Mexicans."

But for this change of names in the baptism of the Indians, the young man who has just comé out of the Academia de San Carlos and gone on up the street would have to be presented to you by some such name as Axayacatl, or Xolotl, or

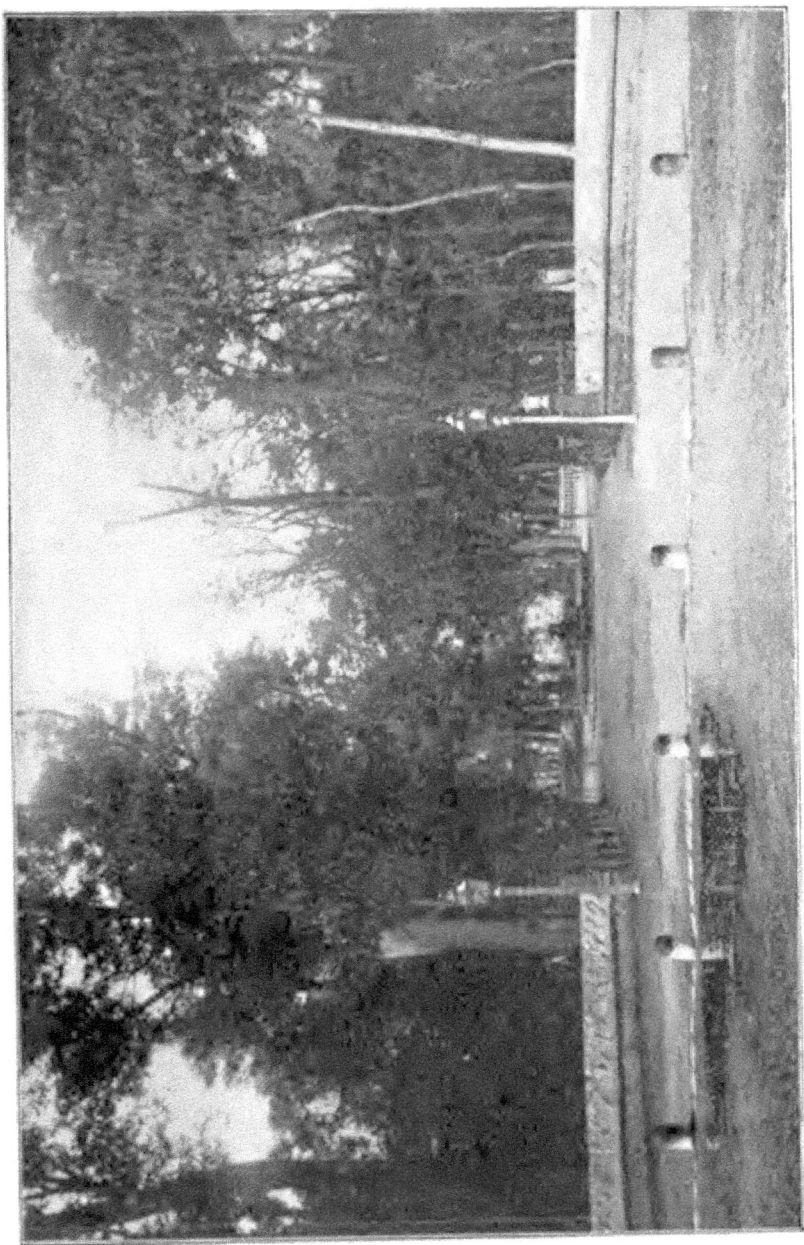

ENTRANCE TO THE ALAMEDA. (Page 191)

Ixtlilxochitl. But, thanks to the "holy Fathers," he was called Teodoro Martinez.

One fine summer morning, about twenty-two years before the time of which I write, two ladies, in black dresses and Spanish *mantillas*, and carrying missals and rosaries, came out of the church of St. Hipolito and turned up the street to go to their homes. They were on one of the bloodiest battle-fields of Mexico, as they might have been reminded if they had looked up at the molded arms and martial figure on the stone pillar on the corner of the high wall of the churchyard. It was along here, then a lake filled with islands, united by bridges, that the Spaniards under Cortez retreated from Tenoctitlan, now called the City of Mexico, followed by the Indians, fighting in the darkness like demons of vengeance.

Sometimes when one passes along there all the busy life of the street, the rattling of street cars, and the crying of hucksters, dies away, and one hears in its stead the clash of arms, the panting of pursued and pursuer, the splashing of the water as the bodies of the dead and wounded fall into it, the groans, the cries, the shouts—all the sickening terror of that Sad Night.

A few blocks farther on up the street is a tiny yard full of grass and flowers and vines. This is the place of Alvarado's Leap; and farther on, perhaps two miles out of the city, is the Tree of the Sad Night, under which Cortez wept over the destruction of his army.

So it was historic ground; but these good ladies, having known all this from their childhood, thought nothing of it, but being come out of the church and turned to go up the street they lifted up their eyes and beheld a sight which made them look at each other and smile for pure and un-selfish pleasure as well as through amusement; and then they looked about them involuntarily to see if there was any one else near to enjoy it. Their eyes met those of two men who stood at the door of a little pawn shop, and they, too, were smiling, for they had seen the sight; and they had looked about them for the same reason.

13

Then the ladies, ashamed that they had been betrayed into
looking and smiling in the street at men whom they did not
know, put on demure countenances and went on their way a
little more rapidly.

Down the middle of the street in the broad light of the day
came two Indians, descendants, probably of those very Aztecs
who on the Sad Night had pursued the flying ancestors of these
two ladies. One of them was a young man in shirt, pantaloons
and sandals; the other was a barefooted girl in a very ragged
dress, her bare shoulders and arms partly covered by a cotton scarf. Each held the hand of the other; they were not
walking nor running; they appeared to glide on the air; they
saw nothing, heard nothing, knew nothing but that each
loved the other and that they were near each other. Somewhere up the street they had encountered each other, their
hands had touched, their eyes had met, and the story was told.
Then the strength of the love that was in them had impelled
them to motion, it mattered not whither, and with clasped
hands, swinging them like children, they started down the
street. Seeing them one hoped they would soon reach a
secluded corner in a tenement house, or some deserted alley,
where he might put back her stringy black hair and kiss her.

I have never obtained any reliable information on that
point; but a few days later the happy couple took up their
abode in a little, dirty, smoky hut on a vacant lot. No marriage ceremony had intervened. They were not averse to
marriage; on the contrary, they would have been married if
they could have paid for the Church marriage, but that was,
of course, impossible; they would willingly have been married by the civil law but for the fact that the Fathers, who
ministered at the altars and held the fate of their souls in
their hands, taught the people that that was not marriage,
that those who were guilty of such blasphemy against the
Church were excluded from her fold and hence lost all hope
of salvation.

A little more than a year later, if our ladies of the *mantillas*
had passed along a street near the one in which they first

saw the enamored pair, they might have seen them again. She stood by a wall with a tiny baby bound on her back with a cotton scarf. She was saying, in a high, hysterical voice:

"O, if you just wouldn't turn me into the street! if you would give me somewhere to live, just any hut!"

He, having the policeman in his mind, replied in a low tone, though angrily. And so the voices continued to alternate for some time.

What was the matter? Nothing. Perhaps he was tired of her; perhaps he had seen another girl whom he liked better. He had not distinctly made up his mind to leave her; he even yielded to her entreaties to the extent of providing her a hut a week or two longer till the owner of the lot turned her out. Then, after she had drifted into one of the great tenement houses, he went there to share with her her small earnings gained by selling vegetables in the streets—went there to drink and sleep and curse and fight, accomplishments in which she soon became scarcely less proficient than he.

This first baby of her own that she ever bore on her back was our acquaintance of the galleries, Teodoro Martinez. In a drunken carousel they had raffled for the name of the infant as it lay crying on the floor.

As soon as he was large enough to lift its weight the least of the succeeding babies was bound on him and only at short intervals during the day was he free to straighten his tired little back without that load. How it happened that he grew to be a straight, tall youth, I cannot tell.

His young life was not, however, destitute of pleasures. He was not always hungry; the baby sometimes went to sleep when he was in the house and then he could lie on the floor and "think," for he had that strange propensity; and sometimes he could slip out to the street and see the carriages pass and the people go by. Once his adventurous disposition led him on a feast day, being lured by the music of the band, to venture a little way into the Alameda. There he saw the great central fountain covered with flowers, arranged in exquisite designs, and the ladies in such pretty dressed that they looked liked so many "Blessed Virgins."

His mother took him once to the Floating Gardens, whither she went for vegetables to sell, returning in the early, chilly morning, that the vegetables might be fresh and tempting. He went with the baby on his back, and leading the child next to himself, while the third one was bound on his mother's back. It may seem that it was pleasure taken under difficulties, but to him it was an occasion fraught with delight. And with good reason, for he breathed the pure, sweet air, he saw the canal and the skiffs and flatboats with their coverings of canes and grass to protect the passengers from the fierce rays of the sun; and he saw the gardens, so green, "so joyful," with many colored flowers. He saw, too, in the distance, the great snow-covered mountains, Ixtacihuatl and Popocatepetl, whose names were not in the least difficult for him to pronounce, for he spoke the language to which they belonged even better than he spoke the Castilian language.

On one occasion his mother took him away out beyond Tabuca to see the Christ crucified. His pleasure in this performance was somewhat marred through the fear that they might kill the man who acted as Christ, and also by the drinking, cursing and fighting of the spectators; for though he was familiar with such behavior in his own home he never lost his horror of it. As many of the people were crowned with flowers, he might have been reminded of a feast of Bacchus, if he had been acquainted with Grecian mythology in those days. But this day's pleasure came near ending tragically for him; for, as his mother was one of those who exercised herself most in wailing and wringing her hands, he came near being trampled to death in the crowd; later she became intoxicated, and she would have left him, but that he resolutely clung to her skirt—that woolen skirt with the horizontal stripes, which I have already described.

He had one pleasure, however, in which there was no mixture of pain. For it he was indebted to a woman named Lupe Rodriguez who lived in the same tenement house. She sometimes gave him *calabasa* (pieces of pumpkin cooked with syrup). He never failed to slip out and give the greater part of it to his younger brothers and sisters, over which wretched, neglected little mortals his heart yearned with an old, pitiful, fatherly yearning; but the little piece that remained was sweeter for this self-denial.

Lupe lived in a little room just back of one of the front rooms in one of those great "whited sepulchers" of tenement houses in the City of Mexico. These houses look well enough from the street, and they are often on good streets. Glancing up, as you pass along, at the large windows of the house, noticing the lace or some other thin material drawn closely over the glass of the shutters you think it is the residence of some family in good circumstances. It would never occur to you that they were the only comfortable rooms in the house. It would never occur to you that back of them, often extending over the whole immense square, is a labyrinth of little, windowless rooms, whose only light and ventilation is received from a door which opens on a tiny *patio*, a space a few yards square, open to the heavens. Two or three families often live in one of these little rooms. They have little or no furniture; all they ask for is space to stretch themselves out at night. Along with these facts, take into consideration the unneat habits of most of the tenants, and you will not be surprised to hear that they are the perpetual haunt of fevers and smallpox.

The rent is as high as can be wrung from such people—"very high," they will always tell you. The landlords, of course, grow very rich; they may be seen sweeping out over the drive in handsome carriages, or flashing their diamond rings over the gaming tables in Baden-Baden, or diverting themselves in Paris,—along with many of the owners of the great haciendas—thoughtless of the miserable thousands who in the morning swarm out of their great tenement houses and crowd in again at night.

Sometimes respectable families, being unable to pay rent in better houses, are obliged to live in these tenement houses, and their souls are much vexed by the character and conduct of the other inmates.

Lupe lived near the front; Teodoro lived far back in the hive. If he had known about such things, he would have thought of those front rooms as the abode of royalty, and of Lupe's room as that of the highest nobility. He always passed very slowly by those front rooms and turned his head as long as he could see anything of the magnificence within, a circumstance which was very annoying to the inmates. If he could only have stepped in and taken a good, long look at the cheap and scanty furniture it might have satisfied him.

Lupe's room differed from the one in which Teodoro lived principally in that she had a bed and a chair and a table, and that everything was exquisitely clean. She sometimes invited Teodoro to enter, and talked with him. She was a queer woman, they said. She spent a great deal of time, when she was not making cravats to sell, reading in a broad, thin book. She read some to Teodoro in that book one day, and one story pleased him very much. It was about a little man who, on one occasion, when the Lord was passing through the streets of a city with a great crowd of people, ran ahead and climbed up into a sycamore tree to see him. Lupe told him it was the story of Zaccheus, the shoemaker.

As he manifested a great curiosity about the letters she taught him to read; and all the time she was teaching him something better than that; and the result was that one day as he trudged along the street with a heavy jar of water, praying to "the invisible God who is everywhere," he came to feel that he would be willing to give up everything in the world, if everything were his, if only he could feel that his sins were pardoned, and that the Lord looked upon him with favor; and just then the grievous burden of sins rolled off his conscience, and first peace, and then great joy, flooded his soul.

Soon after that Lupe, as if her mission in that house was accomplished, went to another, and Teodoro saw her no more; but we may hope that the blessing of God followed her, and that she continued to "evangelize" till the time came for her to enter the shining portals of the celestial city.

Before she left she gave him a New Testament which he read a great deal in his loneliness after her departure. Away back in the dim days of his childhood a realization of the degradation of his family and surroundings had fastened itself on him. It had grown on him till it almost over-whelmed him at times. He compared himself and them with many people whom he saw in the streets—people with gentle manners and in good clothes. But there had now taken possession of his mind the thrilling, inspiring, uplifting thought that God was no respecter of persons. And there grew up in his soul a wish, a purpose, to make of himself such a man that the others of the tenement house would treat his words with respect and attention when he told them of the great salvation.

He sometimes did errands for the Director of a college. Many weeks of this thinking and planning at last gave him the courage to ask this gentleman "if he didn't know no way in which a fellow who had no money nor nothing could get an education." The Director looked him over with attention and said, "We will see." The result of the "seeing" was, that clothed in the cast-off garments of one of the Director's sons, and provided with work by which he might pay for them, he entered a common school. A year afterward he entered the school of his patron.

Five years had passed and he had diplomas for all or nearly all the branches studied by young men, diplomas duly signed by the President of the Republic, Don Porfirio Diaz. They had been hard years; he scarcely knew how he had gotten through them. He had often been hungry and always poorly clad. He had studied his lessons in minutes of leisure, and in the streets as he went about his work, often with a burden on his back and a book in his hand. He did as well, and sometimes surpassed in his studies, the wealthy young gentlemén of his classes who studied walking back and forth in the shady Alameda.

Partly as a consequence of this they often said cutting things to him. "Protestant" and "Pietist" were among the favorite names for him; and one wealthy young gentleman from Guadalajara, the elegant Jose Maria Ortega, whom our acquaintance, the Señorita Frederica, met during a visit to the Capital, inquired frequently, and especially just after having been eclipsed in Latin or Trigonometry by Teodoro, after the health of his mother, using the most elegant formula, "How is the Señora, *madre de Usted*" (how is the señora, mother of your Worship)?

This lady was known to them, for she had insisted, in all innocence, be it said, on selling her vegetables in a street near the college so that her son could carry them for her to the place where she wished to dispose of them.

During all this time the good Director had stood by him. He once or twice spoke of him to the whole college as a person whose industry and good behavior were worthy of imitation. He did so one day when finding Teodoro's deskmate drunk on *pulque* and asleep at his desk he waked him and sent him home, summarily expelled from school, remarking to that youth as he took up his books to leave that this was "a school for boys and not for brutes."

But notwithstanding the kindness of the Director there came very dark days to our hero, through this subtle influence which emanates from the opinions of others and pervades our lives, days when he could not shake off the paralyzing thought that his race was generally considered inferior, nor the more depressing thought of the shameful degradation of his family.

When the thought of his race attacked him he always went to the Pantheon of the church of St. Fernando. At first the sexton, seeing what a shabbily dressed youth it was who was peering through the iron gate would not admit him, but on subsequent visits, noticing his quiet and respectful deportment and the fact that he generally carried a book in his hand, he permitted him to pass the gateway. He then stood in a small, rectangular inclosure surrounded by four walls

the height of an ordinary room. Three of these walls are divided into compartments, just large enough for a coffin to be slipped in endwise. After the coffin is inserted the compartment is closed with a marble slab on which is an inscription. On one side is a room opening from the Pantheon in which are kept the funeral urns. After the expiration of the term for which the compartment for the coffin was rented, the ashes are taken from the coffin by the family or an agent and placed in an urn which is kept in this room.

In the ground of the Pantheon are buried some of Mexico's most distinguished men. But only one of these monuments attracted Teodoro: that of Juarez.

It is a severely simple and elegant structure of stone, about eleven yards long by six and a half yards wide. There are no walls; the roof is supported by columns. On the outside above the entrance is a wreath of artificial flowers bearing the inscription "Honor to Juarez." Above this, in another and an immense wreath supported by the Masonic insignia, is the celebrated maxim of the great statesman: "Respect for the rights of others ensures peace." Within, thickly covering the walls and floors are many wreaths so that if one is so fortunate as to be admitted at all he must step very carefully. There are large and small wreaths of artificial flowers made of glass beads, and even some small ones of silver and gold. They have been presented by every State in the Republic and by the Spanish and French Societies. The flowers of these wreaths are of the most exquisite colors and are artistically arranged.

In the midst of all this beauty, carved in pure white Italian marble, is the representation of the body of the statesman at the moment when the spirit left it. The strong arm has fallen by his side, the head is thrown back; there is the Indian face, the features so familiar to every Mexican. At his pillow sits the bereaved nation, *la Patria*, her young and beautiful face turned heavenward as if she cried after him, "My father, my father, the chariot of Mexico and the horsemen thereof."

Below the monument lie the ashes of the hero, the states-

man, so honored by all the States, the Indian of pure blood,
Juarez. [1]

The boy was accustomed to gaze at it awhile in silence and
then go away calmer in spirit, more patient, more hopeful,
stronger than when he came.

When the thought of the degradation of the family to which
he belonged oppressed him he went to the church of Santo
Domingo, the church of the Inquisition. On one side and
across the street from it and the little garden in front of it,
rises the handsome building in which was held the Court of
the Inquisition. "Here," says a Mexican writer and statesman, Juan A. Mateos, in his novel, "Sacerdote y Caudillo,"
"was administered the torture which was designated by the
palliative title of ordinary or extraordinary torment accord-

---

[1] *Note.*—The stories which are familiarly told about this great leader
are very tender and beautiful. One day, as a Mexican lady and I stood
gazing at this exquisite monument, which I have tried to describe, she
said, her feelings causing her to rise to pathetic eloquence: "When he
lay in state in the *Palacio Nacional* the deep and solemn sound of the
cannon resounded every five minutes through the saddened city. All
the soldiers were in mourning, and often one saw the tears in their eyes.
A high civil officer and a high military officer stood at each end and at
each side of the bier on which he lay: they were motionless as statues
of sadness."

Then, again, this reminiscence: "I saw him once when I was a little
child. He was passing along the street in his carriage, and I was playing before the door. I began to jump about for joy and cry out, 'Mama,
mama, here comes Don Benito Juarez.' He heard me, and he had the
carriage stopped, and he spoke to me very affectionately. He was so
good!" she concluded. She related, too, that at a breakfast, given to
some of his soldiers, one of them approached him and said, "My President, will you permit me to embrace you?" And he, opening his arms,
exclaimed, "My beloved sons, I wish to give you not one embrace, but a
thousand."

The familiar and favorite and most affectionate way of speaking of him
was, and is yet, as "*El Indio Juarez*," "The Indian Juarez."

Among the other distinguished Mexicans, who were Indians of pure
blood, I will mention only a few: Altamirano, an author and a minister
to foreign courts; Ramirez, a very learned man; Du Blan, Secretary of
Finance; General Juan N. Mendez, several times Governor of Puebla;
the son of this General, who was also Governor of Puebla; Juan Alverez,
President of Mexico.

ing to the means more or less active which were used in it . . . . In the hall were the necessary implements for the fearful ceremony: tongs to tear off the flesh, iron gauntlets to put on the hands of the condemned, after having heated them redhot in the fire, ingenious apparatuses to make them imbibe cold or hot water, and even melted lead; cords, instruments, buskins for the horse, and another multitude of apparatuses in which the invention and genius of hell left nothing to be desired."

Sometimes Teodoro stood awhile in the little garden by the fountain which marks the spot where the wandering Aztecs saw the eagle perched on a cactus with a serpent in its talons, which, as the god had foretold, was to be a sign to them where they were to build their city,—stood and gazed on the building where was held formerly the Court of the Inquisition, in which now, having been confiscated to the State, is the National Medical College. Sometimes he entered the church to impress more deeply on his mind the thought of the Inquisition, and sitting down, gazed at the harmonious and softly glowing colors of the gilded pillars of the altar and listened at the sweet notes of the pipe organ which was away off and up somewhere in a loft; or looked pityingly at the kneeling worshippers muttering their prayers, or with scorn scarcely concealed at the coarse images, such as that of the life-size body of Christ "laid out," and the Virgin standing at the head in a black dress of modern cut weeping with a handkerchief to her eyes.

What was there in the thought of the Inquisition that was to some extent a compensation to this young man for the bad blood in his veins? It was this: When his father was drinking and unusually talkative with the neighbors he often alluded to the disgraceful fact that his father's grandfather had been tortured by the Inquisition for heresy. He was fond of describing how his limbs were stretched on the rack and twisted joint from joint, how the bones cracked, how he shrieked and shrieked, till there was no more strength left in him to shriek, and then his cries died away into moans, fainter and fainter, till at last there was nothing left to the "holy fathers" but his mutilated body.

Teodoro had reasons of his own for desiring to know more about this; and once he ventured to ask. But the only reply he received was a blow and the assurance that his ancestor was "just like himself and Lupe Rodriguez." So he was at liberty to hope that there had been at least one among his ancestors who had been a believer in Christ, one who belonged to the nobility of heaven.

Though there was in his mind an abiding sense of the degradation of his family it was only occasionally that it overwhelmed him. He was usually cheerful and hopeful, enjoying greatly his studies and the intercourse with the other young men of the college. He had never left his father's family; in their continual drifting from one house to another he went with them. The Director of the college had advised him to leave them but he had refused. He had always felt that he was one of them; he must stay with them and share whatever fate was theirs; and above all else he feared that if he left them he might lose some opportunity to rescue some of them. He especially longed to save his younger brothers and sisters from being mere bearers of burdens in the streets.

But he was coming to the conclusion that he could never do so by staying with them; perhaps if he could leave them and get a place where he could earn more he could make a sort of home for them—get some better rooms in a more respectable tenement house and induce them to come to him. Then he might teach them in the evenings.

He was thinking of this as he went along the street from the *Academia de San Carlos* to the Cathedral. That look of sympathy from Mercedes had made him think more strongly of it than ever. He felt sure that she would encourage him, that she would think of the plan just as he did if she knew about it.

Just then he was employed to sell second-hand books in one of the stands back of the Cathedral. He liked it because

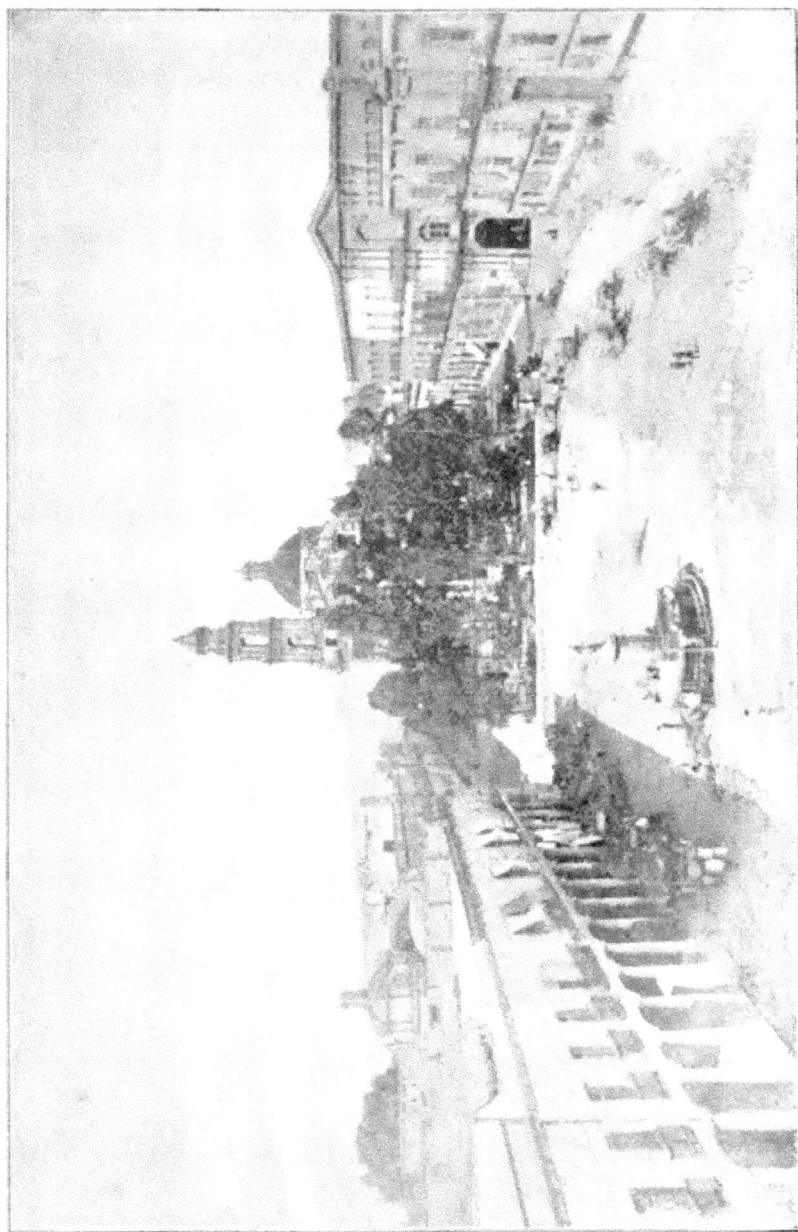

CHURCH OF SANTO DOMINGO.   Page 202

there was leisure to read and plenty of books at hand, but the pay was very little. He must try to find something else.

When he reached his stand he thanked his neighbor of the next one for having kept an eye on his books during his short absence, and slipping Luis de Granada's *Guía de Pecadores* (Guide for Sinners) into its place on the shelf he sat down to think.

CHAPTER XXII.

A DRIVE TO CHAPULTEPEC.

ON the day of Mercedes' visit to the art galleries Don Francisco, having finished his business for the day in the *Palacio Nacional*, came across the street to the Cathedral. He was looking more cheerful than when we saw him last. Since their arrival in Mexico Doña Flavia had said no more about Masonry, and Don Francisco hoped that her opposition to him on that subject and perhaps on some others was growing less. He felt greatly relieved about his daughter, also, for he certainly did not discover in Magdalena any inclination to take the veil. So it happened that it was with very cheerful feelings indeed he crossed the street to the Cathedral that afternoon.

He would have taken a street car for his home, but he saw Doña Flavia's carriage in front of the Cathedral, and though he had not troubled her much with his society for the last few weeks, knowing that it was not agreeable to her, he felt this afternoon that he might safely allow himself the pleasure of driving home with her.

Before entering he passed around to the opposite side of the building and bought a bouquet of exquisite flowers for her, and, as a second thought, another for Magdalena, remembering that she might like them to carry to the concert. He did not at first discover Doña Flavia among the worshippers kneeling before the various altars and images, but presently as he wandered about in search of her, he saw her in a kneeling posture before the images of the Father, Son and Holy Ghost. She arose directly and after dropping three pieces of money into the contribution box which sat in front of the images, glided off to another part of the building

Don Francisco followed thinking he would sit down near her so as not to lose her in the crowd and wait till she had finished her devotions. She passed into the chapel of the "black saint," and frozen with horror, he saw her hang a ribbon across his arms, and kneeling before the image, begin to repeat prayers with unusual fervency even for her. Not even the appearance of Mercedes at the other door aroused him sufficiently to move away.

Presently Doña Flavia arose and turned to leave, and husband and wife stood face to face, and looked each into the eyes of the other. Then with a sudden movement as if she were shaking off a paralysis she swept by him into the nave of the Cathedral. On she went, not rapidly, but steadily, past the Altar of the Three Kings, past the chapels, among altars and images and kneeling worshippers and deformed beggars at the door, through the garden with its flowers and ruins of the Aztec temple, till she reached her carriage and entered it. The maid servant, who all the time her mistress was engaged within, had waited, sitting near the door—after having repeated a few Pater Nosters and Ave Marias for her own soul's comfort—followed her mistress into the vehicle. Doña Flavia gave some direction, she never knew what, to her coachman.

She must have told him to drive to Chapultepec, for thither he drove. The carriage went flashing along among the others which vied with it in speed in San Francisco street, then swept out into the broad drive toward the setting sun; on and on into that cloud of golden dust which looked as if the celestial city were there and all those swiftly moving, dimly seen chariots were rushing into it under its uplifted gates. On past the statue of Charles IV., sweeping around the lofty statues of Gautemozin and Columbus, darting past those of the Mexican heroes on either side, past the moss-covered ruins of the aqueduct, and into the Woods of Chapultepec, drove that coachman as if he were fleeing from an evil conscience, or were trying to save his mistress. But none of these objects I have mentioned flew by his carriage

faster than by the others.   It is a way they have in the City
of Mexico—that rapid driving.

They passed the caged animals near the gate, then Montezuma's Tree and Bath, the statues of Apollo and Venus, the
monument to the youthful defenders of the Castle during the
"Mexican War," and the Castle perched high up on the hill,
and plunged into the dim, enchanted woods.

Doña Flavia was conscious of nothing till the carriage
turned to go home.   She must go, there was no escape from
it, but who should defend her from the wrath of her husband!
"God help me!" she exclaimed; and then to the servant's
surprised question, "What is it, Señora?" she replied, "Nothing," and held her silken fan more closely before her face.
Her progress toward vengeance was as swift as her flight
from an evil conscience.

It was dusk when the carriage stopped at her home.   Don
Francisco came out, opened the door, and assisting her to
alight, drew her hand on his arm and led her into the house,
and up the stairs to her own room.   He could not have been
more gentle and courteous if she had been his bride of
yesterday.

He shut the door and turned the key in it that there might
be no interruption from the children, and then again they
stood face to face and each looked into the eyes of the other.
Doña Flavia clutched the back of a chair with her gloved
hand to keep herself from sinking on the floor.   During her
drive she had been seeing as if by successive flashes of lightning how her deed would look to her husband, to his friends,
even to some of her friends, to the world in general.   For
though that proceeding had the sanction of the Holy Apostolic
Church, and she knew that she should have the approbation
of the priests and the sympathy of many of her lady friends,
who would not fail to observe pityingly: "Poor Flavia Salizar!
to such a strait as she is reduced in her efforts to save her
children from her husband's influence! such a good woman,
too, and so devoted to the church!" though she had seen it in
this light only before she met her husband's eyes in the
chapel, since then it had looked somewhat different.

CASTLE OF CHAPULTEPEC   [Page 208

She was a woman of the world, a proud and gracious figure in the highest society; she knew that she was to a great degree indebted to her husband's popularity for this enviable position; she could not be indifferent to the fact that if his friends should come to know of this insult to him she should become to them an object of contempt, tolerated only for his sake. And her husband! she had found that she cared more for his regard than she had thought she did. Then, as if by another lurid flash, she saw the probability that he might divorce her now, and so she should lose everything—respect, her children and all.

There was no relenting in that stern, handsome face at which she gazed as by a terrible fascination, in those eyes that seemed to be scorching her soul as if he read every thought in it. Oh, if she could only sink down on the floor and cover her face from his sight!

"Flavia," he said slowly, at last breaking the dreadful silence, "I have little to say to you. I have learned the uselessness of using reason to a woman who is led blindfold by unscrupulous priests. They and your own superstition have brought you to the verge of the commission of a crime, to the actual commission of it in your soul. It is likely that they will lead you further. There is only one step more to the actual perpetration of the deed; the priests would absolve you; the history of the priesthood is full of such as that,—your superstitious soul could easily be persuaded that you were doing God service. You are in a fair way to bring shame and ruin on yourself and your children, and all who are connected with you. I shall take measures so that if I die suddenly the matter may be fully investigated and justice done to the guilty parties. That is all I have to say to you. You are not the woman I thought you were."

He looked at her, it seemed to her, a full minute longer, and then went out and shut the door after him.

With a low cry she sank on the floor. It seemed to her that she was dying. She half hoped that she was. Her soul cried out against his injustice. She had never thought of

14

that other. She had only tried to free her children from his influence by supernatural intervention. If God should permit the "saint" to remove him, would it not be right? "What God did not permit the saints could not do." She should never have thought of the other; she, Flavia Salizar! to be spoken to about a crime! To be spoken to as a criminal! In her humiliation she wished she could sink out of sight forever. He was unjust, he was cruel, mean! But—and there was another flash of lightning—it was no wonder he thought of it in that way. Suppose she knew that he had, when she was sleeping her peaceful *siesta*, measured her exactly and had carried the ribbon as an offering to a saint, praying for her death! It would have been a relief to her if she could have shrieked.

"You are not the woman I thought you were;" those words burned themselves into her soul. "That means he would never have married me if he had thought I was capable of this. Oh, Flavia Salizar, what have you come to!"

A great wave of hatred toward the priests swept over her soul as she remembered how they had led her on, telling her that any means were justifiable that might be necessary to keep her boys in the fold of the Church. Even the good, the elegant bishop had told her that. It seemed to her in that awful moment that a veil slipped off him, and she saw him as he really was, a monster of iniquity, a smiling hypocrite.

' And she should have to confess all this to him, she should be risking her soul if she kept back anything! He would give her absolution and his hearty approval, she knew; but she would rather die than tell it to any one; and it seemed to her that absolution from such a man, an accomplice in crime, would only increase her guilt.

Lower and lower she sank in the slough of humiliation. Let us go out and leave her. But one word before we leave her, ladies. Lest we judge this woman too harshly let this reflection occupy our minds: "Who has made us to differ from another, and what have we that we have not received?"

Suppose that we had inherited Roman Catholicism from

generations of ancestors; suppose we had never known any-thing else; suppose we had lived under the daily influence and claims of priests whose powers and claims we had no means of disproving; can we be sure that we should have been better or clearer-minded women than she? Which of us is endowed with a nobler, more generous character than Isabella of Castile? And yet, influenced by her confessor, she banished the Jews from her dominions, and introduced the Inquisition into Spain.

Don Francisco took Magdalena to the concert that evening. He felt that there was strength enough in him to do anything that evening, to go to any theater or ball, to make the greatest speech of his life in the Chamber of Deputies, to denounce the Pope to his face as "the man of sin and the son of perdi-tion," as the Protestants called him—to do anything! You would have thought so if you had seen him enter the National Theater, with his head proudly uplifted, his eyes shining, bowing and smiling to acquaintances, showing every grace-ful attention to the beautiful, happy girl on his arm in deli-cate evening dress and white opera cloak. He was very proud of her, very happy to have her by his side. "I am not dead yet," he said to himself, lifting his head a little higher, as he listened to her pretty prattle and watched the fluttering of her pink fan. She carried no flowers; her father had thrown them away.

Did he think of his wife, as she cowered before him? If he did, it was to say to himself: "Let her suffer. She deserves it. It may do her good."

CHAPTER XXIII.

CHRISTMAS.

IT was the evening of Christmas Day. In Don Francisco's brightly lighted dining room a large party of children and young people were assembled, and among them were about two dozen people of middle age.

The whole city was keeping Christmas. But there had been no giving of gifts, no making of Christmas trees, no hanging up of stockings in joyful anticipation of the coming of Santa Claus or St. Nicolas. If you mention them to a Mexican and explain to him that they give gifts to the children, and ask if the custom is the same here, he will reply in a vague way: "No; I don't know who you mean, unless it is the Holy Child; the *pastores* (shepherds) give gifts to him."

These saints are worshipped here, but not in connection with Christmas.

For nine nights, that is from the 16th to the 25th, there had been in the churches representations of Bethlehem, with Mary, Joseph, and the Babe; and there had been processions, carrying the images of these personages from one part of the church to another and asking for lodging for them. This had been a favorite play in the private houses, also. The procession, bearing the images before them, had gone from one room to another, or from one suite of rooms to another, if more than one family lived in the same house. Some of the inmates, to carry out the play, refuse them admittance, telling them there is no room for them in the inn. But happy the family which at last receives them, for presently will come along the gay *pastores* (a band of boys who at this season go about the streets singing and shaking their decorated staffs) and they will stop where they find the image and sing and recite poems, going through a simple theatrical performance in honor of the Savior's birth; **and** they will present gifts to the Holy Child.

Now and then a man makes **a vow that if he** succeeds **in** this or that undertaking he will devote so much money to the training of *pastores* and to **the** buying of presents for the Holy Child, or it may be that **he has** committed a sin and he does this by way of expiation.

The evening before Christmas there **was a gathering of** friends **at** Don Francisco's house. They **had dropped in** after supper to wait with them for the **midnight mass (the** Misa del Gallo, the Mass of the Cock). **They** had amused themselves with music and conversation, and the young people **with** games, had eaten the Christmas supper of *bunuelos* (a kind of cake) and **syrup,** and when the bells began to ring at twelve o'clock they **had** gone to church and heard high mass till **day**light. Then, the 25th being a fast day, this good Catholic family had kept it as such.

A fast **day** in a Roman Catholic family reminds one of Mark Twain's description of a French duel. There **are so** many dispensations that the result is that everybody eats **as** much as he wants. If one does not **feel well he can** eat of forbidden dishes; children **can, because** they are growing and need **the** food; those who **work can,** because they **could** not work if they did not eat.

This good family, therefore, having ostensibly done without breakfast, according to the manner prescribed for keeping the fast, had **partaken of an** elegant dinner, then they had fasted till supper time, unless the dispensations were in their favor and permitted them the *merienda*.

But now the terrible fast was **over,** and to-night, as last night, there **was a gay** gathering in Don Francisco's dining room. Those who came early, they being for the most part elderly people, had supped with them, the remainder of the company had come in after supper. The festivities in which they had been invited to take part were more suitable for the dining **room than** for the parlor. **The** table had been removed and extra seats had been brought in and placed around the walls.

Through the wide doorway, leading into an adjoining room, was discovered a gay and beautiful scene. Every visitor, after the usual salutations, passed into this room. It was illuminated by a hanging lamp, whose prisms sparkled and threw back many colored lights. The gay flowers of the carpet seemed to laugh in one's face for very joy. Around three sides of the room had been constructed a sort of counter of two steps, and on these and on the walls above them evergreens were skillfully arranged. Among these gleamed all sorts of toys so disposed as to represent various phases of life. There were country houses, with their trees, gardens, fowls, horses, cattle, and servants engaged in their occupations; the families of little people were there also; there were lakes, made of glass, with swans and ducks, and fishes in them; there were forests, with animals in the shade of the trees, and bright birds, some of them singing birds, in the boughs; there were towns with coaches and carriages and railway trains; there were processions of pilgrims; there was, of course, in the place of honor, the Virgin, on a donkey, with the Holy Child in her arms, and Joseph by her side; just below these were two large and beautiful French dolls, one of them a lady in a bright ball dress, who fanned and raised a bouquet to her nose, the other, a gaily dressed man who played the violin and "really made music." There were, in short, toys of all kinds; there were vases and pictures—everything that could make it bewildering bright and pretty. It was a children's paradise—this *nacimiento* made in honor of the birth of the Holy Child.

Magdalena and Mercedes had been very busy making it, and even Doña Flavia had been less sad in seeing the happiness of her children; and the children had said that there was nothing like the making of a *nacimiento* to cure mama's headaches. And they were still happier now, to-night, since papa could be with them, for during the last week his business had been so pressing that he had had to go out early and return late, dining at a restaurant, and "had scarcely seen poor mama, though she had not been well."

Don Francisco's "business," however, had permitted him to be with his friends last evening. He had accompanied them to the church, walking with some of the gentlemen, and leaving Doña Flavia to the company of the ladies. As they were to go to their respective homes at the close of the mass he soon slipped out and returned home, leaving his wife to return with Magdalena and Mercedes.

One who knew all the circumstances would have thought this Christmas evening that he was trying to impress Doña Flavia, as she sat among the other ladies, that he "was not dead yet;" he was so gay, so genial, so courteous, the master of ceremonies for the children, the very life of the party. That thought did occur to him sometimes. He had not relented much towards his wife during this week that had passed since their encounter in the chapel. He had not, however, spoken to any confidential friend with respect to a possible sudden departure from life on his part, placing him under oath to keep his shameful secret.

He had thought he was not excited when he announced his intention to do so, but he found afterward that he could not speak to any one about so disgraceful an occurrence. Mercedes, watching them both, Doña Flavia pale and quiet, Don Francisco with, she thought, a touch of defiance in his good humor toward all others, while he left his wife alone, wondered sadly what the result would be. Would she repent? and if she did would he forgive her? Or would she be led on to take other steps, "divorce or something," to keep her children in the church?

Mercedes was by this time so far blinded herself by superstition that, though she thought of Doña Flavia's deed with horror and sometimes exclaimed to herself: "What kind of a woman is she? Who would have thought she could have done such a thing!" she yet had a good deal of sympathy with her about her children. There was no salvation out of the Church; were not then almost any means justifiable in

order that a mother might keep her children in the Church?
Not such means as this, of course—but any lawful means.
As for this, the deliberate procuring of the death of another
even in this indirect and religious way was dreadful; it had a
hint of murder in it.   Could it be right? and yet the church
sanctioned it.   Sometimes she wondered as she debated this
question if she were going crazy.   To-night she was making
a desperate effort to put it out of her mind and be gay with
the rest.

Don Francisco felt a new delight in the society of his children; it was a new and exquisite pleasure to him to find himself necessary to their happiness.   He had even gone with
his little boys to help them select the *piñatas* and candies for
this occasion.

One of these *piñatas* now hung from the ceiling.   It was a
great doll, a representation of a woman gaudily dressed in
pink and blue tissue paper, with staring eyes and grinning
mouth.   The dress concealed a thin earthenware jar, and in
the jar was a pigeon.   This emblem of innocence was placed
there "to make the children innocent."   Each child in turn
was blindfolded and, after having been led about the room
till he was confused, struck three times at the *piñata* with a
long stick.   The blundering efforts to strike it afforded great
amusement and were attended by shouts of laughter.   At
last one little fellow broke it, and the poor little frightened
pigeon, with its head sadly bruised, fluttered off across the
floor toward the group of ladies.   Doña Flavia took it up in
her arms and caressed it, and presently sent it out of the
room.   Out there in the dark it suffered alone and perhaps
died, having to the best of its ability fulfilled its little mission
of "making the children innocent."

The succeeding games, however, had no such objectionable
feature.   Another gay and hideous *piñata* was hung up, this
time a man.   The jar, which his gaudy clothing concealed,
was filled with candies.   When the jar should be broken and
the candies should fall the children were to scramble for
them.   All the children had in turn struck at it, then the

young **ladies** and young gentlemen. At last Don Francisco's **turn** came **and** it afforded great amusement to all that he should break **it**. Down came the fragments of **the** jar and the candies were scattered on **the** floor. Don Francisco nimbly extricated himself **from** the crowd of children who rushed about him **to** snatch the candies.

This scene of gay confusion was at its height when a servant came to Don Francisco's side and said to him that a young gentleman wished to speak to **him**.

"Bring him in," he **replied, and** then forgot all about **it as** he watched the children.

The servant brought in the young man and left him at his master's side. Presently **Don** Francisco turned, and seeing him there, remembered the message.

"Ah, yes," he said, abruptly, and then smiling pleasantly, he extended his hand to the young gentleman. "Excuse me. I had forgotten. They have brought you into a noisy scene."

"A very gay and pleasant one," was the response. "Perhaps, though, I should not have called on business this evening. As the *piñatas* have arrived before me I will give way to them."

"O, no, that will not be necessary—that is, if I can attend to the business here. I should be sorry to leave my friends, the *piñatas*, unless the business was very pressing."

"It can be easily attended to here," replied the young genman, producing **a letter.** "The director of the college of which I am an alumnus gave **me a** letter **of** introduction to you. He said he thought you might need **a** secretary, and that possibly I might fill the place satisfactorily."

Don Francisco opened the letter and read it. It was from his esteemed friend, Don Eduardo Recio, recommending this young gentleman, Teodoro Martínez, **for** the **place** of secretary.

"I am grateful to my friend, **Señor** Recio, for sending you to **me,**" said Don Francisco, with his usual courtesy, as he folded up the letter. "We **will** see about it; but just now **I** am too much engaged in these important matters to decide.

You will remain awhile, though, will you not, and see some more of these fine ladies and gentlemen demolished?"

Teodoro thanked him and accepted the invitation. That was just what he wanted, as much, it seemed to him just at that moment, as he wanted the place of secretary. His eyes had been wandering hungrily about the room, trying to discover Mercedes. Presently he saw her standing in a group of girls, talking.

"How strange it is," he said to himself, "that in a week after I first saw that young lady I should be standing here in her home, talking to her father!"

It had come about in a very simple way. The evening on which he saw Mercedes he returned to the bookstand, as I said, and sat down to think. He had been engaged in this occupation about half an hour when he saw Mercedes and her companion hastily leaving the Cathedral. Now he had read some novels in his life, and perhaps if he had not had that privilege something in his southern blood would have suggested to him that he follow this young lady who had impressed him. He did so, keeping at a safe distance from her, on Plateros street. When she and Maximiliana entered the street car he was near enough to gain the platform just as it moved off. He saw the house which Mercedes entered. She belonged, he knew from the handsome house, to a wealthy family. He lingered, walking up and down the street for a little while, and was rewarded by seeing Don Francisco enter.

He remembered him as a gentleman whom he had often seen going in and out of the *Palacio Nacional.* The next day he inquired his name of one of his companions at the stands.

"He? Why he is the Señor Urbina, a Senator from one of the northern States."

"Is he a Conservative?"

"No, he is a Liberal."

"Do you know anything more about him?"

"Why, yes, a little more. He is as fierce against the priests as Juarez himself, they say. He seconded heartily the motion to banish all the foreign priests from the country, and even gave some pretty strong hints that if he had his way most all of the native ones would go too or change their way of doing. He is a strong man in politics and very rich, they tell me."

Teodoro thought that he was very fortunate in having gained so much information about "her father." He inferred, too, that so sensible a girl as she must be would follow her father's opinion in politics and religion.

It must be told of him, for a historian must relate the facts, however little they may be to the credit of his hero, that this romantic youth had already, in this one week, twice visited the house in San Cosme street, and stood for an hour or two before it, gazing at a window through which he saw a light. The first night he was painfully doubtful as to whose window it might be, but, the second, these doubts were resolved in what was to his mind the most happy manner: the young lady herself appeared at the window between the parted curtains, stood there a few moments, with her face sharply outlined against the bright light behind her, and then closed the blinds.

It was Doña Flavia's room, and Mercedes was in there receiving some directions about the next day's employment, or the amusement for the children, but our young gentleman remained in blissful ignorance of that fact.

"Am I in love with her!" he had soliloquized fiercely the second night in the street, "of course I'm not in love with her. I wouldn't be such an idiot! What an insult it would be to the daughter of one of the richest men in the city for one of the Indians of the street to fall in love with her! I'm making a fool of myself, of course, but that concerns nobody but myself. There is no law to forbid my looking at the Infanta of Spain, or even falling in love with her, if I don't let her royal mother nor any of her people know it."

And so, secure in the thought that none of this young lady's "people" would know of it he was giving pretty free rein to his thoughts about her. Yet he was loyal enough to sometimes strive against it. "He had no right to be thinking of a wealthy and accomplished young lady who would never think of him except as of one who was to be pitied in a philanthropic way," he said to himself.

But thoughts are not easily controlled and he generally concluded with the reflection that no girl need be insulted that a man of pure morals, good education, and philanthropic ideas in his own humble way, should choose to make her an object of reverence or even of love so long as he did not trouble her with his foolish notions. "He didn't intend to sing any songs under her window, nor recite any poems, nor throw her any letters. He was not Quixotic enough for that," he said defiantly.

But his mind was principally occupied with another and more absorbing subject in these days. He must try to make a place for his two young sisters and induce them to come to him. If his mother would only come too,—all of them—to a more respectable place and let him help them to lead better lives! But he had no hope for any of them but the two girls, and very little for them. Nevertheless he had set his heart on this plan. It was his prayer night and day, and there was not much of submission mingled with the thought that he might fail.

These other thoughts were only a relaxation from this great anxiety. The thought of the young lady was restful because of the belief that she had sympathy for the poor.

He had made every effort he could think of to find more lucrative employment, but without success. When at last he was almost reduced to despair it had occurred to him to go to his teacher for advice. When this gentleman had mentioned among two or three other suggestions that the Señor Urbina might want a secretary he had immediately decided to try that plan first. The result was that on Christmas evening he stood by the side of the Señor Urbina watching the breaking of *piñatas*.

Now it is not to be supposed that this young man appeared in Don Francisco's dining room in those clothes in which we saw him in the art galleries. Fortunately he had better clothes, else how could he have received his diplomas in the National Theatre from President Diaz' own hand? That was a question that had greatly troubled the good Director and his amiable señora a few weeks before.

The Director had sometimes in his speeches in the National Pedigogical Congress when it met in the handsome Iturbide Theater, referred to this young man, "a son, Señores, of the very Aztecs of the street," as a proof that this race was capable of the highest improvement.

It would have impressed the fact on them more deeply if he had led his pupil out on the platform before them in the costume which he usually wore in the college, a costume which was very little better than that of the remainder of the male portion of his race, and had required him to show off his accomplishments in the various branches; and no doubt the idea of the capacities of the race would have sunk still deeper into the minds of the audience on the day of the Distribution of Premiums if he had received his diplomas and the medal or two which were awarded to him in that garb.

"But we don't do things in that picturesque style in these last years of the nineteenth century," replied the Señora Directora when her husband had smilingly stated the advantages to be derived from the course I have mentioned. [1]

[1] *Note.*—Several weeks after I had written this an acquaintance happened to tell me of a scené which he witnessed in the National Theater in the City of Mexico. It was the evening of the "Distribution of Premiums" of all the Preparatory Government Schools. President Diaz and his Cabinet and several prominent literary men were on the platform. At a certain stage in the proceedings Señor Manuel Rubio, a distinguished statesman and writer, announced that an Indian belonging to the humblest class would address the audience and afterwards receive his premiums for proficiency in his studies. He had completed the course of the preparatory schools, finishing such studies as trigonometry, Latin, and preparatory Greek. He had attended only the night school, being obliged to work, like other youths of his class, during the day. When, after the remarks of Señor Rubio, the young man arose, dressed as men of his class, in coarse white cotton pantaloons and shirt—the best

"Well, I don't know what is to be done about it. We can scarcely afford new suits for all our own boys for that occasion;—especially if we are to save anything to send Carlos and Timoteo to the Military School next year, and give Tulis better musical advantages," replied the Director, whose heart was always bigger than his pocket book.

"Well, something must be done," said the sweet-faced Directora; and when she spoke that way the good Director was always pretty certain, as the thought of it crossed his mind in the midst of his many cares, that the needful thing would be done.

The clothes of a neat pepper and salt design, were triumphantly laid before him on the day before the Distribution of Premiums.

"Where did you get them?" he exclaimed.

"O, I went to several wealthy ladies of our acquaintance and told them the story and took their subscriptions, and then I went and bought them. Aren't they nice?" And then the Director kissed her, but that was an act that was not very unusual with him.

It was in these clothes and with a new hat in his hand that he now stood in the Senator's dining room. When he had put them on that evening he had made some desperate efforts to get a view of his person in a mirror that was not much larger than the palm of his hand. He had found time to think a good deal about his personal appearance in the last week. "I wish I could wear such clothes as these all the time," he had said.

Another *piñata* had been hung up and the children were striking at it. Magdalena tripped up to her father, and clasping her hands over his arm, said, archly:

---

he had—and went up through the vast audience and made his graduating speech there were gentlemen even in the audience whose eyes were moist. "The teachers would have given him better clothes for the occasion," said the gentleman who related it, "but they were anxious to impress on those who should see him graduate that the very Indians of the street were well worth educating." So the Señora Directora was mistaken. Things are done in that picturesque way sometimes.

"O papa, you did look so funny and awkward when you were striking at the *piñata*."

"Ah, Magdalena, you are a naughty girl to say your papa is awkward," he replied, patting her cheek.

"So," reflected Teodoro, "there are two grown daughters. I do wonder what *her* name is. Some people would say this one was the prettier, but I don't think so." Then he decided that *she* was the elder, perhaps because she was a little taller. "I like the way she dresses better, too," went on his thoughts. "That black and white dress is so simple, and she has on no jewelry at all but that little pin."

Just then Mercedes came toward them. She was going to blindfold a little girl. When she was near them Don Francisco said:

"Mercedes."

"Señor," she replied respectfully, stopping.

"Be careful to arrange the handkerchief well. I think Pedro could see."

"Yes, Señor," she replied, and passed on. But she had done what from time immemorial young ladies have done intentionally or unintentionally for the benefit of young gentlemen who are in love with them: she had dropped her handkerchief. What happiness for Teodoro to step forward, pick it up, and hand it to her, saying:

"Here is your handkerchief, Señorita."

"Thank you, Señor," said Mercedes, with a little blush as she took it, her blush deepening as she glanced at his face and recognized him, notwithstanding his improved appearance, as the young man she had seen in the gallery.

And so he knew her name, and she had looked at him again, and he had touched her handkerchief, and had done her a service, and she had blushed when she looked at him, from which he knew that she remembered the day at the gallery. Each of these things was great gain, especially the first and last; if, indeed, any distinction could be made between them.

He lingered at the side of the Señor Urbina that evening as long as he thought it would be pardonable in a stranger who was there under such circumstances, and then took his leave, promising to call the next morning at the *Palacio* to hear his decision.

When he called that gentleman told him he did not need a secretary, but he thought he could get him a place as copyist. This he said, wishing to do a favor to his friend, the Señor Recio.

Soon afterward, therefore, Teodoro was engaged as a copyist. In this employment he had to wear his good clothes all the time, though he did not know how more were to be gotten when these were gone. But he "trusted" that he might be able to get more. He had a way of trusting about all these things.

He took a room in a better tenement house, a long way from the part of the city in which his parents then lived, a very poor room, to which there was a very poor little kitchen attached, and then he persuaded his two sisters to come to him. He could do extra work at night to pay for the two rooms and their scanty furniture. They could make rag dolls for sale during the day and study the lessons which he would prescribe and which they could recite to him in the evenings.

Such was his plan, the plan that his mind had been working on for years. They consented for the novelty of it.

They had been with him about two weeks, making few dolls and studying no lessons, when the remainder of the family took up their abode with him, and by their drinking and fighting disgraced him in that house. They were turned out by the request of the other tenants; and when he found rooms for himself and his sisters in still another house they told him they "would rather stay with mother." By persistent persuasion and promises he induced them to come to him, and the result was the same as before. It was evident there was no use to try that plan any longer. He found a room for himself in another part of the city, keeping his whereabouts concealed from them. He paid a respectable neighbor 25 cents a day for his meals. She always spread a coarse but clean napkin on the table for his plate and served him "like the señor he was."

CHAPTER XXIV.

AT THE OPENING OF CONGRESS.

IT was the evening of the opening of the National Congress. Doña Flavia, Magdalena and Mercedes sat together in the third gallery of the Chamber of Deputies, or as it is still often called, the Iturbide Theater, because during the reign of that sovereign it was the royal theater. The bust of the gallant and handsome, though too ambitious, emperor still looked down on the republican gathering from above the tribune.

The Chamber of Deputies is quite handsome. Around four of the sides run six narrow galleries. On the tribune, or platform, are three large crimson chairs. From the center of the ceiling hangs a splendid chandelier for candles; there are several other chandeliers for gas.

While they waited for the President to arrive the two girls amused themselves by imagining which box the emperor and his family, "the empress and the princes and princesses of Mexico," as Mercedes said, had been accustomed to occupy.

The floor and the first two galleries were reserved for the congressmen and the foreign ministers. In one box they recognized the minister from Venezuela and the minister from England.

The congressmen were arriving. They greeted each other with quiet courtesy and cordiality, and then seated themselves to converse. There was none of that excessive ceremony which foreigners sometimes observe among the Mexicans. Now and then two gentlemen embraced, after the Spanish custom. They were elegantly dressed in cloth, and some of them were in evening dress.

Two or three short speeches were made and the minutes of a previous meeting were read. The senators arrived and

15

the deputies arose and remained standing till the former had seated themselves. Soon after a gentleman, escorted by two others, ascended the tribune and took the oath of senator before the President of the Congress. There was an admirable brevity and simplicity in all these proceedings.

Mercedes watched everything with breathless interest, while the pretty Magdalena fanned and tried to recognize the few ladies in the galleries, and Doña Flavia looked as if she were suffering from chronic *ennui*.

Two young gentlemen sat near them. They were handsomely dressed and elegant in their manners, and one of them possessed great physical beauty. They watched the proceedings with interest. One of them, however, the more handsome one, frequently turned his eyes furtively toward Magdalena.

"Well," observed he, looking at his watch with great satisfaction, "it is time for the President to arrive."

"What did you say, Ortega? Excuse me."

"It is time for the President to come."

Just then the music of the band was heard outside, and the President and his staff entered. Among them was a portly gentleman, wearing a magnificent uniform—so magnificent was it that one could not imagine where another brass button or bit of gold cord could be tacked. In his hand, with all possible dignity, he carried his cap. It was gilt, and covered with the most beautiful snow-white ostrich plumes.

"Of course he is the President," thought Mercedes, as she watched eagerly, while this gorgeous being seated himself. She had eyes for no one else, although she knew that one of the number had ascended the tribune and was reading or speaking. She thought that was only a preliminary speech till Magdalena whispered:

"Can you understand what the President is saying?"

"The President! Then who is that in the uniform?"

"O, that is the Minister of War."

"Why does he dress with such magnificence, more than any of the others?" said Mercedes.

"O, I suppose it is to give us to understand what a terrible thing war is. That is nothing to the way he dresses sometimes. You ought to see him on the 16th of September, when all the soldiers and cannon go through the streets. I saw him once on the 16th."

But Mercedes had turned her attention to President Diaz. He was seated in one of the crimson chairs, reading his annual message. He was a portly, handsome gentleman, in evening dress, white kid gloves and a sash or badge of the national colors, red, white and green, across his breast. She was so far from him that she could not understand all of the "message," but she caught something about the improvements in the way of schools, railroads, mining and other public enterprises.

"Mama," said Magdalena, "did you bring the opera glass?"

"No, dear, I forgot it," replied that lady, listlessly.

"O, what a pity! I want to see the President."

"I should think you had seen him often enough not to grieve because you can't see him this time."

"But you know I never did see him reading his message before; and I want to look down there at papa, among the senators, and see if he is pleased with the message."

"Will the Señorita do me the honor to accept my glass?" asked the gentleman who had been addressed as Ortega.

Doña Flavia looked around quickly at the speaker, then extending her hand with a "many thanks," took the glass and handed it to her daughter. But Magdalena had not been oblivious to the admiring glances which the handsome young gentleman had been casting at her for an hour. She, the pretty coquette, slyly thanked him too, with her eyes. Doña Flavia saw the glances which were exchanged, and after that her manner lost much of its listlessness.

"Well," Ortega," whispered his companion, as he turned his face again toward the tribune, "I must say you are fortunate. She is a beauty. I haven't seen a prettier girl in a—week."

"Why don't you say in your whole life! She is an angel.

I'll give it up: I've completely lost my heart, and that before
I've been back here in my beloved country two days."

"No doubt she will go to the ball from here. I heard her
say something about her father's being among the senators.
A dreary time you will have waiting till near daylight to
follow her carriage home, unless you happen to be invited to
the ball yourself, among the other senators and deputies."

"Look what an arm she has, and what a neck! I didn't see
a prettier girl in all Paris than she is! She is the girl for
me. I'll marry her," he concluded with decision.

"You would better quit looking at her. Her mother sees
you."

"I wish," said Doña Flavia restlessly, as the reading of the
message was concluded, "that we could leave now to avoid
the crowd."

"You heard that? I wonder," said Hernandez, "you don't
offer your services to conduct the ladies to their carriage."

"I would if I dared," replied Jose Maria Ortega, "I'm desperate enough for anything."

A few remarks were made by another member at the conclusion of the message and then they adjourned. Immediately after the roar of cannon announced to the city that
the proceedings of that evening were over, and that Congress
was "open."

Doña Flavia and the two young ladies arose. As the former returned the opera glass to the young gentleman, saying,
"I thank you, Señor," he said, in his most faultless manner:

"Will the ladies allow me the pleasure of escorting them
to their carriage?"

"Thank you; you are very kind, but my husband will be
here in a moment." And Jose Maria, a little discomfited,
followed his friend to the street. He had arrived two days
before at Vera Cruz. The remainder of the family had preceded him by two or three months. They had left him,
hoping he would pursue his studies in France; but that young
gentleman did not find studying in Europe any more agreeable to his mind than it had been when he was in the college

of which the Señor Recio was the Director. He was, however, fond of popular literature, and there was no danger but he would always make a good impression in society. Though he was a nephew of Doña Flavia neither she nor Magdalena had seen him since he was a child.

He did not have to keep a dreary vigil that night before the building of the Jockey Club, where the grand ball was given. As soon as they reached the street a number of friends bore Hernandez away to the meeting of a club. He invited Jose Maria and was much amused that he should refuse to go. The latter was waiting to see the lady and her two daughters get into her carriage. Presently he saw them, and to his astonishment his uncle, Francisco Urbina, was with them. "But no, that taller girl is not my cousin; she must be a visitor. The other is—what is her name? how this tumbling about Europe does knock even one's kinsfolk out of his head! Magdalena! yes, I remember now that is it. Well, Magdalena, my cousin, I have begun to worship you tonight!" and Jose Maria really thought he was paying quite a compliment to his cousin from the obscure little town of Salta; for was not he the handsome, wealthy, traveled, and courted Jose Maria Ortega?

The next morning he sat in one of the best rooms in the Iturbide Hotel. The furniture was handsome and old-fashioned; it was probably some of the same that was there when this building was the palace of the emperor, whose name it bears. There was a knock at the door, and obeying his "Come in," his companion of the night before entered.

"Come into my arms, Hernandez. Do I look like a fellow who has watched all night in front of the Jockey Club?"

"No," replied Hernandez as they embraced. "But, tell me! Have you given up the pursuit of your Dulcinea so soon?"

"No, certainly not. I saw them get into their carriage, and it was my uncle who was escorting them, so I knew that the young lady was no other than my cousin, my first cousin, Señor, Magdalena Urbina."

"Your first cousin! That is bad."

"Why? I don't mind marrying **my first cousin.**"

"That is all very well, but **you know you will have to pay**
for a dispensation—that is if the young **lady and her relatives**
accept you," replied Hernandez, **watching the effect of the**
latter part of his speech on his friend. **But Jose Maria was**
too much impressed in his own favor to **take notice of** such
doubts.

"There is nothing more agreeable to the sacerdotal **mind,"**
continued Hernandez, passing a cigarette to his friend, **and**
lighting **one** himself, "than **the** settling of the degrees of
relationship, and the estimating how much can be **wrung out**
of an unfortunate lover for a dispensation. The **eagerness**
with which the zealous 'father' rushes in to **take the declara-**
tion of the contracting parties is **supremely ridiculous."**

"**Well** there is no doubt about **the getting of a dispensation**
to marry a cousin, you know."

"O, **of** course not, if you are **willing** to pay for it. **Didn't**
one of our illustrious compatriots **wash** out whatever of **moral**
wrong there is in a marriage between a **half-brother and sis-**
ter by paying $30,000 to the Pope?" replied Hernandez, with a
jerk of his head in the direction of a palatial residence a little
way up the street. "And another, **with whom I have the**
honor to be acquainted, paid $16,000 for a **dispensation to**
marry his niece. If you wanted **to marry your own mother**
I've no doubt you could get a dispensation for the purpose
from His Holiness by paying—much or little, according to
your ability. And if our spiritual Head should find out
through his devoted emissaries, the priests, **how many**
shekels your Honor can command, he will make **a nice little**
fortune out of you," and he leaned back in his chair and
puffed his cigarette with the complacent air of a man who is
bearing some one else's trouble.

"It does go against the grain to pay out a great sum of
money in that way. But what is a fellow to do? And after
all 'it is for the Church, you know,' as my mother would say;
and a clear conscience is worth something." But there were
two reflections in his mind which were more comforting than

either of these: **one was** that it was aristocratic **to** pay for
dispensations; the other was that he, **Jose Maria Ortega,**
could afford to pay a much larger **sum** than most young men,
epecially than Hernandez, for **instance.** It would be a nice
thing to have the cost of **the** dispensation mentioned along
with the *trousseau* which he should **present** to his bride.

"Why don't you be married **by the law and** let the Church
marriage go?"

"Have some wine, Hernandez," **said Jose Maria, not con-**
descending to reply.

"**Thank** you," said the gentleman, taking the **glass and**
holding it between his eyes and the window, "but you have
not answered my question, Ortega. I **am** surprised that so
sensible **and** traveled a fellow as you should retain any respect for **the** superstitions of this corrupt institution we call
'The Church.'"

"I don't **suppose** you think I would be married in any but
a respectable **way.** Even if I myself were willing to cut
loose from **all** respectability, by omitting the religious marriage, **do you** suppose that any young lady whom I **would**
have would consent to it? No, I'm no reformer; **and besides**
I believe in the Church. I'm not among those who set themselves to pick flaws in the **management of religious matters.**
I suppose they are all right **or they would** not be so. At any
rate, if they **are not** I'm not called to set them right. You
should go **to Europe,** Hernandez, **and see** how much Catholicism has contributed **to** the advancement of the world. All
the great artists were Roman Catholics. And in the **Dark**
Ages the monks were the only ones who thought of preserv-
ing the literature of former centuries. Roman Catholicism
is ancient and aristocratic; but Protestantism, think of it! the
mushroom growth of yesterday!"

"O, I'm not making any defence of Protestantism; though
I may be permitted to refer to the fact—one that you must
have observed in your travels—that the Protestant nations
are more prosperous than the Catholic nations. As, for my-
self, I am an Eclectic; I believe in examining all religions

and choosing the best from each one. However, I suppose if
I were going to be married I should be married by the
Church, especially as it is as you say—that no respectable
girl would take me without it. And I'd pay for a dispensation, too, if it were necessary, and I liked her well enough.
But as to the rest of it—the kneeling, and rolling up my eyes
to images and confessing to these villainous priests—when
it comes to that, excuse me."

"You would have to confess to the priest before you could
be married by the Church."

"Well, thank fortune, I have no idea of being married
soon. But, Ortega, you won't buy the dispensation before
you ask the girl to marry you, will you?" said Hernandez as
he deliberately sipped his wine.

"I see no use to be in haste about any of it."

"You spoke to your uncle last evening, and then drove
with them to the ball, did you?"

"No, I didn't care about the ball. One finds everything in
Mexico stupid after Paris. I strolled about the streets
awhile and then came up here."

"When is the campaign to begin? I have a dagger here in
my cane," he said, drawing out a long, slender, shining blade,
"with which I can defend you from the dogs and all rival
lovers while you and my lady converse at her balcony. And
if you need any original sonnets, command me."

"Thank you, if I need assistance I will call on you."

Then the conversation of the young gentlemen wandered
back over their school days. Jose Maria was eager to hear
what had become of "the boys" during the year and a half he
had been in Europe. At last Hernandez said:

"By the way, Teodoro Martinez graduated this year. You
would be astonished to see how he has come out. I met him
the other day on Plateros and he looked so well that I—well
I was overcome with recollections of old times, and I asked
him into a restaurant and we dined together. I've no idea
he was ever in such a place before, or ever dined at a respectable table, but you can't imagine what good manners he

has picked up somewhere. He may take a higher place among the senators than any of the rest of us yet. He wouldn't be the first Indian who had done that."

Jose Maria laughed heartily. "How could you, Hernandez? Didn't you think of his mother while you were dining with him?"

"No; I tell you I respect the fellow. His staying in school notwithstanding all the ridicule he had to bear showed that he had the right metal in him."

"Ah, Hernandez, you are too democratic. Blood will tell."

"What about Juarez and Ramirez and Altamirano and some of the rest of our distinguished countrymen who are Indians of pure blood?"

But we will not follow the conversation of these young gentlemen any farther.

Doña Flavia indulged in some gloomy reflections about the young gentleman with whom Magdalena had exchanged glances on the evening before. She did not want her to marry soon; and even if she had she would not have contradicted the traditions of her nation by failing to throw obstacles in the way of a suitor, and trying to make him believe that it was with reluctance she gave up her daughter. "If I could only tell all this to Francisco," she thought. "It is so hard to bear everything alone and have no one of whom to ask advice."

As she sat thinking of this Don Francisco entered the room. She was a little startled, for he had avoided her ever since that sad day when he had said, "You are not the woman I thought you were."

He had begun to feel that a reconciliation on any terms would be better than the constraint of the past few weeks. Making an awkward effort to seem natural he said, "Good morning," and asked if she was feeling well.

"Not very well, thank you. We stayed late at the ball and I could not sleep this morning."

This led to some remarks on the elegance of the ball, and after a few minutes of this forced conversation he arose to go, saying by way of excuse for having entered:

"Flavia, do you know where my handkerchief box is?"

"Yes; it is in the top drawer of the bureau, in the right hand corner," she replied in a low voice. She knew now why he had come; at any time during all these weeks he would have bought new things rather than to ask her for anything.

"Francisco," she said tremulously as he turned to go.

She had risen and as he looked at her she dropped her face into her hands and burst into tears.

"O, why will you treat me so?" she sobbed. "You know I didn't mean—you know why I did it," she exclaimed, changing her declaration.

He noticed the change and it cut him to the heart. He realized in his disappointment how fully he had hoped to forgive her. But he would take what she could give and be thankful for that. He went back to her and putting his arm around her said gently,

"Don't be troubled, Flavia. I know you would never have thought of any of it but for the mistaken ideas you had gotten from the unprincipled, ly—I mean from the priests," he said, biting his tongue.

She drew a little away from him, and then leaned on him again. The hope of reconciliation was too precious to be lost.

"O, Francisco, if you only would do right! if you only would do what would be for your good and the children's!"

From his heart he pitied her. "She really believes it, poor thing!" he said to himself; and again he cursed the priests in his heart. But he did not forget that it was useless to reason.

"These weeks have been very sad for me, Flavia. Let us forget it all."

She shrank a little closer to him. "If you care for me how can you refuse to be what I so want you to be, a true son of the church?"

"We will not talk about that, dear; I have my convictions about that; let us not mention it any more; we have plenty of other things in common."

There was a long silence. Doña Flavia was deciding that it was useless to mention the subject of religion again at present. Then she said:

"I wanted to talk to you about Magdalena. I am troubled about her."

"What about her?" he asked with a violent start. Did she want to enter a convent? No, that would probable not trouble her mother.

"There was a gentleman in the gallery last evening who looked at her a great deal and she looked at him."

"Is that all?" he said, his face breaking into a smile, as he sat down on the sofa and drew her down by him. In spite of an effort she laughed, too; it was so sweet to talk to each other about the children again.

And so the reconciliation, such as it was, was effected. There was never any other such serious trouble between them as this in which the "black saint" had played a part. But she went on, in her way, trying to save her children for heaven, and he, in his way, tried to save them for his country. He never dropped back into his beautiful habit of former days of sitting by her with his hand on her shoulder; he always sat a little way from her, and the little children, with their sweet, innocent faces, flitted between them. They both suffered; she a victim of a false religion, and he— was not he a victim also?

That same morning Magdalena entered Mercedes' room in a loose dress, her long, brown hair hanging loose. Mercedes looked up from the book she was reading as she entered.

"Mercedes, I came to talk to you, but you must never tell I said anything to you about it. Did you notice that young gentleman who looked at me so much last evening?"

"I don't know. There were two near us I believe."

"It was one of them; and I looked at him, too, sometimes, of course, when mama was not looking. I'm sure I made an impression on him, and he is so handsome and I'm sure he is nice and everything. I'll meet him again at the balls somewhere. Think of dancing with him! It would be just splendid to have a flirtation with somebody."

"Is it right to have flirtations and think about such things so much?"

"Right! Who ever heard of its being wrong? If you had been shut up with nuns as long as I was, amusing yourself by reciting prayers and studying the catechism and embroidering robes for bishops with the sisters trying all the time to get you to take the veil and become just like them, you would think a flirtation was the finest prospect in the world. But I'll go if you have no sympathy to offer me. Adios."

"What a pity she doesn't appreciate her opportunities!" thought Mercedes as she returned to the history of the miracles and glories of Mary.

CHAPTER XXV. .

THE STRONG DELUSION.

ONE bright Saturday afternoon, in the latter part of
March, Mercedes and Maximiliana sat together in a
street car in the *plaza* in front of the Cathedral. They were
waiting for the car to start to the village of Gaudalupe
Hidalgo. This is the most sacred place in Mexico to the
Catholics, because it was here that, it is said, the Virgin appeared to the Indian, Juan Diego, and announced herself as
the patron saint of Mexico. The village has another historic
interest for Mexicans, but a sad one; for in it was signed the
treaty of peace between Mexico and the United States which
gave the latter nation New Mexico and California.

During the few minutes that they were waiting not fewer
than a half-dozen men, women and boys, agents of the various
lotteries, entered, and thrust their tickets before their faces,
persistently assuring them in rapid, singsong tones that here
was their opportunity to win five thousand, ten thousand, a
million dollars. They all wore the wretched, feverish, anxious, eager expression of gamblers.

Maximiliana was not in a good humor with her friend. She
had fallen into the habit of watching her apprehensively, as
we watch persons of whom we say that they are "not quite
right." She had reason to do so. Mercedes had, indeed,
given no signs of mental aberration, but she was becoming
too strong a Catholic to suit her independent friend.

A few days before, Maximiliana had taken her to visit the
monastery of San Fernando, or rather the comparatively
small part of it that still remained, for much of it had been
torn away to open streets and build business and dwelling
houses. "It extended away over yonder to the depot," she
said as they stood in a passage in the second story and looked

from a little window over the tops of the surrounding houses.
The part that was left was used as a tenement house and was
occupied by very poor people. They wandered about through
long, narrow, dark passages, upstairs and downstairs, glancing into the little cell-like rooms, each with its tiny window
to make the darkness visible.

"You remember seeing in the National Library great piles
of old books, thousands and thousands of them, a great many
of them written in Middle Age Latin? They were taken out
of this and other monasteries when these buildings were confiscated to the State."

"And the monks used to study them in these dark little
rooms!" exclaimed Mercedes eagerly. "I wonder what they
are about!"

"I don't know what they are about; metaphysics, I suppose," replied Maximiliana, with a touch of impatience in her
tone.

But Mercedes was thinking, "What pure and soul-stirring
treasures of wisdom those books must contain! What knowledge of 'the plan of salvation!' No doubt they would answer,
oh, so many puzzling questions."

"O, Maximiliana," she exclaimed, her voice trembling and
her face illuminated with the thought, "how sweet it must
have been to spend the time here studying such books and
only going out to help the poor and sick, and those whose
souls were troubled."

"You seem to have a queer idea of the monks. There may
have been monks of that kind in the world a long time ago,
but the Mexican monks were not hurt with goodness. I
don't know anything about them except what I have heard,
and a little that I have read, for that order of things passed
away before my day; but my mother remembered seeing
them when she was a young girl. They used to go up to
Salta from Guadalajara on their missions. It was long before the days of railroads, of course, and they would go that
thousand or more miles in long processions of carriages.
The monks always rode in the front carriages and the nuns

in those behind. She said the nuns' carriages were always closed, and when they were not in the carriages they were always heavily veiled, because, forsooth, they were too holy to be looked on with by unsanctified eyes. The monks wore hideous, long, coarse robes, to impress the people with their holiness, and under those, when one happened to see, bless you! they were dressed like personages of the highest distinction. And that was the way they were about everything—grand hypocrites."

But Mercedes only thought, "Maximiliana is so prejudiced!"

After that they had visited a convent. It was a large, irregular building, varying in height, and in the most capricious way, from one to two stories, and looking as if it were a pile of blocks that giant children had thrown together. It wandered around several courts. The rooms were small and dark, many of them receiving their only light from their doors or from a small iron-barred window far above their heads. Respectable families lived there, and before their doors were flowers, and birds in cages, and happy-faced children; all of it a strange contrast to the former things.

There in those tiny rooms were buried alive—not a few—but thousands of girls, many of them daughters of the most aristocratic families. With hearts as pure as Mercedes' own they had entered on that life, dressed like brides, for they were to be wedded to religion, and it was announced that from that day they were too pure to be looked on, even by their nearest relatives. The disappointments and trials and longing for liberty we can only imagine.

When they came out of this convent Mercedes exclaimed: "Maximiliana, I have resolved to be a Sister of Charity. You need not stare at me. Isn't heaven worth all that one can do to win it? Even if he must spend long days of fasting and nights of penance and prayer? Think of the blessed privilege of helping the distressed! Think of what it would be to help these Indians! Look at them yonder, mere bearers of burdens; how sweet it would be to go into their homes and teach them to be women, to love their children and care for them, to love and reverence the Holy Mother of God! And even if there were no pleasure in doing all that, how is one to attain the salvation of his soul without good works? They might kill me, too, in one of those terrible tenement houses, and then I should be sure of heaven."

"Well," replied Maximiliana, after a long pause, "I have nothing to say to all that, of course, if you have made up your mind to it."

"I was too much astonished, and I hadn't the patience, any-how, to say a word to her!" she had exclaimed, after she had related it all to Tomas. "I promised to take her to the Village of Guadalupe, but I'm so disgusted I've a mind not to do it!"

"Yes, I would, if I were you. I would not break friend-ship with her. Maybe you can persuade her and show her the foolishness of such a course," Tomas had replied to his impetuous helpmeet. And so it happened that they were on the way to the most sacred shrine of the Virgin.

A few other persons entered the car and soon it started over "the broad old road of humiliation, prayer and penance. Along all these weary miles of scourges and suffering, thou-sands and tens of thousands of the devotees of the Romish Church have knelt and wept and crawled, praying for the expiation of their sins, in obedience to priestly decree, or superstitious sense of duty."

But nobody does that now; it seems to have lost its virtue. When the wife of the President and two hundred of the other principal ladies of the City of Mexico went to this shrine a short time ago to implore the intercession of Our Lady of Guadalupe that the cholera might be averted, they did not go on their knees.

So strong was the crying in Mercedes' soul for peace it would have been a relief to her to kneel and weep and crawl and scourge herself in the old fashion all the way from the Cathedral to the shrine of the Virgin.

When they arrived at the village they went first to the spot where, it is said, the Virgin appeared the fourth time to Juan Diego. There is nothing imposing about the building. The railing in front of the altar is of solid silver, covered with gold. It is about one and a half inches thick. But it is not of fine workmanship, and the pictures representing the appearances of the Virgin have no merit as works of art.

There were several well-dressed ladies, kneeling and reciting prayers to one or another of the images or pictures. Among them went a woman with a dust pan and a broom, busily sweeping the floor.

Mercedes having recited her prayers here, while Maximiliana sat on one of the benches and looked on, they went to the tiny chapel where the Virgin appeared the second and third times, and where she gave the flowers to the Indian. In the anteroom is a large and strongly boiling spring of chalybeate water; it was created by the Virgin and therefore has miraculous properties.

Once a year thousands of Indians come on pilgrimages hundreds of miles to pass here the Day of the Virgin of Guadalupe, to drink of this water and to engage in the great dance in honor of Our Lady, and buy the little cakes made of this holy earth and stamped with her image, which cakes have virtue to cure them of any or "all the ills that flesh is heir to."

Mercedes and her friend drank from one of the little leaking copper buckets, the former remarking, "You know, of course, I don't believe that this water has any miraculous power, nor those cakes either. I leave all such nonsense as that to the Indians."

"The Infallible Church teaches it. If you accept one of her doctrines you ought to accept all."

"That does not follow at all. It is necessary to teach the Indians a religion that is within the grasp of their intellect. We are not expected to believe it."

At last they ascended the hill to visit the holiest place of all, the little chapel which marks the spot where she appeared the first time. There is a wide stairway of stone steps from

16

242 MERCEDES, A STORY OF MEXICO.

the base to the top of the hill. The tiny church on the summit is, like all the others, adorned with many images and pictures, all of them of little or no artistic merit. On slabs in the stone floor of the chapel are inscriptions marking the final resting place of those whose riches have secured them the privilege of burial there. In the paved space in front of the chapel there are other and similar inscriptions, and behind the edifice there is a small cemetery with many rich and curious monuments. The eyes grow tired of looking at the heavy, silver chains with which they are adorned. Here, under a plain marble slab, sleeps Santa Anna, his fever-ish life ended. He rests here in the most sacred of the burying grounds, but "unwept, unhonored and unsung" by the Mexicans. But they speak no evil of him—no more than they do of the unfortunate Maximilian.

When they had reached the summit of the hill Mercedes had turned her head for an instant and caught her breath as the landscape burst upon her vision. But duty called her, and she entered the chapel to count her beads and repeat Ave Marias and Pater Nosters as rapidly as her girlish voice could slip over the words; then to the cemetery, and duty was ended.

When they came back to the front of the chapel the land-scape again swam before her eyes, and she exclaimed: "How beautiful, beautiful!"

There in the distance was the amphitheater of purple mountains; and from the circular range arose the snow-cov-ered volcanoes, Popocatepetl and Ictacihuatl, the Woman in White. They were giants once, and husband and wife; but the Great Spirit became enraged against them and turned the woman to stone. When, in former years, Popocatepetl roared and poured out lava, the Indians said it was in grief and rage for the death of his wife.

One who has ever seen a corpse covered with a sheet will never forget how the sheet sinks down over the still body, showing every outline. Well, yonder it is, that sheet, "white as no fuller on earth could whiten it," sunk down over the corpse of the giant Ictacihuatl. It is all there, the "decent composure" of the figure, the head, the folded arms, the feet. Her long black hair streams down the mountain side. Along the whole length of the mountain she lies, the dead giant wife, and by her side, but at a little distance, as if he would not, through reverence for the mystery, approach too near the dead, stands the giant husband, his hoary head among the clouds.

At their feet lies the Valley of Mexico, green as emerald, and dotted with little silver lakes and patches of yellow flowers. In the distance smiles the broad peaceful surface of Lake Tezcuco, now silver, now blue, in the soft sunlight. In the midst of the valley sits, like a queen, the City of Mexico.

I have seen much of the beauty of mountains and of valleys. I have seen the mountains when an ethereal, purple veil hung over them, so near it seemed I might put out my hand and touch its silken folds, if it were tangible. I have opened a door sometimes in winter and started back because the mountains seemed to stand at the very entrance, like great, brown, grim giants. I have seen range on range, covered with glittering snow. I have seen them gorgeous in autumn foliage. I have stood on the mountains and seen the white fog rolling and heaving and tossing, like the ocean, they said; and then it would break and roll away, and there below would be the green valley and the silvery streams and the peaceful farm houses, with the blue smoke curling upward from their chimneys. I have stood on Lookout Mountain and gazed on the city below, the winding river, and that magnificent semicircle of country, and far off into the adjoining States. But never in my life have I seen any panorama that for beauty and sublimity was equal to the Valley of Mexico and its encircling mountains.

Mercedes gazed, speechless. The past arose before her and she "saw a vision." The tribes were coming over the mountains from the North—Ah! whence did they come?— and they descended into the lake of islands and built a city, for so had the god commanded them. The centuries swept by and over the ocean came some great white-winged living creatures, and out of them stepped Quetzalcoatl, the Fair God, so long foretold and expected, and with horrible cruelties he and his followers taught the worship of the true God to the dwellers in the beautiful valley.

Then she remembered that the Virgin had appeared on this very hill in all her celestial majesty, beautiful as Venus when she appeared to Æneas, as he looked down on the rising walls of the city of Dido; and again she remembered that she had read in a book of Castelar's that the English poet Byron had believed that he saw in the twilight, "on the border of the horizon, beyond Venice, gliding over the waters like the stars of heaven, the Mother of the Word, with the moon under her feet, and with the mysterious white dove fluttering its wings on her forehead in that sublime hour of prayer and of love." "Oh, what manner of man in all holiness of life and of heart must have been that poet Byron ever after!" she exclaimed.

"Why might not I see a vision of the Virgin Mother?" she asked herself. She had resolved now as a last resort to give up all the hope and joy and brightness of life, and it was no small sacrifice (and the sobs choked her, and she wrung her hands as she thought of the giving up of life); she had resolved to shroud her young form in mourning, to spend her nights in prayer and penance, and her days in fasting and in good works among the most degraded, to give all her thoughts to the worship of God and of his "Holy Mother." She had struggled long to know the truth; she had walked in darkness and had no light, she said to herself; forgetting for the moment that when she had been forced to face the question, she had felt in her heart that if she knew the Protestants had the truth she would not accept it from them.

She fell on her knees and clasped her hands, as she gazed at the snow-capped mountains and the lake at their feet. If she could only—could only see for one instant the fair Virgin Mother with the Babe on her bosom gliding over those waters, then she should know that she had done right; then she should know that the Roman Catholic Church was the true church. That should be a sign to her. Could it be denied? Was it not reasonable and right that the "Queen of Heaven," the "Holy Mother of God," should give her a sign now that she might no longer walk in darkness, but might enter on this new life with confidence that she should in it and by it win salvation? Her soul demanded it.

She watched a long time with intensest gaze. There, near the mountains, on the border of the blue lake, did not something move? She pressed her clasped hands on her bosom and gazed—and gazed—till, with bitterness of soul, she knew it was nothing.

Then she arose. "What was she that she should ask a sign from heaven! She, who, as yet, knew nothing of fasting and prayer and scourging! She, who had come easily and luxuriously to worship at the shrine of the Virgin! It was not to such that signs and visions were granted."

She drew her black scarf over her head, mechanically brushed the dust from her plain black dress, then entered the chapel and spoke to Maximiliana, who sat there waiting and resting; and, saddened and silent, both of them, they went down the hill and to the station, and to the city.

That night, when the house was quiet, Mercedes locked her door and then went to a small piece of furniture, that is called in Mexican homes a *buro*. It had a drawer, and below it a door which opened on a case of shelves. She knelt and drew out the drawer slowly, for there was something in it which made it heavy.

And there lay the things, dark, heavy things, horrible-looking things, coiled and folded, on the bottom of the drawer. She had borrowed them secretly from an old woman who sometimes came to the house, and who had happened to tell her of them one day. Night after night she had knelt there and looked at them, and then closed the drawer and lain down on her bed and slept, or tossed till day.

To-night she took up one of them. It was a belt closely woven of iron half-links, with the two sharp points of each link turned on the same side of the belt. She hooked it about her waist, next her flesh. Then she took up two instruments like soles of shoes. There were sharp iron points on them. She fastened them on her feet, with the points next the flesh. After that she lifted up from its coils a leathern scourge of three thongs, furnished with sharp points of iron, and having bared her shoulders, she scourged herself with it till the blood flowed; and at every movement the belt digged into the flesh of her waist and the sharp points into her feet. When this was ended she lay all night on the bare floor.

Do you think I have exaggerated this? Do you think that nobody does this now that we are almost at the end of the nineteenth century, unless it be some fanatic in a convent? You are mistaken. A few days ago I read in a secular paper, published in the City of Mexico, that two young ladies in Yucatan, one of the States of this Republic, had killed themselves by the *exercises*, that is the scourging and other mortifications of the body, to which they subjected themselves by way of preparation for the Holy Week, which is just past. In many cities and towns of Mexico the people shut themselves in the churches at night, the women in one part of the church and the men in the other, put out the lights and scourge each other with the leathern scourge, the *disciplina*, as it is called, and with thorny sticks, as a preparation for the taking of the eucharist during Holy Week.

The Church invented penance in order to sell dispensations, but there are people who have a better opinion of the Church, and they think the prescribed mortifications are for the good of the soul.

While Mercedes scourged herself there stood in front of the house a young man, looking at Doña Flavia's window, that young man to whom years before Lupe Rodrigues had taught the truth as it is in Jesus.

CHAPTER XXVI.

THE GOD CUPID.

THERE is no image of him in the temples among those of the other gods, but his influence is none the less potent for that omission.

Jose Maria Ortega had "opened the campaign." Had he called at his uncle's house and made the acquaintance of his aunt and cousins? Did he call afterward on Magdalena alone? Did he take her to parties, theaters and operas? Did he drive with her? By no means; that is not the way courting is done in Mexico.

He might have called at the house but for the fact that the idea that Doña Flavia did not like him had somehow introduced itself into his head. But there were other ways to make known his feelings to his pretty cousin. He knew that she, like all other fashionable young ladies whose papas were so fortunate as to own carriages, would drive with her mama in the afternoons; so he, too, frequented the drive. He rode horseback, and he was not less handsome on horseback than in any other position or occupation—a fact of which he was as fully aware as anybody else.

Sometimes he swept along the drive among the flying carriages and other horsemen in a magnificent equestrian costume, that which is called "the national costume," more because in has been adopted as such than because of its general use. It consisted of a jacket and pantaloons, ornamented to the highest degree with silver cord and buttons; a broad-brimmed, bell-crowned hat, heavily adorned with silver cord and the Mexican eagle; immense spurs, inlaid with silver; a large saddle, ornamented with the same precious metal, and reins, because of whose silver decorations,

> "When he rode men might his bridle hear
> Jingling in the whistling wind as clear.
> And eke as loud as doth the chapel bell."

A shawl of fine material, and of all the colors of the rainbow, lay behind his saddle and swept nearly to the ground on either side. So radiant was the picture, so handsome and proud-looking the man on that magnificent, prancing horse, that one could not think of anything else but a Spanish Hidalgo of the Middle Ages.

This costume was a sort of advertisement, a refined and conventional one, of course, that Jose Maria was the owner of a costly hacienda. Those who guessed that this gala attire cost $500 were not mistaken. But our young gentleman did not display himself in this style often nowadays. He had been to Paris. The consequence was that he had a good-natured contempt for all things Mexican. He generally took the air on the *Paseo de la Reforma*, dressed in the latest Parisian style.

He soon learned at what hours Don Francisco's carriage was to be expected, and he was always not far from it. One afternoon, as he galloped along a little way from the carriage, he had the good fortune to catch Magdalena's eye when her mother was not looking. He lifted his hat and bowed, and she returned the salutation. It was the slighest bow imaginable, and then she did not look at him again, but instead devoted herself with redoubled assiduity to the tiny dog on her lap; but he was satisfied. He knew that she would look again when he looked away, and when she thought her mother would not detect her glances, and so away he went on his prancing horse, now far before, now a little behind, with the pleasant belief in his heart that among all those elegantly dressed young ladies in all the carriages who were in love with him, Magdalena was no exception. After that he never failed to catch her eye when she was driving, and bow to her.

In the Alameda, too, whither the *elite* of Mexico resort in their most elegant attire on Sunday mornings, he never failed to meet her as she, with her mother or with other young ladies, "walked the other way."

Once he saw her and another girl sitting alone on a seat.

Presently the latter arose and went off a few steps. When her back was turned Jose Maria, who had been watching for such an opportunity, threw a tiny perfumed note to Magdalena's feet. She caught it up quickly, and concealed it before her companion returned. She was very much fluttered and a little frightened at her own boldness, but it was very sweet and thrilling. When she was alone in her own room she opened the letter and read it. It was a love letter than which none more hyperbolical has ever been written, perhaps. She was his Angel, his Queen, his Rose, his Dove, his Star, etc., etc. It was only the beginning of the letters with which he honored her. The chirography in all these letters was pretty as a picture; several kinds would be displayed in the same letter; sometimes it leaned to the right, sometimes to the left, and sometimes it stood straight up. In the more advanced stage of his feelings he bribed a chambermaid to convey these letters to Magdalena; but that was after he had at last called at the house and introduced himself to Doña Flavia as her nephew, that he might have the privilege of calling often on the family.

Then came the serenading under her window. And often he came to her window when he did not serenade, but only gave a low whistle which her attentive ears recognized. Then she went out on the tiny balcony upstairs and talked with him as he stood in the street below. A pretty picture they made, he wrapped in a long, handsome black cloak, looking up at her as she in the daintiest and softest of dresses, and with a silken shawl thrown carelessly about her, leaned over the balcony in the moonlight. So common is this Romeo and Juliette method of courting that there are few people who have spent any time in Mexico who have not seen more than one such tableaux.

Doña Flavia and Don Francisco watched Jose Maria closely during the evenings which he spent in their parlor. There were some reasons for which he would be to both of them an acceptable son-in-law; among these, of course, were his wealth and his aristocratic origin, for, as Doña Flavia would have said, "He is one of our family, you know." But each of them had some objections to him.

They suspected that the serenades were his, but of the interchange of letters and the secret meetings they knew nothing. They, like all other parents in Mexico, would have said that such proceedings were "very ugly;" but if they had come to their knowledge they would have taken no extreme measures. Their own courting had doubtless been done in much the same way. Such evasions of parental authority were to be expected under the circumstances.

Mercedes had come to know of the conversations by moonlight. She had discovered that much of the secret by chance. Magdalena was glad she did know, as she threw no obstacle in her way, for she had an aversion to concealment.

There was a strange contrast between the two girls in those days. Magdalena was radiant in her new-found happiness, looking forward to wedded bliss, with little or no more thought of the destiny of her soul, than if she were a descendant of those Preadamites who, they tell us, were in every respect like other human beings except that they lacked the immortal part.

Mercedes was sad, full of doubts and of gloomy apprehensions of the future; desperately trying to find consolation in the thought of ministering to others, for the terrible sacrifice which that privilege was to cost her; wondering if, after all, that course of conduct would secure her entrance into heaven; spending her nights in prayer and penance, and by day dragging her lacerated body about her ordinary duties.

Magdalena's prospects made her, too, think of marriage. Might she not some time love some one, some one who loved her. But for this feeling that she must sacrifice everything to earn salvation it might not be necessary to pass through life lonely and unloved. And so it happened that Magdalena's happiness caused her to pass through a new and in some respects the fiercest struggle of all, before she could say in her heart: "I will be a Sister of Charity."

CHAPTER XXVII.

HOLY WEEK

HOLY WEEK came for the privileges of which all this doing of penance and confessing of sins to the priests was done. The only days that are observed are Friday and Saturday. As the laws against religious demonstrations in the open air are regarded to some extent by the public officers in the capital, there were few processions in the streets. Doña Flavia remarked to the Señor Bishop, who had come to spend the week in the capital, that it was melancholy to see how different it was from the way in which these days were observed in Salta; and he replied that there was always more true religion in the small, out-of-the-way towns than in the great centers of population.

But if the processions were forbidden in some of the streets of the great city the days were observed with sufficient zeal in other ways.

It was a trying week for Mercedes. To make it worse her mind went back to the "Day of the Dead," the 2nd of November, which they had observed in Mexico, having arrived only two or three days before; and she lived over in her imagination all those scenes, so excruciating to a sensitive soul.

On that day they went to the Cathedral and knelt in the great congregation and listened to the masses which were being said for the repose of souls in purgatory. After they left the Cathedral they went into the *plaza* where the toys peculiar to this *fiesta* were sold. Everybody was very merry. "Here, Señoras," cried a woman as they passed, "don't you want to buy a little corpse for the children to play with?" offering a coffin, the length of a hand, with a corpse that would fly up when the coffin was pressed. There were tiny hearses with their coffins and ghastly corpses in grave

clothes; there were skeletons for the children to play with;
there were skulls, and there was a facsimile of the image of
the soul in purgatory which they had seen inside the Cathedral on a contribution box, red flames, contortions and all—
with the difference that this one was made of sugar and was
for the children to eat, while that was intended to secure
liberal contributions.   Is it strange that the finer sentiments
of Roman Catholics should be blunted?

In the pantheons the graves were decorated with flowers,
and burning candles were placed on them.   The central fountain in the Alameda was covered with flowers in the most
exquisite designs, and there the high society of the city,
after the ladies had visited the churches and the pantheons,
amused themselves as is their wont during *fiestas.*

Mercedes' soul took up on that day the cry of all the noble
souls who have found themselves in that communion: "The
Church needs reforming." And now she was to see again the
ceremonies of Holy Week in connection with the Savior's
death, with all their attendant levity.   It was with the feeling that her teeth were already on edge that she entered on
these days of religious observance.   There was some comfort
in it however: she was to partake of that mystery, the
eucharist; she was to take into her sinful mouth the real
body of the Lord, which was to "preserve her soul and body
unto everlasting life."   If it occurred to her how many other
things she had done according to the prescription of the Infallible Church which were "to preserve her soul and body
unto everlasting life," she put away the thought as sinful.
It was right somehow.

No bells were rung; the people were called to church by the
sound of the *matraca,* an instrument of wood or metal which
makes a loud and disagreeable noise.   The whole city resounded with the *matracas,* for every toy, expensive or cheap,
that was sold on those days contained one of those instruments.

The morning of Good Friday thousands of the common
people went to the Floating Gardens to see the bearing of

the cross and the crucifixion. During a part of this performance Pilate and others of his court appeared on horseback.
The drunkenness, cursing, fighting and stealing were appalling. The priests presided over this performance.

The bishop preached in the morning at the church, which
Doña Flavia and her family attended, on The Twelve Stations, that is the twelve pauses which they say that Christ
made as he bore his cross from the judgment hall to Gol-
gotha. In the afternoon, at three o'clock, he preached with
great fervency, owing to the liberal quantity of wine of
which he had partaken, on the seven expressions of the Lord
on the cross. At the end of the sermon, amid the moaning
of the organ, the wailing and shrieking, writhing and wringing of hands of the kneeling multitude, the veil was drawn
from before the crucifix and the image was taken down and
borne to the glass case in which it was to rest till the feast of
Corpus Christi. By the side of the casket stood the Virgin
Mary, properly dressed in black, and with an embroidered
white handkerchief in her hand; and ever and anon she
stooped and looked at the body. There were women in the
congregation who declared afterward that "for their part
they believed there was a hinge in the Virgin's back," that
is, they did not believe that that stooping was miraculous.

When the people tired of this bodily exercise they went out
into the *plaza*, and with the tears still on their cheeks, and
laughing and talking in hoarse voices of balls, theaters, bull-
fights and other such diversions, they bought candies and
diverted themselves as if they were at a picnic.

Doña Flavia, Magdalena and Mercedes wept and sobbed
and wrung their hands with the rest, but quietly, as refined
women will do, over the good bishop's sermon and the crucifixion.

Then came Saturday, and the tragic end of Judas Iscariot.
In the afternoon the Judases were burned. They are made
in the shape of a man, but are as hideous as possible, often
having the head of one of the lower animals. Fuse is made
to run all over them. They are suspended on wires that are

stretched across the streets. As it is not now considered a religious ceremony it is permitted that this diversion should take place in the open air.

Several of these Judases were suspended across San Francisco street. An immense crowd gathered near the first one; they waited till it exploded and then rushed, with screams and frenzied zeal, to trample on the pieces, to scramble for the shoes or hat, which are often new, and are given by some person with the benevolent purpose of making the scrambling more violent. The pennies which were thrown by the people in the balconies also added much to the confusion.

Jose Maria had invited his aunt and cousins to witness this spectacle from one of the balconies of the Iturbide Hotel.

On the wires which had been extended from this hotel to the opposite building was a large Judas on horseback. When the sweating, howling mob of common people arrived at this one the fuse was lighted. Horse and rider contracted every limb as if in horrible agony; they writhed, sank, rose, burst, and fell; and then the mob in their rage against the betrayer of the Lord rushed to trample on the pieces. Jose Maria, Magdalena and the children scattered pennies on the heads below.

"That is dreadful," said Doña Flavia to Mercedes, "I am afraid some one will be crushed to death in that crowd."

But Mercedes did not hear. She was standing at the corner of the balcony looking down on the crowd. At that moment she had caught sight of a young gentleman who was standing near the wall, a little apart from the others, as if he had just stepped out from the door of the hotel. She should not have noticed him but for the fact that he was looking at her, had been looking at her, it seemed, all the time she had been watching the wild scene below. There was a look of hopeless devotion, of reverence, in his face which astonished and startled her, and she turned quickly away. Where had she seen that face? She tried to recall it among the faces of all her acquaintances. It was only after days of haunting thought that she remembered it as the

face of the young gentleman who had picked up **her** handkerchief on Christmas evening, **and** dimly connected it with that of the young man who had looked **at** her so strangely in **the** art gallery.

As I have said Mercedes was **comforted in the midst of** all the shocking scenes of this **week by** the thought that she was to receive **the** eucharist. It **was** with much awe that **she** arose from her place in **the** kneeling congregation, **and,** advancing to the railing of the altar, knelt and put **out her** tongue **to** receive on **it the tiny** wafer from **the** priest's **consecrated hand;** for his **voice** was exhorting **her** to believe **that this was not** only the true body of Christ, and all **that** pertained **to** the undivided integrity of the **body,** such as bones, nerves and blood, but **also that** all of **Christ** was in this sacrament, the divine **and human** natures, and **all** that pertained to both of these **natures. And** not only that all of this was in the consecrated **bread and wine,** but that all of it was in each particle of **it, so that in** that tiny bit of bread on her tongue were **contained all the** things that have been enumerated. **And,** furthermore, that notwithstanding the testimony of **taste,** sight and smell, there was nothing left of the nature **of** bread in it.

And besides all this he assured her **that her** soul was **to** be comforted, and was to grow with this divine food, that through it all slight past **sins** were to be pardoned; she was **to** be preserved from committing future sins, and that it was to open to her **the** doors of eternal **glory.** [1]

She swallowed **the wafer, making a** desperate effort to believe all that she **had heard, as she** arose and moved away from **the altar.** But in the depths of her soul she knew that this communion had **no more** conferred on her a title to heaven than had her **baptism,** or her confirmation, or the thousand **indulgences that she** had purchased in **one** way or another.

"One thing after another turns to bitter ashes in my mouth," she said sadly. "It must be because I lack faith."

---

[1] *Note.*—These declarations about the eucharist are from the Decrees **of the** Council **of Trent,** the **highest au**thority among Roman Catholics.

Doña Flavia and the bishop were naturally delighted that Mercedes was to become a Sister of Charity. The latter repeated to her much of Cardinal Gibbon's eloquent description of the life of a Sister of Charity, and Mercedes was more impatient than ever to enter on so heroic a life.

"It is a great pity that there are no convents in Mexico now as there used to be," observed the Señor Bishop one day as he and his hostess discussed this subject in the presence of Mercedes. "But, as it is, she will have to go to another country to take the veil. I think it would be best for her to go to the United States."

"I—I thought," stammered Mercedes, surprised and confused, "that our legislators considered it best for the country somehow that there should be no convents here, and that it was for that reason they were abolished."

Dark clouds had gathered on the brows of the Señor Bishop and his religious hostess. So insulting is it to mention the law to zealous Catholics!

"They are not permitted by the impious laws of the land," replied the Señor Bishop. And then he added, as if to himself: "If we could only have them in spite of the laws!"

"But is it not wrong to disobey the laws of one's country?" asked Mercedes, betrayed by her astonishment into still greater boldness of speech.

Darker grew the clouds on the faces before her; the bishop's eyes flashed lightning, and Mercedes thought Doña Flavia was going to order her to leave the room. "I dare her to do it!" she exclaimed mentally, though she did not add the penalty which would accompany such a breach of respect for herself. "She is a lady I have no great liking for anyhow—and the bishop—I don't even know about him now."

But they composed themselves, and the bishop, after muttering something angrily between his teeth, went on discussing the subject of where she was to go without taking further notice of her question.

After that incident Mercedes fell into the habit of watching the Señor Bishop very closely. There were still other things

HANGING OF JUDAS (in Guadalajara).   Page 253.

in the conduct of this worthy representative of the Church that greatly puzzled and troubled her. Instead of devoting her nights to penance and prayer she spent them in the consideration of these new doubts, which were yet only the revival of old doubts.

The elegant, the good Señor Bishop had so little respect for the laws of the land in which he lived that it was an insult to mention them to him. He had told a falsehood one day in her presence and evidently without the least scruples of conscience. There was no doubt that Doña Flavia had been prompted by his remarks on Masonry and his counsels to have recourse to the "black saint" for the removal of her husband; and last, but certainly not least, she had more than once known of his being more than half intoxicated.

Now she would be guilty of none of these things herself. Could she confess to such a man and receive absolution from his hands? Could she take for her spiritual guide a person who was worse than she was?

But worst of it all was that he was considered by all one of the best of his class;—then what kind of men were the rest?

Doña Flavia had sometimes said to her that when she became a nun one of her principal occupations and pleasures would be to confess. That had surprised her, for she had thought that her principal occupation would be to minister to the distressed. She turned with horror from the thought of confessing to such priests.

Maximiliana had said to her one day, quietly, sadly, like one who utters words with no hope of their making an impression, "Mercedes, child, you don't know where you are drifting."

She had turned toward her friend a ghastly face with a momentary realization of her danger and exclaimed. "Maximiliana, am I standing on the brink of a precipice?"

"Yes, that is just where you are standing. May God draw you back."

And so it was that through the lonely nights her disconnected thoughts went all tending toward one resolution: She

17

would never again confess; therefore she could never be a nun—a Sister of Charity.

The day came when she announced her change of mind to Doña Flavia and the bishop, braving their wrath and the prospect of being sent from the house. She gave them few reasons; but one of them was sufficient: She thought she "could be a better woman by not being a Sister of Charity."

After she left the room and they had discussed the question at length, they decided that there might be hope for the girl yet; they would have patience with her.

That very afternoon Mercedes went to Maximiliana's house, and went in and fell down on her knees by her side, and clung to her, as great sobs tore themselves out of her throat. "O! Maximiliana, I will never, never be a Sister of Charity. I have been so blinded," she said.

Maximiliana put her arms closely about her and cried with her. And presently Tomas came in and heard the story and rejoiced with them.

"O! I feel free as a bird! It was dreadful, dreadful to think of such a life anyhow; and now I feel as if I had been snatched back from the brink of a terrible abyss."

"The more you examine them the more you will be convinced that the teachings of the Roman Catholic Church are false and degrading," said Tomas, kindly.

"I believe it—I begin to believe it," replied Mercedes.

CHAPTER XXVIII.

A LAST LOOK AT HER WINDOW.

ONE day Teodoro **Martinez,** descending one of the handsome stairways **of the** Palacio Municipal, saw the tall, slender figure, and **thin,** kindly face of **the** Director of the **college** coming up. **They** embraced, and then the Director said:

"I was coming up **to** talk with you **a few** minutes, Teodoro. If you are going out we can talk **as well in the** street **as** here, and better."

When they **were in the** street he turned **a** radiant face to **the** young **man, and rubbing** his hands with pleasure, said:

"I **have a** magnificent chance for you, my son. I could **scarcely wait** till after school hours to tell you of it."

"**You are** very kind, Sir. **What** is it?" replied Teodoro, trying to arouse himself to interest and gratitude. He had had a feeling all these last weeks that it **made** little difference what became of him; he could not save his family; he could **not win** the girl he loved.

"I received **a letter** this **morning** from a friend of mine in one of the **northern States, asking** me to furnish him a competent teacher **for the school in his** place. The patronage will be good, **he says,** and the salary **is** good. Now what better could **a young** man of your abilities and tastes desire? You might even **in** time **become** superintendent of public instruction **for the** State." And the kind-hearted Director rubbed **his hands** vigorously in his delight.

"I should have—should have **to leave** the city, and not return for months, for years, perhaps," stammered Teodoro, scarcely knowing what he was saying. but feeling the necessity of speaking.

"**Yes, my son,**" said the Director, looking at him curiously, "but why should you mind that? It is not so interesting a place, not so large, nor so handsome a place, of course, but—"

"O, it is not that, Sir," said Teodoro, interrupting him hastily. "It's nothing, only there are people here whom it would be hard to leave; that is all. I will go, of course. I am very grateful to you." And he hoped the Director would think it was himself and some of his schoolfellows whom it was hard to leave.

"Teodoro," said the teacher gently, laying his hand on the young man's arm, "it is natural for you to feel some regret at leaving your parents and the others. But it is better to do so. For that very reason I have rejoiced the more that this opportunity is offered you in a distant town. I know of your efforts to save them, my boy. It is noble of you, and I am glad that you have it in your heart to do it. But it's of no use; you can't do anything with them. It is better for you to leave them and make a man of yourself."

"I know that, Sir. I was not thinking of them. I have done all I can for them, at present, at least. I've tried for years, but I've had to give them up at last. I—I was thinking of some one else; but it's no matter. It's a mere fancy, and there is no hope in it. You won't say anything about it, please," said Teodoro, not supposing that many other young men of twenty-one guarded a tremendous secret of unrequited love.

"I appreciate your speaking of it to me, my son. But if there is no hope in it it is best to go away." But the sensible philosophy of age was chilling, as it always is, to young hearts.

"When shall I go?" asked Teodoro very quietly.

"I think it would be well to go as soon as possible to look after the school; say the first of next week."

"Very well, Sir; I shall make my arrangements accordingly. I cannot express my gratitude to you for your kindness. It is just like you. I owe everything to you," he said in a choking voice.

"Tush, my boy. It isn't worth mentioning. But I am very

proud of you. You have made a man of yourself, notwith-standing the obstacles. By the way, the Señora Directora told me to ask you to dine with us to-morrow, and we shall expect you to stay for the little musical entertainment after-ward. You will come?"

"Yes, Señor; many thanks."

"Well, adios."

"Adios, Señor. Salutations for the Señora."

And the Director went on his way, smiling, but with pity in his heart, as he thought:

"Poor boy! He feels like it is all over with him. It hurts while it lasts, of course, but he'll get over it, and all the sooner for being in a new place. We all have to have these ups and downs. How many Dulcineas had I been broken hearted over before I met Julia. But after I met her I was glad I couldn't win the others. He'll get over it."

Teodoro went home and left his supper untasted, and sat, with his elbows on the table and his head on his hands, so long that the good woman who prepared his meals was dis-tressed with the thought that "the Señor" must be sick.

After awhile he put on his hat and went out. He would go and look at her window for the last time. He had indulged himself in that way several times in these weeks. Twice he had stood out there in the rain, with a borrowed umbrella over him, looking at Doña Flavia's window. He had said to himself every time that it would be more sensible to be at home studying; but no doubt there have been times in the lives of the wisest men when, under the influence of such feelings as Teodoro's, they have failed to obey the dictates of common sense.

It was all over now, he knew; he should never be happy any more. He had never had any hope of happiness from it, of course, he had only been indulging in foolish daydreams, and even they would have been insulting to the young lady.

Realizing this he need not have taken such a terrible heartache over a communication which Hernandez had made to him a few days before. He had met his good-natured, "democratic" classmate in the Plaza de Armas, and had, at his invitation, "given a turn" with him, listening to the music of a band. After some conversation about indifferent matters Felipe had said:

"Have you seen Ortega since he came back?"

"No, I thought he was studying at some university in France."

"He study! Not much of it. He completed the course over there very soon. He was in a university a few months, and to hear him tell it he did wonders, and astonished all the professors by his attainments. But he spent the rest of the time traveling or amusing himself in Paris. It is really edifying to hear him express his contempt for everything in Mexico, now, and contrast it with Paris."

"What is he going to do now? Devote himself to politics? or look after that *hacienda* of his that he used to tell us about? I don't suppose, though, he would do that."

"No. I don't know what he will do. Nothing, I suppose; he is rich enough to live without work. He is in love now; of course, nothing is to be expected of him till he gets over that. It is all arranged, he says. He will have a good deal more property after he gets her, for her father, Don Francisco Urbina, is rich."

Teodoro started, but Felipe had turned away to light a cigarette, and did not notice it.

"Which one of Señor Urbina's daughters is he going to marry?"

"The eldest one. Quite a fine girl she is; worth the winning if she were not so rich. I have seen her a few times at balls and such places. Jose Maria always was a lucky fellow."

This communication had added new gloom to Teodoro's reflections. It was a bitter thought to him that the enemy of his school days, who had often stabbed him in cold blood, stooping over him, as it seemed to him, with his handsome, smiling face, to turn the knife in his heart—it was a very bitter thought that this enemy should win the girl he loved. "He is not half good enough for her. How could she like him!" he **exclaimed**. "But she **doesn't** know him. Ten to one she will be miserable with him when she gets acquainted with him. But it will be too late then."

As he went along thinking **thus** with himself he had approached **quite** near to the **house** of the lady of his thoughts. Looking **at the casket which** held that jewel he had not noticed **that** some one **was** approaching him. It was Jose Maria Ortega. They **met in the** white radiance of an electric light.

"Ah! Good evening, **Martinez**," he said, without **offering his hand.** From **what he** had heard **from** Hernandez he **thought** there was danger of this fellow's becoming presumptuous. Somebody **must** check him. Such duties devolved on **men** of Jose Maria's position; and he believed he could perform such public services more gracefully and **more** efficiently **than most men**; it was a duty, moreover, from which he **never** shrank. He was a little surprised, too, **to see** him **there** gazing at that house.

"**Good** evening, Ortega," replied Teodoro.

"Fine night, isn't it?—for lovers **especially.** **Have you set your** heart on some pretty **chambermaid over** there that **you** come out to watch the house?" and he **looked** at Teodoro with **the same** expression on **his face with which** he used to insult him **at** school. Teodoro **involuntarily** clinched his fist and **half raised it.** He **longed to strike him a** blow **in** the face and leave him **lying full length in the mud of** the street. But there was **no danger of his actually** striking; **there** was nothing of **the brute in him.** He dropped his hand, and **look·**ing full into the **face** before him, with **his** own white **with** rage and scorn, exclaimed:

"Jose Maria Ortega, **I hope I** may **never see your** face again while I live!"

The young gentleman addressed, bowing and smiling as he tossed the cape of his cloak over his shoulder so that the crimson plush lining set **off his** complexion, replied carelessly:

"Adios, then, **and** my **regards** to the Señora, mother of your Worship," and crossed the street to the gate, which was quickly opened by some one inside, and then shut behind him. Teodoro went back to his room and sat, with his elbows on the table and his head on his hands, far into the night.

A half an hour before this encounter in the street took place, Magdalena had entered Mercedes' room, dressed as if for a party.

"Mercedes," she said in a happy whisper, and with a look of great mystery, as she knelt beside her, "I have something to tell you, but you must keep it from mama, will you?"

"I don't know, Magdalena. I'm afraid it isn't right to be keeping things from your mama this way."

"O, Mercedes, it's not wrong. I've no doubt mama did just the same way when she was in love with papa. She just says it's ugly now because she thinks it is prudent to say that before us girls."

"What is it you are going to tell me, Magdalena?" asked Mercedes anxiously.

"I promised Jose Maria to meet him in the garden to-night, under the vine, just outside the dining room door. The servants are gone, so they won't hear us talk. But I wanted some one to know about it; I can't bear to keep things. And you are another girl; you can understand how I feel about it," she added pleadingly.

"Magdalena, you are sweet and good," replied Mercedes, putting her arms around her, "but you ought not to meet him secretly. You and he can talk in the balls."

"O, the balls!" said Magdalena. "We are never alone for one instant in the balls. He asked me to meet him in the garden, and I promised, Mercedes. How can I disappoint him! You wouldn't if you were in my place!" and Magdalena put her arms around Mercedes' neck and dropped her head on her shoulder with something very like a sob.

"Magdalena," said Mercedes at last, "if you will stay with him just a half hour—"

"O, Mercedes, such a short time! Just think of it! I'll stay just an hour."

"But it isn't right, Magdalena. Now promise me, just a half hour; then I'll make a noise at the window, and you can come in. And then I won't say anything about it. But don't promise to meet him in the garden any more; please don't, Magdalena."

"O, well, I promise not to stay but a half hour. But it is cruel of you not to let me have more time;" and she tripped out of the room to listen for the low whistle which was to summon her to the side of her lover.

Mercedes listened, too, and after she heard it she timed them by the little school clock. At the end of the time she slipped out and along a corridor till she came to a window which was just above their heads; then she thumped loudly on the glass. But when she went to the window fifteen minutes later, there in the shadow of the vines in the checkered moonlight, still stood the tall dark figure, and the slender graceful one in the light dress and the snowy opera cloak. She knocked again on the window and watched till she saw Magdalena start away from him, while he held her hands and kissed them two or three times.

When she knocked the first time Jose Maria was saying to her, gayly:

"I had a little adventure in the street awhile ago. I met a fellow out there in front of the house who used to be in the same school with me. He was a curiosity; he was always dressed so shabbily. In fact he was one of the Indians whom you see in the streets carrying burdens on their backs. His mother! she was one of the most ridiculous looking creatures you ever saw. She used to sell vegetables near the college, and he actually carried them out there to the street for her as he came to school," and Jose Maria paused to laugh at the recollection.

Magdalena laughed, too, just because Jose Maria did, but she said in a puzzled and timid way: "But wasn't it good of him to carry them for his mother? She was his mother, you know, no matter how she looked."

"O, yes, he was no better than she was, of course; but you

ought to have seen what a grotesque-looking couple they were! But the Director was a cranky old fellow, and he somehow carried that beggar clear through the course of the college. And now that he has a sort of education and wears good clothes his presumption is intolerable. He was really insulting to me awhile ago."

"How was it?" asked Magdalena in an indignant tone.

"He was staring at the windows of this house, and I asked him if he was thinking of some one of the servant girls here, and he actually clinched his fist as if he wanted to strike me, and said he hoped he might never see my face again. Think what impudence!"

"It was very ugly of him to talk so," replied the gentle Magdalena. "What is his name?"

"Teodoro Martinez. I've seen somebody hanging around the street several nights, looking up at the windows, and since I think of it I know it was he. I wonder what he can be after?" and there the subject dropped.

After he was gone Magdalena again entered Mercedes' room, flushed with happiness.

"How could you make me come up so soon?" she said, gayly. "I would have come when you tapped the first time, but Jose Maria was telling me something," and she repeated the story to Mercedes.

"I've been thinking of the name ever since," she went on at the conclusion of the narrative. "Do you remember a young man who came here to see papa Christmas evening, and stayed a good while looking at the games, and picked up your handkerchief? Well, his name was Teodoro Martinez. I remember it distinctly; I asked papa after he left; and he said that Don Eduardo Recio had recommended him to him for a secretary. And Don Eduardo was Jose Maria's teacher here; I have heard him mention him often. So I know that the young man who was ugly to Jose Maria in the street was that very one. I am glad papa didn't employ him. Well, good night. I must go now and try to recall everything Jose Maria said to me."

After she was gone Mercedes sat a long time in her low chair, with her elbows on her knees and her head on her hands, thinking of what Magdalena had told her. It was a revelation to her. Even if she had never heard again of the young man whom she had seen in the gallery she should sometimes have thought of him, recollecting that look of soul recognition, and should have wondered vaguely where he was and hoped it was well with him; but remembering the expression on his face when she saw him from the balcony on Saturday of Holy Week, she could not doubt that it was on her account he haunted the street and watched the house. Whatever ideas he had of her he had gotten them at the gallery. She tried to recall every word.

"It must have been because the tears came into my eyes when that gentleman said that beautiful thing about the artist, Señor Ramon Sagredo. I understand, now. The young man has been very poor, and he is now, I suppose, and he thinks I have sympathy for the poor. Well, I have reason to have. But how lonely and destitute of sympathy his life must be that he should care for that little expression from a common, ignorant girl! He must be noble and good to be so kind to his mother. I dare say Jose Maria was insulting to him. He is rich and proud and doesn't know how to treat poor people. Teodoro Martinez—he has a good face; I remember it well. It is all very curious!" And from that night that face was remembered with more distinctness and with the tender, pitiful thoughts that each of us has of those whom he knows are lonely and in need of sympathy, and especially of those who, he knows, care for *his* sympathy.

But she had other and more important things to think of. It is not to be supposed that because she had realized that she could never again confess, and therefore could never be a nun, that she turned against all of Roman Catholicism at once. Her's was a slower and surer nature.

But the scales had fallen from her eyes, and as the weeks passed she studied the Catholic religion in a new light, with the help of Tomas and Maximiliana, whom she occasionally

visited. Often she slipped books into her room, and keeping
them hid during the day, read at night the passages which
Tomas had marked for her perusal. They were generally
histories, and the marked passages showed the influence of
Roman Catholicism on the nations. Especially did she learn
of its degrading influence in Mexico.

She did not study it in the light of the Bible. They had
none to lend her; they scarcely thought, if at all, of the Word
of God in connection with it. They offered her no religion
in the place of the one they were taking from her. Unlike
her they did not feel the necessity of a religion. But in their
own way they helped her not a little toward the attainment
of freedom.

Nevertheless, she decided the question for herself. Night
after night she sat, with her hands clasped so tightly that the
blood stopped in the finger tips, and the perspiration stood
on her girlish forehead, as she tried to settle that—to her—
so difficult question: "Is the Roman Catholic religion the
true religion?"

There went on in her mind a fierce dialogue of insinuating
questions and defiant answers:

"I would rather have no religion than a false one. If the
Creator should give a religion to his creatures it would be
one that would make them better and happier. We believe
that instinctively. We can not separate the idea of benevolence from the Creator. But how do we know that our in-
stinctive beliefs are correct? We receive them directly from
the Creator; if they are wrong it is not our fault. But, after
all, how do we know that there is a Creator, or even that we
exist? How can we be certain of anything?"

With a terrible struggle she would fight back this sugges-
tion, and her spirit would grasp again its belief that there
was a God. And always, inevitably, she went back to the
consideration of that fact that has been fatal to the Romish
Church in the minds of so many other people, of most Mexican men of education, of some Mexican women even—that
the religion that the Creator would give would make people

better and happier; the Roman Catholic religion had not done that, therefore it was not the true religion.

That settled the question in Mercedes' mind at last. The day came when she said to them, speaking from her heart, "I give it all up. I am no Roman Catholic."

That same day, with a terribly desolate feeling in her soul, she knelt by her bed, and stretching out her arms across it, dropped her head between them and repeated the "Our Father, which art in heaven." But the heavens were like brass above her; she knew the prayer was not heard; she knew, as she arose from her knees, that there was some preparation of soul needed before she could approach the great King; but she did not know what that preparation was, and she had no hope of being able to make it. There was even, away down in her heart, unacknowledged by herself, an unwillingness to make that preparation.

CHAPTER XXIX.

THE TWO MARRIAGES.

IT was arranged that Jose Maria's and **Magdalena's** marriage should take place soon after their **return** home.

As I have intimated there were reasons why both Don Francisco and Doña Flavia objected to **Jose** Maria as a son-in-law. The latter objected **because he was a** Mason. He had **joined** that fraternity, **not because of any** appreciation of the liberal principles **which they** inculcated, but because, **as** the president of the **republic** and other prominent men were Masons, it was popular **to be a** Mason. When he found that it stood in **the** way **of his marriage** he withdrew from them, with the distinct understanding **in his** own mind that he would **return** to them as soon **as his marriage** was consummated. I **have** heard, however, **that the Masons** were so unreasonable and obstinate as to **refuse to receive** him again.

Don Francisco objected to him because he was a member of the Clerical party, **or** as it is sometimes called, the Conservative party. **But he** managed to quiet his uncle's scruples as **to his** politics **by** intimating that he thought very favorably indeed of the **Liberal** party; that, in fact, it was very probable that he would cast his vast influence on that side as **soon** as he should have studied their principles a little **more.**

Mercedes, **too,** had reasons of her own **for having some** humble scruples about the approaching **marriage.**

She had a high **opinion of** Jose Maria. **It is** not to be supposed that she was acquainted with **several of** the characteristics to which, as a historian, **I have called** the attention of the reader, such as conceit, **insincerity, and** an overbearing disposition. In fact it **is rather** appalling to the historian himself to see **the cold, hard words written;** just as it would be disagreeably **startling** to hear **various** characteristics of his own or of his intimate friends expressed by their most concise names. It would be unjust, too, would it not? for, along with the unpleasant qualities are often found good ones which go far toward counterbalancing them. Jose Maria was benevolent in his careless, high-bred way; and it even sometimes happened that he gave to the poor without any thought of the connection between such acts and his own salvation. He was condescending with inferiors; and, notwithstanding his aristocratic ideas, he had always been very pleasant with Mercedes in the parlor, treating her as if she were of the same rank as Magdalena. If there was now and then in his manner a slight recognition of his own superiority it was passed over by all as a matter of course, a thing inevitable in one who *was* so superior as Jose Maria.

In the evenings in the parlor Mercedes had quite as much conversation with him as Magdalena; and when he told of his travels in Europe, of the cathedrals, art galleries, palaces, ruined castles and the like, she was a far more interested and appreciative listener. Though his health had never been in danger from overstudy he had read a good deal, in an idle way, which he considered becoming to a young gentleman who had nothing to do but amuse himself. He liked to talk about what he read, too.

But Magdalena read nothing, not even the mass book. Indeed, her mother sometimes remarked, with a sigh, that she feared she did not even know what the holy mass meant. She could only sit by in pretty silence and admire Jose Maria as he held forth on his favorite topics. It was not strange, under these circumstances, that he should fall into the habit of directing most of his conversation to Mercedes. It made her uneasy, and she sometimes attempted to avoid joining the circle about Jose Maria on account of it; but Magdalena quieted her fears by saying often, as they went to their rooms for the night, slipping her hands, in a pretty, enthusiastic way, over Mercedes' arm, and looking at her with her great, innocent, happy eyes:

"O, isn't he just splendid, Mercedes? He is so intelligent!

and I know you enjoy hearing him talk. And, O, he is so handsome, now isn't he?"

And Mercedes always replied, "Yes, he is quite handsome," but she thought to herself, in her girlish, somewhat tropical enthusiasm for a being who was superior in her mind to any one else she knew: "He is beautiful as Apollo!"

"I think," she would add sometimes, standing a little way from Magdalena, that she might admire her beauty, "that he looks better when he sings with you, just you two together at the piano, than at any other time. It would make a beautiful picture. You certainly do suit each other." And she was sincere in it. She was jealous for Magdalena if Jose Maria's glances wandered away from her, even to herself, for to her Magdalena seemed the most lovable of girls.

One evening the conversation turned on *Les Miserables*. Don Francisco, who happened to be passing to the other end of the parlor, paused a moment behind Magdalena's chair to remark:

"I was in Paris the day Victor Hugo was buried. I was in that immense procession that followed him to the pantheon."

"*Les Miserables* is a very fine book," observed Doña Flavia, when Don Francisco had turned away. "I have read it; it is the story of the good bishop."

A look of amusement gleamed for an instant in Jose Maria's eyes, as they quickly sought Mercedes', and involuntarily the twinkle of enjoyment was reflected in hers; then she lowered them in shame and self-reproach. She knew that Jose Maria was thinking, just as she was, that Doña Flavia had read no more of the book than the part in which the "good bishop" figures. Fortunately neither Doña Flavia nor Magdalena had seen the interchange of glances. After that she did penance for a week by refusing to go into the parlor in the evenings.

Jose Maria felt that evening more distinctly than ever before that Mercedes could "appreciate" him more fully than Magdalena. But what aggrieved him most was that she did not show so much disposition as he thought the subject de-

manded, to fall down and worship him; she enjoyed his
stories and liked him as Magdalena's lover; that was all.
But that was far from being satisfactory to a young gentleman who saw no reason in the fact that he was engaged to
one girl and expected to marry her why he should not love
another and talk love to her, too, if he had an opportunity.

Just before they left the city Mercedes and the younger
children spent a week with a sister of Don Francisco's, in one
of the most elegant homes in that suburb of splendid homes,
Tacubaya, while Don Francisco, Doña Flavia and Magdalena
visited Puebla, Cordova, and other cities.

One evening, near twilight, she was wandering alone
through the spacious grounds in the midst of which the house
stood, admiring the gleaming of white statues and the flashing
of fountains among the dark green foliage. The twittering of
birds in the trees, the falling of water in the fountains, the
scent of orange blossoms, and the faint light of the dying
day, all contributed to make it a perfect evening.

Presently she saw coming up the broad carriage drive a
tall, dark figure. It turned aside into the winding path and
came toward her; it was Jose Maria. She was very much
surprised to see him, for he knew that Magdalena was not
there. "But, perhaps," she thought, "he has not heard from
them, and he has come to hear through me. But he ought to
have gone on to the house. If I go up to the house with him
they will wonder how long we have been talking in the
grounds, and I certainly can't stand here and talk with him.
But, perhaps, he will only tell me good evening and then go
on alone to the house."

She went to meet him, and in spite of her perplexity there
was a welcome in her bright young face, for she said at the
last moment: "He is only so eager to hear from Magdalena.
He will go on in a moment."

But he did not go on. He held her hand and looked into
her uplifted face, and when she attempted to withdraw her
hand he held it more closely and said:

"Are you glad to see me, Mercedes? You have no idea
18

how lonely I have been since you came out here.   I hoped to find you in the grounds," and his handsome face approached very near hers in the twilight.

She snatched away her hand and started away from him. stammering:

"I—I thought you came to hear from Magdalena.   I—I am going to the house."

"No, Mercedes, don't go.   Stay and talk with me a little while.   We shall be separated soon and not see each other any more; and you know I love to talk to you better than to any one else."

"You are engaged to Magdalena and you ought not to want to talk to any one else; it is treason to her," and she fled from him, among the trees and shrubs, to the house.

Fluttering like a bird escaped from the fowler she sought her room.   "I never thought of its coming to this," she said to herself as she dropped into a chair.   "I never thought of his being faithless to Magdalena.   But he does mean to marry her; he said we should be separated.   And yet he as good as said he loved me best.   But if he thinks he can make love to me while he intends to marry some one else he is mistaken," she added proudly.

But as the days went by she forgave him and pitied him; and she pitied Magdalena not less than him.   Would it not be better for Jose Maria to break his engagement than to marry Magdalena under such circumstances?   Sometimes, too, there arose before her dazzled vision the life she might live with him, and she contrasted it with the life of poverty and hardship that probably lay before her.   But she had a wretched feeling that every thought of Jose Maria was unfaithfulness to Magdalena.   She carefully avoided seeing him during the remaining days that they passed in Tacubaya, after the family returned.

They came home in June, leaving the beautiful Valley of Anahuac in all the luxuriance of a tropical summer.   It was happiness for them to be at home, to go through the familiar rooms, feeling again the tender associations; to see the faces of friends and hear their words of welcome.

"Come, let's see the bath," cried Magdalena, seizing Mercedes' hand; and they ran together to the old bath which the Marquis constructed in the orchard. A swift, deep current of crystal water ran through it. It was so swift that it would sweep a man off his feet if he were not cautious. An iron ring was suspended from the strong rope which hung from the temporary roof of the bath. In those first summer days at home the two girls learned to plunge through the stream by seizing the ring. Sometimes Don Francisco, coming in from a walk in the orchard where he had been hearing the girlish screams and laughter, would say to Doña Flavia:

"It makes me very uneasy to know those girls are in that bath; it's dangerous." But nothing came of it, and morning and afternoon they plunged into it, their pink bathing dresses growing pinker, and their bare arms and feet flashing in the water. And Magdalena was scarcely more gay than Mercedes in those days; it was so easy and natural to be light hearted and gay.

Then came bevies of cousins, young ladies and young gentlemen from Monterey and other towns, and the large, old house was full to overflowing, so full, they declared, that there was no room for the ghosts of the Marquis and his family. It was like a cage full of twittering birds. There were amusements from morning till night.

In the afternoons there was always a horseback party. The girls donned riding habits of the latest Parisian style; each gallant young gentleman rode by the side of a fair cousin. It was worth one's while to watch them as they passed through town in a gallop, and swept out over the broad, yellow, country road. In the evenings there were always games, music, and dancing.

An event of great importance was the arrival of Magdalena's handsome *trousseau*, including everything from the daintiest white garment to the foamy veil and wreath of orange blossoms, all of them selected by Jose Maria's mother

and sisters, and paid for by himself; and you may be sure
that the young ladies did as much rapturous exclaiming over
them as any young ladies of the United States could do. [1]

Jose Maria and a half dozen friends from the capital and
from Guadalajara joined the party a few days before the
marriage was to take place.

The day of the civil marriage came. A few intimate friends
from the town joined the party that gathered every evening
in those days in Don Francisco's parlor. They engaged in
conversation till the hour for the marriage arrived. Jose
Maria and Magdalena, followed by the bridesmaids and
groomsmen, entered the room. The bride was very lovely
in a pale pink silk dress. They stood side by side, a goodly
couple, he radiant as Apollo, and she fair and rosy as Diana.
Then the Judge and the *Alcalde* and the two witnesses, and
all the people, stood up, and with patriotic thoughts of the
"Citizen Benito Juarez," and of the good days that had succeeded the evil days, the Judge united them in marriage.

And it was so much better than going into convents,
thought the old people who were present, remembering their
own daughters and their probable fate in former years. And
so the young people rejoiced, and the old people rejoiced
more, and thanked God for Benito Juarez. And they kissed
the bride and congratulated them both. But Don Francisco
thought all that evening of his other daughter, as fair and
lovable as this one—the one who was in a convent in France.

After the marriage there was more conversation and music,
and at an early hour the company dispersed. The lights
were extinguished and the house grew quiet, and all of them,
from the sweet bride, for the last time with the other girls in
her "own room," where she had dreamed so many happy
dreams, to the little girls who were to carry the train of her

---

[1] *Note.*—Sometimes the young couple, accompanied by their parents,
go to a city together and the ladies of the party select the bride's wardrobe, the promised husband, of course, paying for it. But it is quite
common, now, as it is more convenient, for the husband-to-be to give the
money to the bride, so that she may herself select the *trousseau.*

bridal dress, thought, waking or asleep, of the marriage that was to be on the morrow.[1]

It was near noon of the next day when about a dozen carriages drew up at the side of the pretty little plaza in front of the church. A carpet had been spread from the stopping place of the carriages to the church door. Don Francisco, Magdalena and two of the little girls were in the first carriage; in the second came Jose Maria, Doña Flavia, and two young ladies. The procession formed, Don Francisco and Magdalena leading the way. Two little girls in white dresses and wreaths of pink roses carried the long train of her white satin dress. Next to them came Jose Maria and Doña Flavia, and after them the bridesmaids and groomsmen, the former in pale cream-colored dresses, and with tiny white veils over their heads and fastened on their bosoms, but without flowers.

Jose Maria joined Magdalena in front of the altar. The groomsmen took their places by his side, and the bridesmaids stood by her, all of them on the handsome rug, which extended from the platform far down in front of the altar. Before the groom and bride and each groomsman and bridesmaid lay an exquisitely embroidered cushion of white silk, all of them furnished by the groom. On these they knelt and awaited the entrance of the Señor Cure. He advanced to the

---

[1] *Note.*—Sometimes, after the civil marriage ceremony is performed, the company dance all night, and at dawn or before dawn of the day go to the church where the religious marriage takes place. But it is now considered more elegant to have the civil marriage at night, making little ado over it, and the religious marriage the following day, accompanied by all the festivities which are common in weddings.

"Are there many people now who consider that the civil ceremony is not valid, and that therefore the parties are not married till the religious ceremony is performed?" I asked of a bright-faced Catholic young lady who had been giving me a vivacious account of an elegant wedding in which she had been one of the bridesmaids.

"No, only a few old people think that now. Sometimes the religious marriage takes place first, but in that case," she added, laughing, "the civil authorities fine the Señor Cure, because they say the religious ceremony is not marriage. He has had to pay a good many fines for doing that, but he doesn't mind it: he will perform the religious ceremony first every time he gets a chance."

front of the altar, accompanied by two acolytes, one of them with the golden censer of incense, the other with the high cross.   As the Señor Cure was to say high mass he was in robes suitable for the occasion.   The sacristan held the vessel of holy water and the hyssop with which it was to be sprinkled on the contracting parties.

Jose Maria, Magdalena and the bridesmaids and grooms men arose and stood before him.   The usual questions were asked and answered; then the rings were exchanged, the thirteen pieces of money, "the pledges," were poured by the groom into the hands of the bride and returned by her to the Señor Cure, and they were sprinkled with holy water.   They then knelt, and the first bridesmaid lifted the veil of the bride and drew it across the shoulders of the groom; the Señor Cure wound about them the silken cord which typified their union, and the sacristan gave to each of them and to each of the attendants a lighted candle, which they held while the mass was being sung.   This being ended they returned to the house where they received the congratulations of their friends.[1]

The remainder of the evening was spent in conversation, games, *meriendas*, music, and dancing.   There was a splendid supper and a grand ball in the evening.

The next day, accompanied by a large party to the station, seventeen miles distant, Jose Maria and Magdalena left with the friends of the former who had come with him, for his parents' home in Guadalajara.   There, admired and admiring each other, they enjoyed the balls, receptions and all that go to constitute the life of fashionable people in the first weeks after their marriage.   Then they went to housekeeping in the City of Mexico.

---

[1] *Note.*—The "tariff," as they call it, of the religious marriage is so jealously guarded by the priests that by no efforts could I get a sight of it.   It matters little, however, except for the suffering from ungratified curiosity, since the charges are, of course, arbitrary, depending on what the happy groom can be induced to pay.   I can only say that the rug, incense, holy water, cross, robes, candles, cord, etc., are each paid for; and if the finer things, such as the "golden censer," the high cross, the silken cord, etc., are used the cost is more.

CHAPTER XXX.

THE GREAT CHANGE.

AFTER Magdalena's marriage the months glided swiftly by in the old house which the Marquis built. At first they were all lonely and sad without her, and the arrival of her letters, telling of her gay life, were the greatest events of the week. But as the weeks passed her place closed over and they learned to live without her.

Mercedes would have considered herself happy in those months but for the certainty which hung over her, like the fabulous sword, that as soon as Doña Flavia was convinced that she could not be induced to return to the Church she should be dismissed; and then how should she support herself? Who would give work to a girl who had been dismissed by the Señora Urbina for want of respect for the Church?

She would have thought she was happy but for this and the haunting unrest, the mysterious, dreadful weight which lay on her spirit. Sometimes she knelt and tried to say the "Our Father," but she knew that the Father did not hear, and often she arose from her knees without saying one word. Instead of being happy she was desperately gay and inwardly defiant against the influences of the Spirit, which were more and more distinctly felt.

At last the burden could be borne no longer; the time had arrived for the consummation of that great change which had been decreed before the foundation of the world, "according to the good pleasure of his will." She herself told the story of this change in a letter to her friend in Mexico:

"SALTA, March 15, 189—.

Sra. Maximiliana Valle de Sierra:

MY DEAR FRIEND: Such a great change has happened to me that I must write to tell you about it. You will be astonished, I know, to hear that I have believed the gospel. It happened two weeks ago, and I have thought of you often since; and this morning I said: 'I am going to write to Maximiliana, and maybe when she knows how good and how true it is the Lord will have mercy on her that she may believe too.'

This was the way it happened: You know I was a strong Catholic, and I confessed to the priests, and I did penance, and said prayers to the images, and I even wanted to be a Sister of Charity; and all the time I was trying to buy salvation with money and good works. But I found no peace in any of these things. At last I happened to see some copies of 'El Faro,'[1] and 'El Ramo de Olivo,'[2] and they made me more anxious than ever about the salvation of my soul. I resolved to see what the Protestants taught about it.

I could not go to the Protestant house of worship right away, because I didn't know how to do there, and I didn't know whether I should be welcome. So I asked Cipriana Gorivar, my godmother, you remember, to go with me one Sunday afternoon to the house of the Protestant minister to try to find out about it. We pretended that she wanted some sewing to do. She does sew for people, but she said she was afraid of their sewing, and she hoped they would not give her any; and they didn't, for they said they had none to hire. Then we waited and waited, for I did not know how to tell the lady what I wanted, and I did not want to leave without finding out how to go to the meeting, and if they would let me go.

At last the lady asked us if we knew anything about the gospel and told us she would be glad for us to come to the services; and she said that everybody was welcome, and that there was nothing to do but go in and sit down and listen. I persuaded Cipriana to go with me that very night. Of course, I did not let Doña Flavia know it; I went from Cipriana's house.

The Protestant house of prayer looked very curious. There was no holy water near the door, and there was not a single

---

[1] The Presbyterian paper.   [2] The Quaker paper.

image or picture on the wall. There were **seats enough for every one, and the** people didn't kneel at all when **they came in, for there was nothing to** kneel to; **they just** walked in and sat down. **There were no censers, nor robes, nor incense, nor** anything of the **kind. They sang a hymn, and then they** prayed without any books **or rosaries, and without seeing** anything to pray to—just **to God, you** know—and then **the** minister read some from **the Bible and explained it. I could** understand the song and **prayer and sermon and** everything—none of it **was** in Latin.

I went three times to **the** church; and I went **to the house, too, and the** minister and **the** lady I spoke **of** first read to me **from the** Word **of God and** explained it **to me.** One night, in **the house of worship, the** minister read and explained a story.

It was about a **rich man** who had **two sons; and one of them** asked his **father to give** him his share of **the** property; and **he** went **away off to** another country. He lived extravagantly; **he** had a *casino* and he gave **balls, and** he belonged **to a** club, and he went tó the **theaters. He spent** all his money so that he was poor, very poor, **and he had to hire to** a man to keep his hogs. And then he **thought about his** father's house and wished **he was** back there.

His father was very **sad because his son was gone; he stood out in the road and watched for him nearly all the time, putting his hands over his eyes and looking. A woman passed and he asked her if she knew anything about his** son. **She said, 'No, I don't; but if I see him** I will tell him that **you want him to come back." A man** passed and he said the **same** thing **to him and he received the same reply.** And so passed many days. **At last the son did** come back, all in rags, but his father knew **him, and he ran and** embraced him and kissed him and took him into the house and put a **fine,** new robe on him; and they noticed that he had **no ring** on his finger, so they put one on **him;** and they **ran** and killed the fatted calf, and they all were very merry. Oh, it was such a beautiful **story!** The minister said that **was** the way the

Lord would receive a sinner if he repented and went back and asked for pardon.

After I went home to Doña Flavia's house I couldn't sleep for the preaching of the minister that was sounding in my ears. All the night I saw myself covered with sin; and then it all slipped away from me, and I saw myself clothed in a robe as white as snow; but I was very, very weak. I was regenerated and made white by the blood of Christ.[1] I am a member of the church now, for I was baptized last Sunday night.

But you don't know, dear Maximiliana, what struggles one who is just converted from Roman Catholicism has with his heart on account of his false education in religion.

I have learned a great deal about the gospel since I believed, for I have read the Bible a great deal. They showed me where it says that we must not have images, nor bow

---

[1] *Note.*—The following account, which Schiller gives of the conversion of Mortimer, is quoted in El Tiempo as a genuine "conversion to Catholicism." "It seems incredible," says El Tiempo, "that one who could speak thus of himself should remain longer sunk in the errors of Protestanism." Mortimer is represented as relating his conversion to Mary, Queen of Scots. He says: "I had never felt the magic of the arts; the religion in which I had been educated disdains them and does not tolerate images or anything which speaks to the senses; it wants only the dry and bare word. What then would be my emotion on entering the church and hearing the music which appeared to descend from heaven—on seeing on the walls and arches that multitude of images representing the Almighty, the Highest, which appear to move as one looks at them. . . . . I contemplated with ecstasy the divine pictures of the Salutation of the Angel, the Birth of the Savior, the Holy Mother of God, the Divine Trinity, and the brilliant Transfiguration. I attended at last the sacrifice of the Mass, celebrated by the Pope, who in all his splendor blessed the people. Ah! what are the gold and the jewels of the kings of the world worth compared with so much magnificence? he alone is seen encircled with a divine halo; his word is like the kingdom of heaven, for that which is seen there is not a thing of this world."

Says El Tiempo, "The reasoning of Cardinal Guise finished the work which the splendor of the worship had begun." He "showed him that the eyes must see what the heart ought to believe, that the Church needed a visible Head, that the spirit of truth presided in the Councils." . . . . "I entered," says Mortimer, in conclusion, "into the bosom of the Catholic Church and abjured my errors."

down to them. It is one of the ten commandments. When Father Ripalda wrote his catechism for the Catholics he omitted that commandment and divided the tenth to make ten commandments. The Bible teaches us that we ought to pray to God and not to the saints. We have no formulas for prayer; we just say what we feel in our hearts. The priests can't forgive sins; there never have been any men on the earth who could forgive sins except the holy Apostles.

In our church all is brotherly kindness and equality. We call each other 'Brother' and 'Sister.' Oh, how one does love his brothers and sisters in Christ! Even if one has never seen them he loves them.

Now, my dear friend, I have written you all this so you may go to the evangelical worship, too, and learn the way of salvation. Oh, if you only knew how the burden of sin slips away from one when he believes in Christ!

You are mistaken about their having an image of the blessed Virgin for candidates for admission to the church to spit on and slap. We think of her as the holy Mother of God as she was in truth; but we say that she has no power to forgive sins, for that is what we are taught in the Sacred Scriptures; Christ is the only Savior.

Give many salutations to your husband for me, and accept an embrace and a kiss from your friend, who loves you,

MERCEDES GONZALES.

P. D. Doña Flavia would not let me stay in her house when she learned that I had believed the gospel; my aunt had left Salta more than a year ago, and the Señor Cure threatened not to absolve Cipriana if she took me in; but a good woman, who is a sister in Christ, Doña Susana Espinosa, took me to her house. She is very poor, but I help her make cigarettes. Sometimes, it is true, I do feel like one who is out on the ocean clinging to a plank, and it seems that my fingers are growing numb and slipping off; but when I feel so I get my Bible and read how our Lord Jesus Christ said that our heavenly Father clothed the flowers and fed the birds, and that we were of much more value than they; and so I leave it to him and go on; I would rather live this way than be a Catholic."

In this letter she says nothing of several things which she would have told with enthusiasm if she had sat by the side of her friend. Above all she would have told her of her joy and of her awe when for the first time she held in her hands the Word of God, the revelation of the Creator to his creatures.

We who are so familiar with this revelation, who use these phrases so often—how seldom we pause to think of their import! How wonderful it is to know the mind, the character, of him who created all things, the sun and moon and stars, the Milky Way of suns, and, above all, of him who gave us our mysterious being!

She said nothing of that day when she was called to stand before man for the Lord's sake. When even Don Francisco's strong authority could no longer shield her from the wrath and scorn of Doña Flavia. But there were given her in that same hour some strong, calm, plain, humble words which those who heard her could neither gainsay nor resist.

And at the end of the scene, in obedience to her mistress' orders, she opened, and closed behind her, the great front doors and stood in the street—homeless. She was very, very happy: she now had fellowship with Christ in his sufferings.

There was one instant when her faith failed her and everything grew dark and swam before her; it was when she turned away from Cipriana's door. It was only for an instant. Night was approaching, but again she looked toward the setting sun with a bright face. God would take care of her somehow, in his own way, she knew. She went on down the street, and presently she met Doña Susana Espinosa, a poor woman, whom she had seen at "the house of prayer."

"Good evening, *mi alma* (my soul, equivalent to "my dear"), at your service. Where is the Señorita going?" she said.

"I don't know, Doña Susana, I am like the Lord now, without a place to lay my head."

"May God will it! Blessed be his holy name!" exclaimed Doña Susana, whose Roman Catholicism would cling to her, notwithstanding the new life that was in her, till she entered the gate of heaven. Her pious exclamations were often quite irrelevant. "What has happened?" she continued.

"Nothing but what I expected. The lady I lived with has turned me off because I believed the gospel."

"Has the Señorita any friend that she can stay with?" she asked hesitatingly, thinking of her poor home.

"No, but I am not afraid, Doña Susana; the Lord will take care of me."

The good woman took her to her house. The next day she sent to Don Francisco's for her clothing. Her fingers soon acquired their former swiftness in making cigarettes; but she could not earn enough at it. Day after day the little money that she had saved slipped through her fingers; then she sold some of her dresses. She tried to induce some of the poor neighbors to let her teach their children; but, of course, they would not permit that, for had she not added to her other sins by trying to convince them that her heresy was more acceptable to God than the teachings of the Holy Mother Church? Don Francisco tried to find her employment, but he was no more successful than herself. The minister offered her a temporary home in his house, but she preferred to earn her living, even in the humblest way, to being a burden to any one.

And so the weeks grew into months till three of them had passed, and still she sat, with a painted tray in her lap, and twisted cigarettes. And always there lay by her side a New Testament; and often she read aloud to Doña Susana and they talked of what she read: and thus, slowly, one by one, were corrected the errors in her belief that appear in her letter to Maximiliana.

CHAPTER XXXI.

THE SHADOW OF DEATH.

"YES, *mi alma*, it is better to follow the Lord, no matter how much we have to suffer. In heaven we shall have peace and rest."

"Yes, Doña Susana," replied Mercedes.

"I was a Catholic," went on Doña Susana as she prepared the shucks to receive the tobacco, "and a strong one. I belonged to the Society of Perpetual Adoration. My time to kneel before the image of the Virgin was Tuesday morning of every week. How tired I did get kneeling on the stone floor! The rich ladies that I worked for used to have me go to their rooms and they would read the prayers to me. And when they thought I didn't want to confess they used to take me up in their carriages and carry me to the church. O, they were very good to me in those days!" she said, laughing.

"How did you come to believe the gospel?" asked Mercedes, knowing that the old woman would be pleased to tell her for the twentieth time.

"I was going to mass one Sunday morning, and I met a gentleman in the street. He stopped me and asked me where I was going, and I told him, 'To mass;' and he said, 'Come in and hear me say mass.' So I went into the little room, and he preached the Word of God to me and to a few other people who were there. And the Lord had mercy on me, and the light entered my mind and I believed the gospel. That was ten years ago. Since then I have had a great deal of trouble, but the Lord has been with me."

"I couldn't join the church right away, because I was married to my husband only by the Church. I had to either leave him or be married to him by the law. He was very rebellious and I had a great deal of trouble," she added, with a deep sigh. Then, remembering, she said, "But, poor man! he is dead now. He didn't know any better. It was the drink that ruined him, just as it is ruining my poor boys, that I pray so for every day. If they would only come home from the mines! Ah, God will succor us! After I had saved the money to pay the judge to marry us it was a long time before I could persuade him to be married by the law."

Just then something darkened the doorway, and looking up, Mercedes saw a servant from Don Francisco's house crossing the two thin rocks that spanned the tiny stream of water which ran in front of the house. Seeing her in that humble room, and in that occupation, he did not take off his hat, but, saluting them both in a style which he thought suitable to the occasion, he handed Mercedes a note. It was from Doña Flavia. She had just returned from Mexico, bringing Magdalena and her baby with her. She had found Pepe very sick, and he had been steadily growing worse. He wished to see her; would she be so kind as to come to him? She had evidently tried to write as if nothing had happened between herself and Mercedes, and it had been a difficult task.

A half hour later Mercedes was at the door of the room where the sick child lay.

When she could distinguish objects in the darkness she saw Doña Flavia kneeling by the tiny bed; Magdalena sat at the foot, and a little way from the head sat an elderly lady, a friend of the family. As Mercedes entered Doña Flavia turned her fair, troubled face to the lady, and exclaimed:

"O, Doña Guadalupe, how could I bear it if my child should die!"

"Well, Flavia," replied the low, gentle voice of the matron, "when my son died I said, 'The Lord gave and the Lord hath taken away.' We must all submit to the will of the Lord. What else can we do?"

This was merely an expression of the fatalism that is so prevalent in Catholic countries.

When Mercedes came near the bed Doña Flavia arose and

shook hands with her, saying kindly: "I am glad you have come, Mercedes." Magdalena greeted her with all her old affection.

When she turned to the little bed she saw the wasted form and pale face of her little pupil. A new rope hung on the foot of the bed so his feverish eyes could see it. "He wants it to drive the calves with when he gets well," explained Doña Flavia. "His papa bought it for him. Sometimes he has it hung at the head of the bed so he can touch it. Speak to him, Mercedes. Maybe he will know you."

Mercedes knelt and touched his hand, saying softly:

"Pepe, darling, do you know me?"

He opened his eyes and a smile pursed the thin face, as he said: "Mercedes."

But he was too weak to say more then. After awhile he opened his eyes and said in a slow, faltering voice: "Mercedes, you won't—leave me—any more, will you?"

"Tell him you will stay with him," whispered Doña Flavia, hiding her face, bathed in tears, behind Mercedes.

"Yes, Pepe, darling, I will stay with you."

And she did stay during the three remaining days, and then the end came. But when the "angel"[1] lay in the parlor with the flowers about him she stole out of the house and went back to Doña Susana's. She could be of no further use to them, and they must not think that she wanted to stay.

But the evening after the burial she put on a black dress and a black shawl, and accompanied by Doña Susana, went to the house of mourning. A servant met them and took them through the dark hall, through a dark room, and another in which one candle burned, into a room where sat in darkness, save for the little light which entered from the one candle of the adjoining room, Doña Flavia and Magdalena. They were dressed in black, and had black shawls drawn closely about their faces.

A strange sight it was. Here in this inner room they sat to receive their visits of condolence, and the dark room and

---

[1] Note.—The corpses of children, seven years old or under, are called "angels," and flowers are placed about them to typify their innocence.

the mourning apparel were a fitting expression of the state of their minds.

When Mercedes entered Magdalena arose and threw her arms around her neck, sobbing. When she released her Doña Flavia came to meet her, her old dignity and grace of manner clinging to her in the midst of her deep grief. But her voice was very much shaken, as she said:

"Mercedes, why did you leave? He wanted you to stay; I am sure he wanted you to stay after he was gone. We all want you to stay. Can't you?" The belief had forced itself into Doña Flavia's soul that her child's death was a punishment for her having turned a homeless girl into the street.

"Yes, Senora, I can stay awhile if I can be of any use to you," replied Mercedes.

She came back the next day and stayed. And after several of those sad and quiet days had passed over the household she again gathered the children into the schoolroom and taught them.

Magdalena was sad and quiet as the others. She tried to smile as she showed Mercedes her baby, but it was a pitiful failure. Mercedes noticed with apprehensions of something wrong, that, in contrast with the days of her courtship, she seldom mentioned Jose Maria. Had her married life disappointed her? or was it but natural that she should—not love her husband less, of course—but think less and say less about him because her heart was filled with this great, new mother love?

One day they were walking in the orchard under the grapevines, whose young leaves were pale, golden green in the spring sunlight.

"Tell me," said Magdalena earnestly, slipping her little hand, with its tapering fingers, over Mercedes' arm, "tell me, what do you believe, Mercedes?"

"About what?" asked Mercedes, her heart giving a great leap, and then growing quiet.

"About religion. What do the Protestants believe?"

"Well," replied Mercedes, remembering that the minister

19

had told her she must be very cautious how she began to talk to the Catholics about religion, "we believe just as the Catholics do about some things.   We believe in the Father, Son, and Holy Spirit," and then she was sure that at any other time Magdalena would have laughed at that dignified declaration of her creed.

"But do you not believe in the saints also?"

"No, not as you do.   We have no saints as you understand it."

"O," said Magdalena, wonderingly, "you have saints; you could not have names without having saints."

"O, yes, we can.   Protestants don't name their children for the saints."

"What do you do at your church?" resumed Magdalena.

"We study the Scriptures and sing and pray, and our pastor preaches to us from the Bible."

"You read the Bible for yourselves, too, don't you?" and the shocked tone of her voice and expression of her face were quite noticeable.

"Yes, all of us, every day."

"But do you not pray to the saints at all?" asked Magdalena, going back, after a pause, to that important dogma of the Catholics.

"No, never."

"Not even to Mary, the Holy Mother of God?"

"No, never."

"What do you think of Mary, anyhow?"

"We think that she was a good Christian woman, because she was a believer in the Lord, and that she was highly honored in being the mother of our Lord; but we believe that she was capable of sin, and that she did sin just as you or I or any other woman."

"O, no, no! How can you think so? The Lord made her pure and holy.   He kept her from all sin, from all thought of sin, in order that she should be his mother. She was the highest product of his mind, of his intelligence."

"I know that is the teaching of the Church," said Mercedes, quietly, "but it has no foundation in the Word of God."

"Our religion is so comforting!" went on Magdalena, not noticing the reply.

"But ours is consoling, too," said Mercedes; and she was thinking: "chosen, loved, before the foundation of the earth; casting all your care on him; to be like him at last!"

"But not like ours. O, it is such a comfort to have so many saints to pray to!"

"But I think it is a greater comfort to confess our sins and tell our griefs directly to the Lord."

"But it is this way, you know, Mercedes: An earthly king must have a great many ministers about him, because he can't attend to all the requests of the many people who call on him at the same time. When a poor man comes he must make his request to one of the ministers. So God has appointed the saints to hear our prayers, and the priests to forgive our sins."

"But God is not like a man. He could hear and pay particular attention to each petition if every person in the whole world prayed to him at the same time."

"Ah, Mercedes, it is strange you should think of it that way. But come, I am very tired. Let us go to the house."

Mercedes prayed in her heart as they went on to the house, "Lord, teach me how to teach her." And her heart ached for her worse than ever as she saw how pale and tired she looked in her black dress when she lay down on the sofa in her father's study.

She was not feeling well, her mother noticed. In her grief she had not thought much about any of her children except the little boy whom she had lost.

In a day or two Magdalena said she must go home; she had been away from Jose Maria a whole month and he would be lonely without her and baby. In vain they protested that they would write or telegraph to him to come; she replied that she preferred to go home; she should be better for the change, she thought. And they all thought she was probably right about that. So her father took her to Mexico, and stayed a few days and returned, reporting that she seemed to be better; she would, no doubt, be quite strong and well soon.

But in a few days there came a telegram. It flashed down like scathing lightning into that already stricken household. It was from Jose Maria: "Magdalena was very sick; would her mother come immediately."

Then Doña Flavia, forgetting the impossibility of leaving the house during the months of mourning, went with Don Francisco to her daughter's bedside.

The fever had seized her. It was the same old story; "the old, old fashion of death," for "we are all to die, each in his time, and who can help it!" as the Catholics say.

There was no help in anything, thought the parents and the young husband.

Before the delirium and in lucid intervals the terror of death laid hold upon her. There were crucifixes and burning candles where she could not open her eyes without seeing them, but they gave her no comfort. In vain the priest heard her last confession and gave her absolution; in vain he gave her the Eucharist; in vain he administered the Extreme Unction, putting on her feverish face and hands the oil of olives consecrated by the bishop, and repeating over her the words which he said the "Holy Church of Rome, the Mother and Mistress of us all had received by faithful tradition, 'By this holy anointing may God pardon thee all that thou hast sinned through vice of the eyes, of the nose, the touch,' etc., etc." In vain Jose Maria assured her that many masses should be said for the repose of her soul. All in vain!

But after it was all over and she lay on the silken cushions of the casket in the black *mortaja*[1] in the midst of the burning candles, there were many who said that she looked very

---

[1] *Note.*—Formerly this dress, the *mortaja*, was bought from the priests. They would not bury any corpse without it; and as the burying grounds were all in the hands of the priests it followed that no corpse could be buried without it. The priests, therefore, often charged exorbitant prices for it. Now that the cemeteries belong to the government the *mortaja* is used or not, according to the wishes of the friends; and it is made by the friends as any other dress would be.

peaceful, **and** that there could be no doubt that that sweet, young creature had "died in grace."[1]

Notwithstanding **the** prohibition of the law, **the** double chimes of bells announced the funeral services in the church. There was **sung** the *Misa del cuerpo presente* **(mass** with the body present). Afterward **the** casket **was bound** in the hearse with ropes covered **with** flowers, **and the male** friends of the family followed it **in** coaches, **in slow procession,** to the pantheon. Doña **Flavia** set her heart **on having the** funeral service chanted by the priests **and** acolytes in the **streets, as** the procession moved along. **after** the old fashion, **but Don** Francisco **would** not consent to **so** flagrant a violation of the law.

In the pantheon **the casket** was placed **on** the ground, the priest in his **robes stood by** it, and the acolytes, with the high cross, **the holy water,** and the censer of incense. After their **ceremonies were** over the coffin was lowered, a few shovels of **earth** were thrown in, and then all retired **but the** sexton and **his** assistants.

After the last sad rites were over Don Francisco **and Doña** Flavia brought the tiny baby and its nurse **to their home; and** Jose Maria remained alone.

This last blow almost prostrated Doña **Flavia. She was** rebellious about her daughter's death; if God **had punished** her for her conduct toward Mercedes by taking **her son why** should he punish her still **more, after she had** repented, by taking her daughter? she **said** to herself. Her health gave way under the **strain of grief;** she was not able to care for the baby. Thus **it came to pass that** Mercedes took charge of it and **its nurse. They** slept, **and, in** fact, lived in her room. It was **to this** care for the **child** that Mercedes was

---

[1] *Note.*—All of the dead in Roman Catholic countries who have the privilege of going to purgatory instead of directly to the infernal regions are said to "die in grace." None go directly to heaven; and none go to hell except heretics, infidels, and others who die refusing the offices of the Church, and whose relatives refuse to pay for masses for the dead. Consequently the Church loses no money by admitting the doctrine of eternal punishment.

indebted for the privilege of staying longer in the house; for, but for that, Doña Flavia would have found some excuse to dismiss her and yet retain a quiet conscience.

As the months passed the tiny boy became fat and rosy and beautiful. The dark shadow of death slipped from over the family. The baby was a "well-spring of joy" to them all, even to Don Francisco. Jose Maria came sometimes, and he, too, was gay and playful with his boy. He did not fail to see during his short visits that it was Mercedes who cared for his child, though she intentionally had less to do with it during his stay in the house than at other times.

Her position was far more like that of a servant than it had been during her former stay there. She was seldom invited into the parlor now. The excuse for the omission, if one were needed, would have been that the care of the child occupied her time when she was not in school. But she knew that that was not it, for often they saw her walking back and forth in the corridor while the baby slept and the nurse sat by him.

But she was happier for being left thus alone; she had more time for the reading of the Bible and for prayer.

CHAPTER XXXII.

DUTY.

NOTWITHSTANDING her faith there were some very dark days in Mercedes' life. She knew that the time would certainly come when she should have to go back to the life of poverty and coarseness from which she had been lifted for awhile.

Then, again, it was inevitable that such a nature as hers should feel deeply, now that she stood on a higher plane, and her finer sensibilities had been cultivated, the wrongs that had been inflicted on all of her class by the Roman Catholic Church—the poverty, ignorance, and degradation.

In those days this Mexican daughter of a religious marriage sought to quiet her spirit by reading the eighteenth chapter of the Revelation of John: "Babylon is fallen, is fallen." And her soul took up the cry of "them that were slain for the Word of God and for the testimony which they held: How long, O Lord, dost thou not judge and avenge our blood on them that dwell on the earth!"

A very human instrument was used to help her out of one of these seasons of darkness. It happened that Jose Maria came. He had few opportunities to talk with her in these days; but he sometimes came out and swung the children during the recesses of the school, and then he exchanged a few words with her.

He had for some time been making up his mind that he would like to marry Mercedes. I don't suppose he is the first young gentleman of aristocratic origin and ideas who ever fell into the error of wanting to marry a girl who was his inferior in social position. There was more than one reason which caused him to entertain this extraordinary thought. He loved his child; he wanted him with him. He wanted to know that he was in the care of some one who would always be kind to him; he had rejoiced all this time that Mercedes had the care of his boy.

Besides that he liked Mercedes, liked her very much, because he knew that she admired him.   He remembered her low origin, it is true; but he reflected that he, Jose Maria Ortega, was high enough in riches and respectability to do as he pleased in this matter, and in all matters.   Besides no one would suspect it; seeing her and knowing her, who of the society in which he moved in the capital or in Paris would ask if his wife were the daughter of a peon?

He knew that she had gone off into this strange heresy, and that was to be regretted; but she would soon turn from it under his influence.

Besides these considerations there was another which, if it was not an argument in favor of it, was at least a pleasant thought in connection with it: His marriage with Mercedes would be a terrible blow to his mother-in-law; and Jose Maria had developed that unaccountable, unprecedented peculiarity, that of heartily disliking his mother-in-law.

Giving all these things due consideration he had arrived at the conclusion that after Magdalena he would rather have Mercedes for a wife than any other girl he had ever known.

He was thinking this one afternoon when he came up to Mercedes as she stood in the shade of one of the large trees at the back of the house.   The children were playing a little way off.   After a little conversation he said:

"I wish you would come into the parlor in the evenings now as you used to do.   I would so love to talk to you sometimes."

He said that at the most dangerous time.   She had no thought of courtship, but she was hungry for respect and sympathy.   She looked up at him with half pleading eyes, and said:

"You do respect me and like me a little then?"

Jose Maria had not expected such a reply.   It touched him. He stooped to pick up a pencil that had slipped from her fingers as she spoke, and as he restored it to her his slender, soft hand, with the blue veins in it, lingered on her hand and clasped it.

"Mercedes," he said, as he bent nearer her, "you know I always respected you and liked you. I wish I could be with you often."

Just then the children bounded toward them and she was spared the necessity of replying. She was surprised, but to her, in that strained, suffering state of mind, it did not seem a very exaggerated expression of simple friendship. "It was very beautiful and noble of him to show so much kindness to a poor, humble girl," she thought. So it is often; the words go out from our lips and we know not what chords in the souls of others they are going to strike.

She thought a good deal about it in the next day or two; and as the depressing clouds broke and fled away from her mind she began to suspect, remembering what he had said to her two years before, that he meant more than friendship. And now and then, as one who is crossing the mountains catches sometimes a glimpse of distant landscapes, she saw again the dazzling life that Jose Maria might offer her. Those prospects of worldly enjoyment would have had no attraction for her in the first days after her conversion, but these months of living with those to whom unseen things were as nothing, had told on her spiritual life.

One afternoon she happened to pass through the study, just at dusk. When she was about half way through the room there arrested her, coming from the dark corner where the sofa was, a happy, electrifying, baby laugh. Thinking the nurse was there with the child she started to rush across the room to catch him in her arms and cover him with kisses; but a tall, dark figure arose from the sofa and came toward her. It was Jose Maria. She threw up her hands with an exclamation, then clasped them, saying:

"I—I thought it was only Catalina with the baby."

But Jose Maria came to her side; he laid one hand on her shoulder, and holding her clasped hands with the other, said:

"Mercedes, why do you avoid me? You know I want to be with you! Won't you stay with me all the time? Won't you marry me?"

"O, I don't know. Don't talk to me that way, please. Let me go. Think of Doña Flavia!" and she tried to wrench her hands from his grasp.

But he held them. The mention of Doña Flavia was the thing of all others to urge him on. In fact in the instant before she said that he had been conscious of something very like uneasiness lest she should accept him.

"It makes no difference what she thinks. It only matters what you and I think about it. Tell me, Mercedes."

"I—I can't now. I don't know. I must think about it. I will tell you to-morrow."

With another effort she disengaged her hands and glided out of the room. Jose Maria went back to the sofa and lifted up the baby from the floor. He scarcely knew what to think of Mercedes' conduct. He could not imagine that any girl would refuse him, and especially a girl of her position. "Think about it, indeed!" he said to himself. But no doubt she was only dazzled at the prospect, and she was evidently afraid of Doña Flavia. Then, remembering his feelings when he thought she might accept him, he reflected that even if he were engaged to her there would be nothing to prevent his breaking the engagement if it did not suit him "on further consideration."

Mercedes had before her the task of deciding a difficult question that night. What reason was there why she should not marry Jose Maria? He liked her and she liked him. She admired him even; but she had to own to herself, as she had often done before, that there was something wanting, some earnestness of character. She could not thoroughly reverence a man in whom she felt that that was lacking. And the Holy Spirit had said: "Let the wife see that she reverence her husband." She moved uneasily as she thought of that. But she did reverence him in some degree, she said. She remembered that he had never said anything about loving her, and she had scarcely ever thought of love in connection with him; but, no doubt, now that she did think of it, that was what he meant; and she—well—she liked him. It would be a great pleasure to her always to have the care of Magdalena's child. Might it not be a duty to marry him on that account, that she might give the child a Christian education?

After all the fine things that were said and written about marriage ought we not to exercise common sense about it? The day would come sooner or later when she would have to go out again to that terrible life of poverty and anxiety, a taste of which she had already had. It did not seem so easy and heroic now as it did when she had first entered on it; she shrank from it with an inexpressible shrinking. The life that Jose Maria offered her seemed like Paradise compared with it. How she should be sheltered and cared for! And more and more in the last two years she had been feeling her helplessness and the need of some one stronger and better than herself on whom to lean. Her mind drifted off into thoughts of this new life of ease and wealth and travel. It was so easy and pleasant to think about it. The glittering gift was just before her; she had only to put out her hand and take it.

But she shook off these thoughts and came back to her task. The question must be decided. She had answered with a sophistry one thing that the Holy Spirit had said. It frightened her to think of it. He might leave her alone to do as she pleased; and it is a fearful thing to a Christian to be left alone to follow his own inclinations. There was a fierce struggle, and at the end of it she said in her heart: "I will do whatever thou mayest show me it is my duty to do."

Immediately there confronted her another declaration of the Holy Spirit which she had hitherto refused to consider: "Be not unequally yoked with unbelievers." Jose Maria was an unconverted man, an unbeliever. That was unanswerable; that decided the question. She was exhausted by the struggle, but in her heart shone the soft radiance of the Lord's smile of approval, the "peace that passeth understanding."

The next day when she saw Jose Maria under the trees she did not avoid him. She dreaded very much to answer him. She was not the first girl who ever went, almost breaking her heart with pity, because she must refuse to marry a man who would forget her, and marry some one else within six weeks if he had an opportunity—nor will she be the last.

'She told him that she respected him and liked him very much, but that the principles of her religion forbade her to marry one whose beliefs were so radically different. She was very, very sorry he had ever thought of it, but she was sure he would soon think she had answered him wisely, and would be glad that she had answered so.

He was astonished; then he manifested something very like anger as he made some reply which Mercedes could never quite recall, but which left the impression on her mind that it was not very polite. He turned and walked abruptly away, and the next morning he left, without telling her good-bye, for the City of Mexico.

Well, Doña Flavia found it all out. Eavesdropping servants are a wonderful help sometimes to mistresses in keeping up with the affairs of their households. She was disgusted with Jose Maria; he deserved it, she said. But to think that a girl of Mercedes' station should actually refuse to marry one of "our family!"

She avoided another scene, for she had not enjoyed the first one; but in two or three days after Jose Maria's departure the handsome front doors opened and closed again on Mercedes, and she went again to Doña Susana's for shelter.

As Jose Maria has nothing more to do with this story I will tell you here the little more that I know about him.

He has not yet married again. He pays little attention to the young ladies, and some of his friends opine that he will never marry again; but the young ladies hold a different opinion about this much discussed question. They "think more of him for not being in haste to marry." They think his devotion to his little son is "perfectly beautiful." He has been heard to say that as soon as he is old enough he intends to bring him to the capital and keep him all the time with himself.

He has become very religious, very religious, indeed. He attends the entertainments in the theaters, the circuses and the *plaza de toros* with great assiduity, and he is particularly liberal when any of these are for the cause of religion. It was in the Cathedral that I saw him. He was kneeling on a silk handkerchief, his silk hat on his legs behind him, his hands clasped, and his eyes upturned to an image.

Every year, on the anniversary of Magdalena's death, he pays for a curious performance in the church which she attended. Over the entrance are hung, and gracefully looped back, black velvet curtains. Within, and forming a long aisle that leads toward the high altar, are placed, alternately, evergreen trees in boxes, and long and large candles in tall, handsome candlesticks. In front of the altar, and extending far up among the painted angels of the dome, is built a mausoleum. It appears to be made of brown stone, but, of course, it is of wood or of sôme lighter material. On the front, in large letters, is the name, "Magdalena."

When all these arrangements are completed masses are sung at every altar by the priests in rich vestments.

All this is for the release of Magdalena's soul from purgatory.

CHAPTER XXXII.

"THE COURSE OF TRUE LOVE NEVER DID RUN SMOOTH."

TEODORO, as I have said, went to a small town in one of the northern States to teach. He was well received by the best people in the little town and the school began under bright auspices. His salary was good and he soon began to indulge in some little luxuries, especially in books which he had long coveted. He had not been in the town long before he heard that evangelical services were held there. He sought the service hall; he was much pleased by what he saw and heard, and afterwards attended regularly the two Sunday services and the week-day prayer meeting. After some weeks spent in examining the doctrines of the church in the light of the Scriptures he became a member. He had never had a church home before, nor had he ever known anything of the communion of the saints. If he had not been separated from Lupe so soon after his conversion it is probable that he would not have been deprived so long of these privileges.

When it became known that he attended the heretical meetings two or three of the "best" families took their children from the school. After he joined the church it became evident that he was far less popular with the others; but he was a good teacher, a much better one than any other they had had for some time and they did not like to lose this opportunity of having their boys well instructed at home. But when, after the first year he "took to preaching," all but a few of the youngest and poorest pupils left the school; then Teodoro resigned, and it was closed. He had known all the time what would be the consequences of his course, but he was one of those people who will do their duty uncompromisingly and leave the consequences to God.

As to his call to preach the gospel, he said of it, as every other true minister of the Word has said since the time of Paul: "Woe is unto me if I preach not the gospel."

Soon after he gave up the school he was employed by a missionary society to take charge of the church in that town.

About this time he left the hotel and went to board in a private family. The wife of the master of the house, Refugio, was a member of the church, and so was her mother, Doña Benigna Cadena. The life in that orderly, Christian home was like a foretaste of Paradise to Teodoro.

Doña Benigna was of middle age; she was tall, with plain features and a kindly expression. Her black hair was always parted in the middle and combed smoothly back from her forehead; her dress was simple and scrupulously neat. She was gentle and kindly in her judgments of others. She had been trained to strict honesty and truthfulness in her childhood. "My mother," she would say, talking to her little grandson, Pancho, "always told us children that if we found anything in the street to take it into the house in front of which we found it and ask if it belonged there. And if the house was closed we were to lay it in the window. On no account were we to keep it if it were no more than a pin, unless the owner could not be found."

She loved to tell of her conversion. The history of one's conversion! Is it not the new song which the believer sings on the earth, a song which no man can learn save him to whom the Lord teaches it?

Sitting around the dining table, when Refugio had removed the plates, and the napkins on which they sat, she told it with much gesticulation to Teodoro one evening, soon after he took up his abode in the house.

"It was about fourteen years ago," she said, "I lived in a little town not far from Zacatecas. My husband was away from home, working in the mines, and I and my daughter, Refugio, lived in a house with another family. They were very kind people. They were so kind they made me uncomfortable; they would take my work and do it for me before I could get at it. They would get up early and get my breakfast and bring it to me. It made me very much ashamed, and I told them so, but I could never keep them from doing it. So at last I said: 'You are so kind and good that I can't live with you.' So I went to the house of a near neighbor and rented a room from them. Now they were Protestants, and I knew it, but I didn't care for that. I thought I would let them alone and they could let me alone.

"They did let me alone; they didn't say a word to me about their religion, except one day when Doña Luz and I were in the kitchen together (for we used the same kitchen), she said to me: 'You are very good, Doña Benigna, and I like you very much, but I think we can't eat together any longer.' Then I said: 'Why?' and she said: 'Because we like to ask a blessing at the table, but you would not like that; so we will have to eat separate.' Then I said: 'But why can't you ask a blessing before me? I don't mind that. My father and mother always asked a blessing both before and after the meals.' There are very few Catholics who do that, but my parents always did. So after that we went on eating together.

"The man, he was the preacher of the Protestants there, and he had worship in the house where they lived. But I never went in; I only heard them singing as I sat in my own room. The first thing that touched my heart was a hymn. I don't remember what hymn it was, but it was wonderful sweet and tender. After that I began to go to hear the sermon; then I began to ask about this new religion, and to compare it with Romanism. I asked about it all, the mass, the perpetual adoration, the priests, purgatory, and everything; and they showed me that none of those things were taught in the Sacred Scriptures.

"They offered me the Bible to read, but I wouldn't take it because I thought I couldn't understand it. I remembered when I saw the Bible that my mother had had a Bible when I was a child, and that she and my father used to read it. It was a large old book bound in leather, and there were leather straps that buckled around it. But they never had any one

to explain it to them, and I knew when the preacher and his
wife were explaining it to me that that was why my father
and mother always remained Catholics—they never had any
one to explain the Bible to them.

"Well, there was something in my heart all the time that
wouldn't let me rest day nor night till I believed. O, my
conversion was wonderful! It was miraculous! The Lord
just laid hold on me with his right hand and he wouldn't let
me go till I had submitted to him. And I did believe on him
after many weeks.

"My husband did not oppose my believing. After that I
took a long journey to bring home my daughter, for she was
at my father's house. When I reached there I told them
what had happened to me, and they were all very much troubled; and my mother said that was the first stain of shame
that had fallen on any of her people. And she said that was
what had befallen me, because I had wandered in foreign
lands, instead of staying there in the ranch where generation
after generation of my people had lived and died. My father
came in, and when he heard about it he upbraided me very
much. One night I went out into my sister-in-law's room,
and while we were talking my mother came in and began to
talk about the new religion. She said I must give it up; and
when I told her I couldn't, she stood up and stretched out her
hand toward me and said: 'Unless thou wilt give it up thy
mother's curse shall rest on thee all the days of thy life.'

"That was awful, awful to me. It made me very much
afraid, too, for I thought there must be something in a
mother's curse. I took Refugio and went home. When I told
Doña Luz about my mother's curse she opened the Bible and
showed me where it is written that we must love the Lord
more than father or mother. At that word of the Lord peace
returned to my heart and I was comforted."

"What became of your husband?" asked Teodoro gently,
for he knew he might be touching a tender chord. "Did he
believe also?"

"No," she replied very quietly, "he turned to the evil ways

20

of the world. He refused to be married by the civil law; so I took my daughter and came away."

Honesty and sincerity were written on every line of Teodoro's face. The people loved him, for he was lovable. He believed in people; he believed what they said, and he attributed to them good motives. His faith in them inspired them to be what he thought they were.

His voice in preaching was clear and sonorous; in conversation it was low and pleasant. And if "a low voice is an excellent thing in woman," how much more excellent is it in man! How it suggests refinement, kindliness, reserved strength!

In his first efforts to preach he blundered and stammered not a little. But the thought with which he himself afterwards encouraged young converts to speak to the church of what God had done for them helped him in those days: it was that as the first lisped words of a little child are precious to his parent, so are the first imperfect utterances of a child of God precious to his Heavenly Father.

His thoughts were forcibly expressed and in pure and simple language. And sometimes the thoughts were beautiful; I remember that he said once in a sermon that the words, "Jesus wept," were a poem. Both the ignorant and cultured said: "How clearly he explains the gospel!" And verily he did explain it like a man who had experienced the power and sweetness of it.

When he was asked if he did not sometimes think with regret of the career he might have had as a lawyer or politician he looked up earnestly and replied with quiet emphasis: "No, the calling of God is higher and more desirable." "I could make more money," he said once, "by devoting myself to another occupation; but I should not be so happy. One who is called of God to preach the gospel can never be satisfied when he is doing anything else. I have often thought," he added, "that I should be happier if I could work and support myself while I preach, but it is not the Scripture plan, and therefore I can't do it."

"I have great faith in private prayer," he said on another occasion. "How many, how many prayers have I seen answered!"

His patriotism was one of his conspicuous characteristics. "May God save our country from that!" he would say sometimes, when a national sin or calamity was mentioned.

When one expressed appreciation of his sermon he would reply quietly: "May it be for the glory of God."

He talked comparatively little, and he seldom, perhaps never, jested, though his conversation was not infrequently brightened by a quiet, refined humor. He would become animated in the discussion of a great question or of a book which pleased him. For the rest, he was humble and earnest, persevering and enthusiastic, hopeful, joyful, and loving. Of course, his work was blessed.

Not long after he took charge of the church he received a letter from Hernandez, which gave him some joyful news and some sad news. In the first part of the letter he told him jubilantly of his hopes of political preferment, and of his engagement to be married to Tulis, the bright, gentle daughter of the Director of the college. Then the letter had been interrupted, and two days afterward he continued thus:

"Could not finish until to-day. I have to tell you the sad news that Ortega has lost his wife. I attended the funeral yesterday. Poor fellow! he seems quite cut up by it. It is a heavy blow."

When Teodoro had read that he clutched the letter tightly and walked on with wide-open, unseeing eyes till he was out of the town and among the hills. Some of the boys who saw his face as he passed them, and noticed that he did not return their salutations, said that "the master looked like he had seen a ghost." He never knew how far he walked, nor where he went, nor by what street he entered the town when he returned; but he became conscious that toward the close of the day he was sitting in his own room, with his arms on the table and his head on his arms.

So it was all over at last. He had tried to quit thinking

about her when he learned that she was to be married,—and married to his enemy. But he had not succeeded in forgetting her; he was continually wondering about her, continually fearing that she was unhappy.

And now she was dead. Was she happy now? She was so gentle and good, maybe she knew the truth and had been saved by it. There were people, he believed, in the Roman Catholic Church who learned the truth through stray Bibles and were saved by it, though the circumstances prevented their ever coming out of that Babylon. O, if he only knew it! if he only knew it!

Then there came a strange thrill of joy: she was no more Ortega's now than his own. In the spirit world marriage ties were dissolved and the petty social distinctions of earth were swept away, and kindred of soul alone was considered. He would hereafter every day of his life visit her grave and lay flowers on it, but she would be nearer to him than when she was living.

As the months passed his grief became milder, like that of a husband who buries his young wife out of his sight, and then through lonely years carries in his heart the loved face—a sanctifying memory.

So the weeks grew into months and the second year of his life in the little northern town was nearing its end.

CHAPTER XXXIV.

THE END WHICH WAS THE BEGINNING.

"Then while I live, and till I die,
And all my life I'll fondly try,
With all my soul, to bless thee."

ONE evening the family were sitting for awhile, as usual, around the table in the dining room after the dishes had been removed. Refugio was resting her hands, tired from sewing, on the table. Simon, her husband, was whittling a toy for Pancho, while Doña Benigna was trying to persuade that young gentleman to read over his lesson so as to know it well for the morrow. The young pastor had taken out of his pocket and spread out before him the Catholic daily, *El Tiempo*, and was busy with a long article on "The Policy of the Holy See and the Catholic Party in Mexico," when he caught the name "Urbina"—Simon was saying:

"They say Don Francisco Urbina recommended her."

Teodoro kept his eyes on the paper, but he listened. Anything that concerned Mercedes or "her people" was sadly interesting to him.

"I shouldn't be surprised," said Doña Benigna, "if she was the girl who taught in his family for so long. What was her name?"

"I didn't notice the name."

"Was it Mercedes Gonzales?"

"Y-e-s, I believe it was. Yes, I remember now; that was the name."

"She is the girl. When I visited Cipriana Vega in Salta she told me about her. Cipriana is her godmother."

"What is it?" asked Teodoro. "Excuse me; I didn't catch the first part of your conversation."

"It was nothing of importance. They told me to-day in L. that Don Francisco Urbina had recommended a teacher for their government school, a young lady from **Salta**, and they had employed her on his recommendation; and mother says she is the young lady who was governess in his family for some time."

"They seemed to think a great deal of her at first," said Doña Benigna. "They carried her to Mexico to teach the children while they were there. But I have heard since—let me see who told me that, why the wife of Polycarp Duran, who came from Salta to see her daughter when she had the fever, three months ago, wasn't it, Refugio? or four months? I believe it was three months ago—that Don Francisco's wife dismissed her because she believed the gospel; though she did say they took her back again afterwards."

All of that was interesting to Teodoro because it was about a "sister," and because she was some one who lived near the Mercedes he loved. It was pleasant to talk about it, and they would never suspect his feelings, he thought.

"Señor **Urbina** had a daughter named Mercedes, I believe?" and he stared very hard at the paper and clinched his hand so tightly under the table that there was danger that the nails would cut into the flesh.

"No, he had no daughter by that name. No; he has one daughter in a convent in France; her name is Ursula. Another one died a long time ago; I don't know what her name was; it may have been Mercedes, now. Then there was his grown daughter named Magdalena; she married somebody from Mexico and died nearly a year ago, and the little ones are named—"

"I thought the one who married Ortega of Mexico was named Mercedes—the one who died," he sat erect, staring with stern eyes and with an expression that seemed to say he would make those people tell him the truth if it killed them.

"No, her name was Magdalena. I know, for when I lived in Salta, before Refugio was married, I sewed for Doña Flavia, Don Francisco's wife, and Refugio did drawn work for her; she liked it very much and always paid well for it—"

But **Teodoro** had pushed back his chair and risen suddenly and stalked through the door and through the court and into the street.

"Why, what is the matter with him?" exclaimed Refugio, "I never saw him act so before."

Teodoro wanted to get out where he could breathe. Sudden joy has killed people. There were two clear thoughts in his mind as he turned his face toward the calm stars: "She was living, and she was not Ortega's wife."

So the people felt in the days of our Lord on earth when their dead came back to life. So the sisters of Lazarus felt; so the widow of Nain; nay, so Isaac would have felt if after he had learned to love Rebecca she had fallen on sleep and then awaked to life and come back to him. Teodoro's soul sang and shouted: "Thou hast given her back; thou hast given me back my dead!"

It was long before another thought came to him, but at last he remembered the mention of the governess of that name. He recalled every time he had seen her; he remembered how simply she was always dressed; he remembered that no one had ever told him that this young lady was a daughter of Señor Urbina; he saw how it all was, now; but he longed to be assured by the voice of another.

Early the next morning as Doña Benigna was winding in and out of some cane lattice work some stray tendrils of the vine that she was training on it, he came out and essayed to help her; but his fingers, usually so helpful, were unaccountably clumsy this morning.

"Doña Benigna," he said, "you say there was a governess in the family of Señor Urbina when they were in Mexico, and that her name was Mercedes Gonzales?"

"Yes, so they told me," she replied, looking at him curiously.

"And you say she has believed the gospel?" That was another assurance that he wanted to hear again.

"Yes, that was what they said."

"Do you know anything else about her?"

"Well, yes; I asked about her because she was a sister in

Christ, you know. Her history is an uncommon one. They said she was the daughter of one of Don Francisco's *peons*, but a German lady noticed that she was a bright girl, and she educated her and afterwards got her this place in Don Francisco's family."

"And after she believed the gospel they turned her off and then took her back again," he said, taking up the narrative where she dropped it, and looking at her keenly as if he were a detective.

"Yes, but I suppose they want to get rid of her again, as he has gotten her this school. Come, Refugio says breakfast is ready," and at the table they talked of other matters.

"Why might I not win her?" he said to himself, tremulous with the thought. "If I could only know her, there might be hope."

As he went on thinking of this, some other facts were suggested to his mind. He knew the people of the town where she was to teach; there was not a little fanaticism there among the Catholics; he knew that the Board of Directors could not have been induced even through Señor Urbina's influence to employ an anti-Catholic teacher if they had known that fact. They would soon find it out and dismiss her, and that would be very mortifying and painful to her. It would be better for them to know it beforehand and not employ her.

On the other hand, the Protestants of his own town had been for some time trying to find a teacher. The salary would not be more than half as large, nor the position by any means so honorable in the eyes of the world as those offered by the government school in L. But would it not be better for her in the end to take this place? If his own feelings had not been so deeply enlisted he would not have hesitated to write to the young lady and advise her to resign that place and accept this more humble one. But now he feared to do so. How did he know what she would think about it? And if she should come to suspect that he had any personal interest in the arrangement it might be fatal to his hopes.

And besides all that, there were compromising Protestants who could adapt themselves very well to the Catholics and get along with them admirably. But he rejected the thought instantly that she could not be of those. If it could only be brought about somehow without his having anything to do with it; or at least without her knowing that he had anything to do with it!

Now he had been intending for some weeks to go over to L. to attend to a little business. Why might he not go now, and it might be arranged "somehow"? At any rate fair and open dealing would be best for all concerned. He resolved to go; but because of his own interest in the matter his susceptible nature suffered as if he were about to do a mean action. He explained it to Simon and the rest of the family, of course suppressing all mention of his own interests and scruples, and they fully agreed with him. But he felt as if he had confessed a crime.

After that he tried to persuade Simon to go and manage in an off-hand way to break the intelligence to the Board; but as he had no business in L. he could not see why he should go and mix himself up in this unpleasant business; why couldn't Teodoro do it himself; he had heard him say that he had to go to L. soon, anyhow. So there was no avoiding it; he went.

He attended to his business; he went around to the bookstore and bought a book or two that he needed; he called at the houses of some of the humble brethren of the place and talked to them and encouraged them in their poverty and trials with promises of Scripture; he took a New Testament from his pocket and read to one woman who was an unbeliever and warned her solemnly of the destruction that threatened her; he did everything that could be expected of him rather than go about the Palacio Municipal, where he knew he should find one or more of the Board. But at last it could be put off no longer. About a half an hour before train time he went up to the Palacio. He met two or three of the Board whom he knew. He talked with them about the weather, politics—anything rather than school matters, till he had to shake hands with them, put himself at their orders and rush off to the train. As he sank back in the seat of the narrow gauge car he could not have told whether he was glad or sorry that he had not mentioned it.

He sat looking out of the window at the mountains as they flew past him, when a hearty voice at his side exclaimed:

"Ah, Martinez, how do you do? Glad to see you."

He sprang up to shake hands with his friend, Don Dionicio Torres, not a member of the School Board, indeed, but a man who was interested in the matter, as he had children to educate. They sat down and talked awhile. Presently Don Dionicio said:

"This question of schools is a troublesome one. We have just employed a teacher who is very highly recommended by Don Francisco Urbina of Salta, but I have been told she is a Protestant. That wouldn't matter to me, you know," he said courteously, remembering to whom he was talking, "but it won't suit some of our people, the mothers of the young people, for instance," he added scornfully.

"Who is the teacher?" asked Teodoro, not knowing what else to say.

"She is a young lady who taught for some time in the family of Señor Urbina; Mercedes Gonzales is her name. Maybe you know her, or know of her? They tell me you Protestants are great people to hang together."

"I have heard of her," replied Teodoro almost faintly.

"Do you know whether she really is a Protestant? It's better for our Board to know it beforehand. You know what their fanatical *señoras* will make them do when they find it out. You know how they broke up that fine school of yours. It's a pity women can't get something in their heads besides religion!"

"I know—y-e-s, that she is not a Catholic."

"Well, you will forgive me, old fellow, if I tell the Board. It's best, you know. For my part, as they say she is a good teacher, I wish they would employ her anyhow."

When Teodoro was saying good-bye, as the train approached his station, he said:

"Will you please drop me a card as soon as the Board decides about the Señorita Gonzales? The Protestants here want a teacher and I think we might give her the place."

"I will, with pleasure," replied Don Dionicio.

So the matter was settled; but Teodoro wished, as he explained it to them at supper that evening, that he had not said anything about it before.

After a few days of feverish anxiety lest the Board should employ her anyhow—for anything seemed possible to him that would separate him from her, even to the Pope's ordering everybody to read the Bible, if that would have that effect—he received a card saying that the Board had dispensed with the Señorita Gonzales' services. Then he induced a member of his congregation to write to her, requesting her to teach their little school. He would not write himself, for delicacy forbade his making her feel that she was under obligations to him for the slightest thing.

There were more feverish days of waiting, then came her letter, saying she would come gladly.

Then Teodoro astonished the family by telling them he would give up his room to Mercedes and find another place to board. No, they must not protest; it would be a great favor to him, and it was the most suitable place in town for her. As she was to come in three or four days he moved immediately.

But he did not move everything. He selected some of his favorite books and placed them on the small shelves in the corner. He even ventured to suggest some improvement in the room. One of the doors dragged badly on the tiles of the floor; it could be made shorter so it would close easily. There was no window; he had always been satisfied with the light from the narrow iron-barred transom over the door, but perhaps it would be better to have some panes of glass put into the tops of the folding doors. He would pay for it if Simon would permit it. So it was done. He objected that the table was too tall for a young lady to write on; his table, now, would suit her much better.   If Refugio would let him exchange he would leave it here and take this one to his room.   So that also was done.   But he capped the climax when he sent up a little rocking chair.

Doña Benigna only expressed the astonishment and curiosity of the whole family when on the afternoon that Mercedes was to arrive, as he stood in the door of the room, after having inspected everything, and fastidiously rearranged some books and a pair of vases with some flowers that Refugio had put in there:

"Brother, is it only the friendship of friends that is between you?"

"I," replied Teodoro, with slightly heightened color, "I don't know the young lady.   I have only seen her, but she is a sister in Christ, and we ought to try to make everything comfortable and pleasant for her."   And the good woman had to be satisfied with that; and she knew he was good enough and had brotherly love enough in his heart to do all that for a woman who was twice as old as himself.   But he strictly charged each and all of them not on any account to let the young lady know that he had had anything to do with the arrangement of the room.

When the hour came for the arrival of the train he walked down to the station with Doña Benigna and Pancho.   But he was not to go back with them; he could not meet her that night; he only wanted to see her.

He stood near a lamp post when the train thundered up and stopped.   He saw her as she descended; he recognized the slender figure in the dark dress, with the black shawl drawn over her head and thrown over her left shoulder.   He heard her low, musical voice as she answered Doña Benigna's question: "Yes, Señora, I am Mercedes Gonzales."   His head grew so hot that he took off his hat to let the night air cool it.

As he stood thus they passed him, and Mercedes, happening to glance up, saw his face clearly in the light of the lamp. Their eyes met. She started violently, then hurried on. It was the very face, the very one, that she had thought of so frequently, and with a strange curiosity and tenderness for nearly two years. She had thought of it especially in these last three weeks as the face of some one who for some reason thought kindly of her. He wanted her sympathy! Ah, how she needed his, or some one's! She wondered vaguely if he were a believer, for that was always her first thought about one in whom she was interested.

When they reached the house she sat down a few minutes in the parlor with Doña Benigna, till Refugio should light the lamp in her own room. It was a long, large room. The tile floor was scrupulously clean. In each of the two corners near the door were corner tables. On one of them was a large plaster of Paris cat with the most phenominal spots imaginable; on the other was a box covered with shells and a few other ornaments which Simon had probably given to Refugio in their courting days. In another corner was a white plaster of Paris pedestal on which sat a gilded bust of Juarez, and in the other corner was a corresponding pedestal with a bust of Hidalgo. On one side of the room was a table over which hung a looking glass in a wooden frame. Around three sides of the room, standing against the walls and as near together as possible, were chairs with rush bottoms. In an unbroken line they stood except where they were obliged to skip the before-mentioned table and pedestals. Subsequent observation revealed the fact to Mercedes that there were thirty-six of these chairs. Chairs, tables and frames were shining with paint. On the walls were a few cheap and highly colored pictures. This parlor was Refugio's especial delight.

Mercedes was very much surprised at her own room. She was much touched, too, when Doña Benigna said: "We tried to make it pleasant for you because you are a sister."

After she had eaten her supper and gone back to her room for the night she went around it, looking at everything. She lingered longest, of course, before the book shelves, taking down the books and looking at them. Who in that house read those books, she wondered. There were some of Castelar's and Altamirano's; there was a translation of Shakespeare, and some translations from French, such as "Paul and Virginia" and "Picciola." There was no name in any of the books, but from some of them the name had been carefully erased.

The next day Teodoro was invited to dine with them. His introduction to Mercedes was the most commonplace thing in the world. When he came into the dining room she was standing there, in a simple, light, summer dress, her glossy, black hair parted and smoothly combed back as she always wore it. "Brother," said Doña Benigna, "this is the teacher. Mercedes, this is our minister, the pastor of the church."

He took her hand for a moment, saying, as he looked into her eyes:

"Teodoro Martinez, at your orders."

"Thank you," she replied, simply.

Neither of them could talk very much during this first meeting, and Simon and Refugio were never great talkers, so that Doña Benigna found herself with the burden of conversation on her shoulders. I don't know how she came to speak of banditti, but presently she was saying, in reply to a question of Teodoro's, for he had felt that he must say something:

"O, yes, Don Sotero was a noted bandit. Everybody knew about him. He was not just anybody, either; he belonged to a rich and highly respectable family. He was the only one of them that ever went wrong. He was rich himself; why he had houses and lands of his own. He was a bandit just because he liked the danger and adventure of it. He was a very handsome young man, they said. He was captain of the band. They had their headquarters in the ranch of R. By seven o'clock all the honest people had to be in their houses, with the doors shut, and the ranch was given up to the banditti, and they drank and danced and fought and killed till morning. They would go off on robbing expeditions and come back with great loads of plunder, and nobody dared say a word. But at last the President sent General M., with a band of soldiers well armed, and they surrounded the ranch and captured them all and killed them—all but Don Sotero; he was not there."

"What became of Don Sotero?" asked Mercedes.

"They caught him afterwards; he was betrayed by a woman who knew where he was, and they hanged him in the door. But they said it was awful hard to kill some of those bandits."

Teodoro observed Mercedes grasp her knife more closely, and he wished he could change the subject of conversation, but he was helpless just because of her presence.

"Another awful murder, worse than that one, happened in this State a few years ago," went on the worthy matron, still moved by the hospitable desire to entertain her guests. "Why the bandits cut off the head of one man and cut out the tongue of another. But I have forgotten the particulars."

Then, as she paused, Teodoro aroused himself at last and said:

"Well, Señorita, the school will begin Monday, will it?"

"Yes, I suppose so. Just as the patrons please, of course."

"I think you will have twenty pupils at least. The school-room is not so nice as you have been accustomed to, I know; but we have made it as neat and comfortable as we could."

"I have no doubt I shall like it. I am very grateful to you all."

Then Simon thought of something to say:

"I expect after all you'll like it better than teaching in L. I was afraid at first when Teodoro broke that up and had you come here that you wouldn't be pleased with the change; specially as the salary is not more than half as large."

Poor Teodoro! If all the poles and canes and earth of the roof had fallen on his head it would not have been much more overwhelming. He could say nothing, and nobody found anything to say for, it seemed, a very long time. Mercedes was too much surprised and confused by the new thought, and Doña Benigna was too much chagrined to make any reply.

Refugio thought it must have been the right thing to say since Simon had said it. After some moments Doña Benigna remarked to Mercedes:

"The brother thought that you would prefer to be among believers here, rather than with the Catholics. For they are said to be quite fanatical in L. They wouldn't have borne with a believer long."

"I have no doubt," said Mercedes pleasantly, anxious to relieve Teodoro, "that it will be much more pleasant here."

Then they went on talking of other matters till the dinner was over; and very soon after dinner Teodoro excused himself on the plea that he had some writing to do.

Mercedes escaped to her own room to study over this new phase of the subject. He had had her come here. Had it any connection with his strange interest in her in Mexico? Then Refugio had let slip the information that he had boarded with them "until—well, until a few days ago, in fact," and then the good little woman had looked frightened as if she had told something she ought not to have mentioned.

Was that a clew to the mystery of this room, to the taste with which the things were arranged, to the books, especially? It was kind and thoughtful of him not to let her go to L. From that day she began to love him.

But Teodoro wondered all the afternoon if he should ever feel like smiling again.

The next Monday the school opened. It was in a small room on the principal street. In the center of the room sat a long and wide table, on either side of which was a bench. They were the only seats in the room, except the chair for the teacher. Here on these high benches sat the children swinging their feet, spelling books and reading books in hand, studying aloud, vying with each other in the exercise of their lungs, for such is the custom of the country. They were not barefooted children; they always wore shoes, though they were frequently without stockings. Every morning the teacher read a chapter of the Bible and they sang a hymn. "What a friend we have in Jesus," or "How firm a foundation," or "Little children who love their Redeemer," or some other.

It was marvelous how often in those days Teodoro's visiting and other duties took him by that noisy little schoolroom. Sometimes, when Mercedes lingered, after all the childrens were gone but Pancho to finish the work of the day or prepare some exercises for the morrow, Teodoro would drop in and ask some questions about the school and hope she was enjoying the work. More than once when she looked up suddenly and saw him standing in the door her face had brightened suddenly with gratitude or something sweeter. But Teodoro was afraid to believe what his eyes saw.

But those calls at the schoolroom were necessarily infrequent and quite short. He often called at Simon's house and talked with her in Doña Benigna's presence. They found that their tastes about other things as well as religion were similar. They would have been happy in those days if each could have been certain—quite certain—that he was loved by the other. But people in that state of mind are very liable to misunderstand each other. Every now and then there was a misunderstanding which was painful enough for both while it lasted, and let them know the joy of reconciliation when a glance, a word, a smile and bow, or something else of like dimensions bridged over the fearful chasm.

One afternoon, after Mercedes had been with them about two months, there was a small social gathering at Simon's house. It happened that the young Methodist preacher was moved that day to talk a good deal to Mercedes. This was very distressing to Teodoro, and he tried in vain, by passing fruit to Mercedes, and by other little courtesies, to attract her attention and induce her to turn from the Methodist brother and devote herself to him. Mercedes understood his motives, but she didn't know very well how to get rid of her companion. Presently Teodoro was driven by despair and resentment to sit down by the silver-tongued Gaudencia and engage in conversation with her, not deigning again to glance toward Mercedes. After that she, hurt by his neglect, took pains to show him that she liked Gaudencia as well as any of the other girls, or better. But she cried nearly all night for fear

21

Teodoro liked Gaudencia better than he liked her. That trouble between them lasted for a week.

It was a month after this that Teodoro planned an excursion to a cave that was about five miles from the town. About two dozen persons went in hacks. I am sorry to have to report that Teodoro did not invite the Methodist preacher; not that that gentleman was aggrieved by the neglect, or even thought of it; but because of the lack of willingness to do so on Teodoro's part. But he was punished, as he felt, for that, and many other shortcomings.

As he sat in the hack with Doña Benigna, Mercedes, Gaudencia, and two or three children, something brought up the subject of Mercedes' not having gone to L., and Teodoro received a more severe blow than the one that Simon had given him at first. It had always been a sore subject for him. He could reason about it and come to the conclusion that, of course, Mercedes would rather be where she was, with believers, than in L., even if she could have stayed there; but she had never said so to him, and her failure to do so hurt him.

Mercedes had wanted a hundred times to say it, but she felt that saying that would be the same thing under the circumstances as telling him that she was glad to be near him; and, of course, she could not do that.

When they drew up in the midst of the wild, picturesque scenery at the foot of the mountain, left the hacks and began the steep ascent to the dark hole, the mouth of the cave that gaped far up toward the summit, Teodoro assisted Doña Benigna, as it was his duty to do.

They reached the opening, and sat down for awhile on the stones to rest; then they entered and began the exploration of the chambers.

Not far from the entrance, the first time they had to descend from one chamber to another, Teodoro helped down all the women, and Mercedes was the last one. She stood above him and looked down at him; their eyes met and their hands touched. After that he thought no more of Doña Benigna, nor of the other women, nor of the Methodist preacher.

On and on they went, up and down the steep places, and
from chamber to chamber. Sometimes, when the others
were not near they went hand in hand; sometimes he drew
her hand into his arm, holding it closely. They spoke few
words; they only looked at each other by the light of their
flickering candles. They noticed neither stalactite nor stalag-
mite; they stood in the room where the white stone woman
clasps the child in her arms, and the light shines down on her
through the top of the mountain, and they saw nothing of it,
cared nothing about it.

At last they reached before the others the Chamber of
Glory. It was here that a thought grew too strong for
Teodoro, and he stood up very straight, with his face turned
a little away from her, and said in a low tone, through which
she heard the cry of pain:

"O, Mercedes, you know how I love you; won't you say
you forgive me?"

Then her candle slipped from her hand and she clasped it
over his as she held her other hand closely on his arm, and
throwing back her head she looked up into his face and exclaimed:

"No, Teodoro, I won't say I forgive you. How could I use
such a word to you; I love you."

He pressed one kiss on her lips, and then they heard the
others coming, and, laughing softly; they caught up her candle and lighted it.

So they went on through the cave and returned to the
mouth of it, and sat down just inside and rested, and ate supper. Then down the mountain and to the town. And when
Teodoro lifted Mercedes from the hack at Simon's door Doña
Benigna heard him whisper, "*Mi alma*," and she knew the
whole story.

They were married a few weeks later. Mercedes wore a
simple white dress, which Teodoro had bought, and in her
black hair some white flowers, which he had selected. Every-
one of the thirty-six chairs in Simon's parlor was occupied
that evening, and there were some who stood up, for the

Methodist brethren and **sisters** were there, **as well** as Teodoro's own people. **After the civil** judge had married them **the** Methodist **preacher—who, by the** way, had never had any idea of Teodoro's **jealousy of himself,** and who **could** have assured him, if he **had been interviewed, that he** liked Gaudencia better than Mercedes—prayed **that** their union might **be** a blessing to themselves and to the **world that lay** in **the** darkness of error around them.

During **the** evening Teodoro and the **Methodist** preacher were observed to cordially embrace each **other.** The hospitable Simon and Refugio served a *merienda* **of** chocolate **and** cake; **and** during the *merienda* they consulted **together about another** teacher for the school.

They **went** to housekeeping **soon.** It was here **that** Don Francisco found them one **day,** having stopped **for the** purpose, and inquired and found **out** the house. He sat **and** talked with them an hour **or two;** and Mercedes observed, with an aching heart, **that he** looked older and more careworn. As he told them **good**-bye he stood, with his hand on her shoulder, and said **to Teodoro, in his** pleasant, dignified way, that he **was** glad so **worthy a young man** had won Mercedes, for he should always **have something of the** interest of a father **in her.** And she, **looking up** into his face, saw, as he **turned away his** head, that **it was** convulsed with feeling, **and she knew that** he was thinking **of** Magdalena. **Then** they **said** *adios*—meaning it—and **they** watched him **as he** went down **the** street in the **golden** sunlight. **In a few** days there came to Mercedes, **from** Don Francisco, **a** beautiful writing desk; "a wedding present," he said **it was in** the note which he **wrote about it,** "though it came **late."**

They had **been married about** three **months** when one afternoon Teodoro, walking **with a** joyful step along the street, came **to** the door of **a humble house.** Some children, seeing him before the door, bounded toward him, and seizing his hands led him through the court **to the** door of a room where sat three **or** four women, and Mercedes in the midst of them with **an** open New Testament in her hand. She had just read and explained to them how that a great king made a marriage feast for his son and sent forth and called them that were bidden; and they would not come; **and** again he sent and called, and they would not come; and then he sent into the highways **and called others** and they came; and when **the** king came **in to see the guests he** found one who had not **on** a wedding garment; **and** he, having nothing **to** respond, was bound hand and foot and cast into outer darkness.

Teodoro entered and shook hands with **them** all, and sat **down; and** taking the book from Mercedes' **hand he** added a **few** words of exortation; then he said: "Let us have a word **of** prayer," and they all knelt down and followed him in prayer. When they had risen up he stood **a** few minutes by Mercedes' side talking; **then,** dropping **his** hand gently on her shoulder, he said, looking down at **her:**

"Come, Mercedes, **it is time to go home.** We must have supper early, **you know; it is prayer** meeting night."

"Yes, **I was just thinking of** that," she replied as she looked up at **him with a bright face;** then, tossing her black **shawl** over her shoulder, she arose. They shook hands with **the** women and went out and down the street, side by side, toward their home.

THE END.